THE POET
AND
THE SILK
GIRL

THE POET AND THE SILK GIRL

A MEMOIR OF LOVE, IMPRISONMENT, AND PROTEST

SATSUKI INA

HEYDAY
50

BERKELEY, CALIFORNIA

Funding provided by the Jonathan Logan Family Foundation—
empowering world-changing work.

Library of Congress Cataloging-in-Publication Data

Names: Ina, Satsuki, author.
Title: The poet and the silk girl : a memoir of love, imprisonment, and
protest / Satsuki Ina.
Description: Berkeley : Heyday, 2024.
Identifiers: LCCN 2023031873 (print) | LCCN 2023031874 (ebook) | ISBN
9781597146265 (hardcover) | ISBN 9781597146272 (epub)
Subjects: LCSH: Ina, Satsuki—Family. | Psychotherapists—United
States—Biography. | Japanese Americans—Biography. | Japanese
Americans—Forced removal and internment, 1942–1945. | World War,
1939–1945—Japanese Americans. | Japanese Americans—Civil rights.
Classification: LCC RC438.6.I53 A3 2024 (print) | LCC RC438.6.I53 (ebook)
| DDC 616.89/14092 [B]—dc23/eng/20230821
LC record available at https://lccn.loc.gov/2023031873
LC ebook record available at https://lccn.loc.gov/2023031874

Cover Art: Courtesy of Satsuki Ina
Cover Design: Archie Ferguson
Interior Design / Typesetting: Misha Beletsky

Front endsheet: Shizuko Ina, San Francisco, April 26, 1942.
Photo by Dorothea Lange, titled "Eviction Order." Courtesy of the National Archives and Records Administration
Back endsheet: Itaru Ina, foreground right, July 1,
1945. Photo by Robert Ross, WRA photographer

Published by Heyday
P.O. Box 9145, Berkeley, California 94709
(510) 549-3564
heydaybooks.com

Printed in East Peoria, Illinois, by Versa Press, Inc.

10 9 8 7 6 5 4 3 2 1

*For my grandchildren, Skyla Sachiko,
Weston Kai, Nora Emiko, and May Kyoko, and to their
children and their children and their children*

Contents

Preface   ix

1. American Citizens   1
2. Non-Aliens   41
3. Disloyals   63
4. Renunciants   97
5. Enemy Aliens   161
6. Deportees   209
7. Internees   227
8. Alien Residents   239
9. Healing   283

Acknowledgments   289
About the Author   291

Preface

My earliest childhood memory is of a train ride. Standing in the aisle, barely able to reach the worn armrests on either side, I lift myself, swinging back and forth to the rhythm of the moving train. The air is hot and musty. My brother Kiyoshi is curled asleep, his head across my mother's lap. The man beside her is a stranger to me. My mother has told me to call him Otō-chan, Daddy. When I cry, he says to me softly, "Shikkari shina-sai. Nakanai de." "Be strong. Don't cry."

I was born on May 25, 1944, in the Tule Lake Segregation Center, a maximum-security prison camp in Northern California, during World War II. When I was a year old, my father was taken from us and held in a separate prison in North Dakota. Finally reunited, after more than four years of prison life for my parents, we were leaving the Crystal City, Texas, family internment camp by train on July 9, 1946. Our destination held an uncertain promise. I had only known life surrounded by barbed-wire fences.

Almost eight decades have passed since that defining moment of American history when over 125,000 people of Japanese ancestry, citizen and immigrant alike, living on the West Coast of the US, were forced from their homes and imprisoned in American concentration camps, euphemistically referred to as "relocation centers." By executive order, Franklin Delano Roosevelt would deny American citizens the civil liberties guaranteed by the US Constitution, to be considered innocent until proven guilty.

Someday my grandchildren will learn that their great-grandparents, Shizuko and Itaru Ina, were taken from their home in San Francisco and forcefully held in six different prison camps from 1942 to 1946. Sadly, they may also hear that their great-grandparents were "disloyal" to America. It's a message I heard in muffled voices when people learned that I was born in the prison camp for "traitors and troublemakers." My father's frozen silence about our time "in camp" added to the shame that I unwittingly absorbed. When I asked my parents why people would say those things, my mother deftly put the problem aside and said, "Just say that you were born in Newell, California." I followed her advice, referring to the little town just outside the prison, but the question was never answered, and like a fly unable to escape from a windowless room, it bumped around in my head for years until somewhere along the way, it stopped—curiosity withered, rerouted, without answers.

In 1994, I joined a pilgrimage to the Tule Lake prison site to commemorate my fiftieth birthday, and as if waking from a decades-long hibernation, the questions came back to life with a fury. What silenced my parents? What secrets were so painful they had to be suppressed? What choices did my parents make? Why am I so haunted by these questions?

By this time, my father was gone and my mother was showing early signs of dementia. I had been a psychotherapist specializing in the treatment of trauma for over twenty years. To understand the psychological trauma of the mass incarceration that seemed to haunt me and other former captives, especially at Tule Lake, I began by researching files in the National Archives. I went on to interview former incarcerees, and eventually conducted more than 110 group therapy sessions with people who, like me, were children in the camps. After five years of holding a series of "Children of the Camps" workshops with Japanese Americans who were incarcerated as children, I produced a documentary film, *Children of the Camps* (2000), with the help of my niece, Kim Ina, and a crew of professional filmmakers.

It was my hope that when former child prisoners observed people in the film revealing their stories and emotions, they would be encouraged to see the benefits of doing the same. Adults who suffered trauma as children often suppress their own direct experience and internalize the narrative of the perpetrator, who, with unlimited power over the bodies and minds of their victims, can distort the truth about the how and why. The kaleidoscopic stories of the Japanese American experience during World War II had been shamefully suppressed by the US government to avoid bringing to light the violation of our constitutional rights. Our artificially distilled narrative had become a typical perpetrator-informed story that blamed the victim. Justification for the mass incarceration was based on race rather than due process, and "loyalty" had become the onus of the victim to prove, after they had already been incarcerated. It was a difficult and often painful process to separate out the real stories from the false internalized stories, and to unearth deeply held emotions of sorrow and rage, especially in the face of the almost universal silence that was a predictable coping response of the traumatized adult victims.

This profound uncovering process brought to light aspects of the World War II incarceration story that I had never heard or read about. Before the war, Japanese Americans were not forced to see themselves as either loyal or disloyal. Most first-generation immigrants had been living in the US for decades, committed to raising children who were American-born citizens. Slowly, the false narratives were carved away as group participants sifted through their own stories, corroborating memories and facts to find previously unspeakable humiliation, tragic losses, deep faith, sacrifice, love, angst, and both large and small acts of dissidence.

Finally, after I completed the *Children of the Camps* documentary, it was time for me to excavate my own family story. I learned from the people who shared in the workshops that family secrets have a way of disconnecting people from their past, often shaping the relationships between parents and their children. A vague sense of anxiety was ever present in my childhood. It wasn't a secret that we had been in camp, but my parents hardly spoke about their wartime experience. Somehow, I knew it was best not to ask questions, thus joining not only my family and my community but society at large in keeping the story of our incarceration stowed away out of awareness, a festering wound, never to heal.

Fear, rather than hope, seemed to drive my parents' desire for us to be successful in the world—to be good students, to behave, to excel in whatever we undertook, and not to bring shame to the family. There was frequently a sense of foreboding when one of us kids would step off the mark and go in a direction that wasn't part of the plan—foreboding so present that all three of us, my brothers and I, would quickly reverse course, avoid risks, and above all else, seek safety and approval.

Something kept my parents, and possibly my entire community, from speaking about "the camps." This something, I believe now, had to do with a deep sense of shame. Shame so choking that it would prevent my mother and father from speaking up when they were shortchanged in a store, spoken to rudely, ignored in restaurants, called racist names, spit on. Shame that was passed down to us children about who we were, how we looked, and what we deserved in life. We learned not to complain, to avoid being vulnerable, and to bear a never-ending need to strive for approval. Mental and emotional toughness was what it would take to endure whatever life brought our way. Looking back now, I realize how my father's repeated message to me, "Be strong. Don't cry," reflected the fortitude that made it possible for my parents to survive the trauma of their incarceration. For me, it would become both the strength and the weakness in my ability to cope with my own life challenges.

Learning about my parents' wartime experience would lead me on a healing journey that would change my life forever. After my father passed away in 1977, my mother and I were sorting through his large, weathered oak desk, where he often sat to compose his poetry. When I reached into the back of the bottom drawer, I discovered a large packet of letters, neatly stacked and tied together with rough brown twine. My mother seemed stunned when I handed the packet to her. As she slowly shuffled the letters in her hands, tears formed in her eyes. She sank to the floor beside me. "I didn't know Daddy saved my letters from camp," she said. She circled her finger around the room, "Somewhere around here are the letters he sent to me."

In the moment, I felt a rush of excitement about the discovery, but when my mother, without hesitation, handed the small bundle back to me without untying the string, I realized that the letters held more than just reminders of past times. They were artifacts of ghostly memories suddenly brought to life. Like the silence that haunted our home, they represented a door she chose not to re-open. She never said what she thought I should do with the letters, but within days, she had unearthed the corresponding mail she received from my dad during that same time period, put both bundles in a neatly wrapped box, and never mentioned them again.

I carried this box around with me for more than twenty years, moving it from place to place, packing and unpacking it, often forgetting it even existed. The letters were mostly written in Japanese, and I sometimes wondered what it would feel like to be able to just open and read each one. But not being able to read or write in Japanese was in some ways a protective guard against knowing what my parents might have endured during their incarceration.

Besides these prison camp letters, earlier ones written during their courtship before the war, along with photographs, diaries, and my father's haiku journals, were waiting to be found in boxes in my mother's apartment. Before she passed away I asked if I could have her permission to make a documentary film about our family story. She shrugged, saying there wasn't much to tell, but *kodomo no tame ni* (for the sake of the children), as well as for other survivors of the World War II Japanese American experience, she consented. It was the impetus I needed to begin to face the letters sitting in the box. Five years later, in 2005, along with the same amazing team that worked with me on *Children of the Camps*, I produced a docudrama broadcast on PBS called *From a Silk Cocoon*. It took several years to translate, research, gather, and connect the jagged pieces of a historical puzzle. Slowly, piece by piece, with the help of my parents' letters and diaries, as well as government documents from 1939 through 1946, their story unfolded before me. I was soon to discover that our family story would not be a part of the dominant narrative about the so-called relocation and evacuation of Japanese Americans, in which the only way to prove one's "loyalty" was by silently accepting government-perpetrated injustice.

It has been twenty-five years since I began this personal journey to uncover, make meaning of, and heal from a trauma that occurred before I was born. The intergenerational transmission of trauma has been the subject of great controversy. How does one tie symptoms of emotional distress to events that occurred in a previous generation? What behaviors and messages were passed on to me, consciously or unconsciously, that I have internalized yet cannot make sense of from within my own life experience? Is there more than just my own direct experience with racism that could explain my reactivity to shame, exclusion, and "othering"?

In my quest, I have turned many times to the work of Dr. Judith Herman, whose writing and research have informed and inspired my own work on the impact of collective historical trauma. It hasn't been easy to write this book about my family's incarceration experience during World War II. Dr. Herman's words in her 1997 book *Trauma and Recovery* have helped me to stay committed to the task at hand: "Remembering and telling the truth about terrible events are prerequisites both for the restoration of the social order and for the healing of individual victims." If healing from trauma, as Herman posits, can be achieved by "remembering and telling the truth about terrible events," this story is about my search for personal healing. If it also helps to make possible a "restoration of the social order," a community claiming its own narrative, then it is at the very least a necessary endeavor.

I spent most of my career as a psychotherapist applying the traditional "micro" approach of individual therapy. More recently, in the past ten years, I have—out of frustration over seeing the constant and massive impact of chronic states of trauma inflicted by personal and systemic racism—shifted to a more "macro" approach to intervention, joining other social justice therapists whose "clinical interventions" have shifted to "community interventions." No longer able to ignore the societal context in which many of my clients, particularly clients of color, suffer common psychological symptoms of distress, I have found it essential to examine and bring into the therapy exchange the systems in which the trauma has been perpetrated. This expanded perspective has led me from my comfortable private-practice office to prisons where Central American women and children have been indefinitely incarcerated, to churches where years of clergy sexual abuse was suppressed, and to pilgrimages where Japanese American survivors of World War II American concentration camps gather for healing.

The forced removal and incarceration of thousands of people of Japanese ancestry during World War II was an aggressive act of oppression legitimized as military necessity. History has shown that there was, in fact, no basis for claiming that people of Japanese heritage living on the West Coast were a risk to national security. Economic and political motives, as well as racist rhetoric inciting hate, were the strategies implemented by a leadership that took the country off course from its professed democratic principles.

Oppression by mass incarceration of an entire community first required the dehumanizing of the targeted people with propaganda that fostered feelings of threat to the dominant society. West Coast Japanese immigrant farmers and fishermen, using traditional methods of their trades along with the diligence and hard work characteristic of immigrants, were seen to pose a threat to the established white agricultural and fishing industries in the Central Valley and coastal waters. Powerful segments of US social, political, and economic sectors pressed for their removal. The "othering" of Japanese Americans as unassimilable, disloyal, potential spies and saboteurs made it justifiable to the majority of the American public to have people of Japanese ancestry disappeared from their homes, farms, and classrooms.

Victims of oppression suffer long-term psychological consequences resulting from deprivation, loss of agency, and humiliation that endure for decades, even generations, after the trauma was first inflicted. Almost eighty years after the government released Japanese Americans from up to six years of confinement with only $25 and a one-way ticket, survivors and their descendants are still unwinding the distorted narrative that was used to justify their imprisonment. In my own journey, I have found that uncovering and reconstructing the true narrative, remembering and claiming our family stories, are necessary for our personal and family healing and for the healing of our community.

Community-focused programs can empower victims to discover their own history, culture, and language, and to organize and educate their communities by sharing their stories. Through their art, writing, speaking, and performing, victims become dissidents actively resisting and ultimately replacing the shame and silencing of the perpetrator's narrative with the clarity of purpose to write their own.

When I first began writing and editing this book, I thought it would be enough to tell the story of my family's experience during our World War II incarceration by publishing a collection of "primary resources"—letters, diaries, photographs, and poetry that, for the most part, came to light after both of my parents had passed away. But after years of delving into the details of the contextual history and wrestling with my own emotions in the process, I was forced by the gentle but insistent prodding from my editors to see the importance of including my own voice in this story. Attempting to avoid my presence in this book was a symptom of my own trauma, a kind of intellectual dissociation, a self-imposed silencing. Learning to break that silence has not been an easy transition.

Only after years of working on this project did I fully realize that telling this story, in all its truth and life, would require not just facts and documents but, more important, a deep empathy for my parents. My avoidance after all these years was a cover for the unconscious fear that the pain of their experience would be more than I could bear.

It took years after my parents passed away before I was ready to find somebody to help me unlock the story that lay silenced in the box in my closet. Although I had used some of the letters and diary entries in my research for *From a Silk Cocoon*, most of the material still remained untranslated. But having decided to move forward, I still had to wait several more years before I would cross paths with the perfect translator, someone I could trust to walk with me through this emotionally uncertain terrain. Iko Miyazaki, a graduate student in the Marriage and Family Counseling program where I was teaching at California State University, Sacramento, was from Kyoto, Japan. Having lived and studied in the US for several years, she had a strong background in psychology, exceptional bilingual skills, and a unique sensitivity to and understanding of Japanese culture and history. She was gentle, kind, and caring, conscious of how vulnerable the project made me feel.

It seemed to me almost magical as she carefully unfolded each letter and began simultaneously reading the letters in Japanese and translating each of my parents' words into English, slowly revealing what had seemed to me unknowable parts of my parents' lives. Iko went beyond direct word-for-word translation, articulating the nuanced tone and unspoken meanings deeply buried in the Japanese language.

While she translated my parents' words from Japanese, I contextualized the history, the personal characteristics of my parents, and the circumstances in which the letters were embedded. Together, over the course of two years, we cotranslated more than 180 letters and diary entries that spanned the war years of 1941 to 1946.

I had initially approached the task at hand with my skill for fending off emotions and getting the job done. My goal was simply to remove the language barrier that kept me from knowing my parents' story. Just a few days into our work, however, I would learn there was so much more waiting to be known.

As I busily typed the words she translated into English, Iko suddenly stopped speaking and grew quiet. I glanced over to see tears streaming down her face. She had been deeply moved by my mother's account of the day of her removal. My response shocked both of us, as a flash of intense anger rushed through me. I leaned over to her, and with the urgency of thwarting danger, I raised my voice, echoing my father's childhood directive to me: "Be strong. Don't cry!"

Iko's tears were my tears. In that uncanny moment of my outburst, a switch was tripped. As if I were roused from a dream, the sadness and longing, feelings I had deeply buried from awareness for most of my life, rose painfully to the surface. Ungrounded and flustered, we returned to translating a letter my father wrote while imprisoned miles away from his wife and children. "As I am writing to you," it read, "a single autumn leaf has floated down by my window." Iko and I both spontaneously turned to see a single red maple leaf floating slowly past the window of my office. In that moment, we could not hold back the tears.

From that moment forward, as we worked together, we freely cried and laughed and raged. I had entered my mother and father's world, but more important, I had allowed them into mine. Through this long and often arduous process, Iko became my compassionate witness, a dear friend and fellow traveler who stood with me to look back at the trauma that previously had no words. Empathic and without judgment, she would come to know me in ways no others would.

It was often a tedious yet lively triangular exchange between my parents, Iko, and me. Two specific strategies became essential. Iko was able to expertly translate Japanese into standard English, but I had to adjust the translation within the context of the setting. For example, what might be translated in standard English as *dining hall* was more accurately described as *mess hall*, or *bathroom* as *latrine*. A second strategy was to clarify the emotional tone of a message. On occasion, the Japanese-to-English translation sounded flat when in fact, the situation being addressed was quite intense and stressful. Iko and I had to negotiate the level of intensity intended in segments of the letters and diaries and poems—is he angry here or just solemn? Is she panicked or just calmly making a request? We found that our cultural orientation influenced how we perceived the writings. Iko, my parents, and the Japanese language tended to be more emotionally restrained, while my more westernized psychologist's perspective led me to question the flatness of the emotions conveyed in Iko's choice of English words. After rigorous discussion, we'd always confirm that what we settled on stayed consistent with what was expressed in Japanese.

Throughout the process, we often had to take time to research or find experts in Japan who could make meaning of some of the archaic kanji characters, or figure out the katakana (phonetic characters used specifically for non-Japanese words). In one letter written during a particularly harrowing period of time, my mother uses katakana to ask my dad whether he needs a *rokuki*. Only by taking time to study the context and circumstance were we able to figure out that she was asking about a "lock and key." The knife cuts of the censors slicing through the letters made communication between my parents unpredictable and sometimes incomprehensible. Over time they developed secret code words to get around the restrictions, which often left Iko and me befuddled.

My parents had to rely on language and labels imposed by the authorities, terminology that distorted the reality of what they were describing. In their letters and diary entries, they referred to their forced arrest and removal as "evacuation," their unlawful deportation as American citizens "repatriation." Although it was painful to witness the manipulation of language used to minimize the travesty of their incarceration, we stayed true to the terminology my parents used.

If what Dr. Herman states is true—"You cannot understand the victim until you understand the perpetrator, and to understand the perpetrator you have to understand the political and intellectual climate of the time"—then writing this book is just the beginning of the work that lies ahead for me, and facing our collective history is just the beginning for my community and my country.

I grew up knowing very little about my parents' World War II experience. Like others who had resisted and protested the injustice, they had been shamed into silence. Over their four years of captivity, my parents lived under assigned labels that created boundaries and definitions of who they were, what they did, and how they would be treated. By birthright they were American citizens, but the war would justify their removal as "non-aliens"; their demand for civil rights would render them "disloyals"; they would respond with despair as "renunciants"; and ultimately they would be designated "enemy aliens" subject to deportation.

The dominant narrative that shaped my limited understanding was promoted by the perpetrator of the injustice, our American government. It was a narrative that was, at the time, perpetuated by leaders of the Japanese American Citizens League and community

leaders whose intent was to curry favor with the authorities by accommodating their demands and urging Japanese Americans to
prove their loyalty by abiding by government restrictions and regulations rather than challenging the unlawful mass incarceration.
Simple dualities of loyal or disloyal, good guys or bad guys have led
to fractures in our community that remain today. It is my intent
to recount my family story, absent the euphemistic language and
self-serving lens imposed by government authorities to distort and
disguise the truth. My hope is that through my parents' first-person
accounts of their World War II incarceration, readers will experience not only the reality but also the humanity of the many whose
voices have been silenced.

As a psychotherapist specializing in the treatment of trauma,
I had to write this book with an analytic eye toward not just my parents' perspective, decisions, and actions but my own as well. The
intergenerational transmission of trauma has been a lived experience for me. Writing, researching, and attending to my parents'
written words and my memories of growing up with them has been
a journey of healing for me. Their strength and determination to
survive a major trauma that didn't end after their unjust incarceration have also served to inform my work with the intergenerational
trauma that has permeated the lives of many families, Japanese
American and otherwise.

I hope that this story, one of 125,284 stories, will give dignity to
all those who found ways to protest and resist the dehumanizing
trauma and staggering injustice of the World War II mass incarceration of Japanese Americans. Perhaps it can inform and, more
important, inspire those who are protesting cruel and unjust incarceration today.

I.

American Citizens

It was the end of March 2000. My mother's favorite wisteria blossoms were beginning to show off their radiant purple hues. Her eulogy had just been given, recounting how she met my father when she came to the US to represent Japan's silk industry at the 1939 World's Fair. The Buddhist minister, with his black robes and shiny, balding head, leaned forward to my brothers and me and whispered, "So, if it were not for the silk cocoon, you wouldn't be sitting here today."

I realized in that moment how little I really knew about either of my parents' lives before their children became the center of their universe. I knew of the major events that brought them to San Francisco, but not the fine-grain moments and emotions that likely spilled over into the person I had become.

As I tried to remember the stories my parents shared with me about their childhoods, I found I could only recall them in short wisps of memory—ephemeral yet incandescent. Their stories were not stored in my brain as a linear, detailed narrative, but more as emotional glimpses held like vibrant butterflies caught in a net. When I sat down to write about their lives as children, I could only

describe what felt like precious memories of their memories flut-
tering out in poetic rhythm, each with a life of its own.

In her tiny apartment, my mother surrounded herself with stacks
and stacks of boxes like protective armor against forgetting. After
my father died, she moved from their rented flat in San Francisco
into a nearby unit upstairs from my brother's veterinary hospital.
After she passed away, my brothers and I slowly cleared out her
treasures from the past, coming across small mementos and early
photographs. With each item we unpacked, we also unearthed
long-forgotten stories, memories my mother had shared with us
when we were growing up. In the rare moments when she spoke of
her early years, a veil of sadness would move across her eyes as she
recounted the painful losses and the life of poverty she endured
throughout her childhood.

My mother, Shizuko Mitsui, was born on February 5, 1917, in
Seattle, Washington. Her parents, Minoru and Aiko Mitsui, were
immigrants from Nagano prefecture, Japan. My grandfather Minoru worked as a section laborer for the Great Northern Railway
along with other issei[1] men hired to do the grueling and treacherous work of repairing tracks and rescuing trains stuck in the snow
in the high mountains of the Northwest. Short and stocky, he was
strengthened from the hard physical labor. By the time I met him,
he must have been in his sixties. His face was dark and weathered, his mustache prominent. He had an air of mischievousness,
his broken English often marked with an enthusiastic "Gondang
songa beech!"

When Shizuko was barely three, her mother died giving birth to
a child who also did not survive. Unable to care for Shizuko and
her elder brother, Isamu, Minoru brought his children to his home
village in the Nagano prefecture of Japan, leaving them behind

---

1. *Issei* is the Japanese word for "first-generation" and refers to immigrants from
Japan to the US. Nisei are their second-generation, American-born children.
Sometimes, those born in the US were sent to Japan to be raised by relatives or to
attend school, in some cases due to poverty, illness, or family circumstance. They
were called kibei, usually kibei nisei.

to be raised by their maternal grandmother, Kisa Nakayama. His plan was to return to work in the US and send money to support the family living in impoverished circumstances. My mother would sometimes refer to herself as a "motherless child," describing the confusion and longing of a child too young to understand the incomprehensible changes in her world.

As she recounted these early childhood days, she would close her eyes and tilt her head, as if listening for the mass of silkworms feeding on mulberry leaves. In the rural villages in northern Japan, many rice farmers supplemented their income by raising silkworms to be sold to large silk-producing companies. Nostalgically, my mother would re-create the sound that must have been so familiar to her, an elongated, "Shaaaaaa . . ." ("like heavy rain shower"). These silkworm caterpillars, plumped up from their voracious

Minoru Mitsui with Isamu and Shizuko.
Photo taken prior to their departure for
Japan, circa 1920.

feeding frenzy, would then spin their cocoons of precious thread to
be woven into Japanese silk fabric, entwining my mother's destiny
with the aching sense of loss that would come and go throughout
her life.

> The old woman
> grieves for her daughter.
> The small child
> searches for her mother.
> Tiny fingers point to the light
> glowing in the next village.
> "Over there! Over there!
> *Okaachan,* Mommy!
> Must be over there!
> Inconsolable,
> the old woman
> offers the child
> her withered breast,
> and they fall asleep
> to the gentle rain song
> of silkworms feeding
> on mulberry leaves.

Shizuko's father steadfastly sent money every month from America, but unbeknownst to Shizuko, her grandfather Nakayama's
gambling debts left Kisa struggling to feed and care for the two
children. Although poverty was the backdrop, unstinting love was
the foreground for Shizuko and Isamu, as their grandmother Kisa
managed to find ways to keep the children fed.

> Rising early and quietly
> as the dew weighs heavily
> on grasshopper wings,
> two children armed
> with coarsely hewn
> chopsticks,
> swiftly snatch them

from green rice stalks
and drop them
into small cloth sacks.
Grandmother waits
with hot frying pan.
Grasshopper *tsukudani* over rice
for the hungry boy and girl.

Shizuko's elder brother was her protector, and the only constant presence in her young life. When he grew ill and died of pneumonia at the age of fourteen, she was left once again with an aching loneliness that would come and go throughout her life. She had told me about him at one point, but I hadn't paid much attention at the time. I didn't even remember his name, but I did remember her telling me that his love for her was always the well from which she drew the strength to endure whatever life brought. Upon discovering a photo of Isamu, I remembered this story:

I watched from a distance
as grandfather
cut the wood
to make the box.
There wasn't room
for him to lie down
so my brother was buried
with his knees
folded to his chest.
Namu Amida Butsu
Namu Amida Butsu
Namu Amida Butsu,
dearly beloved Isamu.

When Shizuko's father finally sent for her in 1930, ten years had already passed since her arrival in Japan. Suffering yet another heart-wrenching separation, she promised to return as she said goodbye to her beloved grandmother. Shizuko returned to join her father, his new family, and an unwelcoming stepmother, who was her mother's sister. She struggled to fit in with her "all-American" half-siblings and white classmates in the small railroad town near Spokane, Washington.

> I was thirteen years old
> in the first grade.
> Couldn't speak English.
> Too big to fit
> in first grade chairs.
> They called me
> "To-ki-o."
> I don't know why
> they called me that,
> I'd never been there.

The stories my mother shared with me were scattered over time as I was growing up. Only later in her life did she talk about her father "drinking too much." She told me that when she returned from Japan at thirteen, living with her father's new family, she felt like an interloper and a threat to her stepmother. My mother made excuses for her father's alcoholism, describing him as a happy drunk who had to escape the tormenting dangers of his job. Feeling the sting of being her mother's child in a family she only half knew, she completed her primary education, and as soon as she could, she moved out, leaving for Seattle to work as a "schoolgirl" (essentially, a high school student serving as a live-in maid) for a wealthy Caucasian family.

> My father married
> my mother's sister.
> They were strangers to me.
> Fermented rice drink,
> hidden from sight,
> swollen with alcoholic breath,
> he clapped his hands and sang,
> calling out
> my dead mother's name.

Stepmother,
worn broom in hand
chased him around
the wobbly green Formica table
as his singing grew
louder and louder.

In 1937, Shizuko graduated at the age of twenty from Garfield High in Seattle, and kept her promise to return to the rural village of her childhood in Nagano-ken to care for her ailing grandmother. Here, I imagine the joyful reunion of grandmother and granddaughter. Although my mother had left as a school-age child and returned a somewhat "Americanized" young woman, their attachment was unwavering. She recounted the reunion and the conversations that followed as they reflected on their earlier life together. Understanding the many transitions my mother went through from early childhood to adulthood has helped me to better understand the deeply embedded fear of abandonment that would continue to threaten her well-being even after she became a mother.

Obaachan! Obaachan!
Grandmother! Grandmother!
Shi-chan! Shi-chan!
Little quiet one.
Are you Japanese?
Are you American?
I don't know,
but I am home
safe with you.

* * *

Remember, *Obaachan*
how you would scold me
and cry with me?
I was afraid
when I couldn't find you.

I would run *dochi-kochi,*
this way and that way
to different houses
in the village.
Holding my breath,
I wet my finger
on my tongue,
rubbing tiny holes
in the rice paper screen
so I could see
your face.

Two years after Shizuko returned to her grandmother's village, the Japanese government launched a national search for two young women to represent Japan's burgeoning silk industry at the San Francisco Golden Gate International Exposition, known as the 1939 World's Fair, on Treasure Island. The "Silk Girls" would demonstrate the reeling of silk thread from the silkworm cocoon while wearing both western dresses and traditional Japanese kimono made of the finest silk. There was a great deal of national publicity for the ramp-up to Japan's entry into the International Exposition, and the selected Silk Girls would represent the beauty and craft of Japan's silk industry.

It was Shizuko's grandmother who urged her to apply for the job. Without legal permanent status in Japan, Shizuko knew she had to return to the US at some point and needed to seek employment to support herself. If selected, she would be well paid and have guaranteed employment for two years. Her travel expenses would be covered, and she would have the adventure of a lifetime. It was the perfect job for my American-born mother, since the silk companies sponsoring the exhibition in San Francisco were anxious to open new markets in the US and impress the world with the elegance of Japanese culture and its fine silk products.

Through all the losses she experienced as a child and the challenge of adjusting to American life as a teenager, she had developed a level of confidence unusual for a young Japanese woman. Shizuko traveled to Tokyo for many interviews and meetings. When I asked her why she thought she was chosen among the ten thousand applicants, she demurred regarding her beauty, and instead was sure she was hired because she was bilingual and familiar with life in America. They needed an English speaker to explain to visitors to the Japan Pavilion the process for making silk thread from the silkworm cocoon.

When I visited my mother's home village in Nagano-ken many years later, I met an elderly farmer who remembered the excitement of Shizuko's unexpected celebrity.

> The old farmer spoke in words
> I could barely grasp.
> His back bowed
> like the scythe
> he carried in his
> leathered hand.
> "Shi-chan, Shi-chan,
> your mother,
> she was beautiful.
> We all gathered 'round
> the one radio in the village.
> She said she would
> do her best
> to bring honor to Japan
> and the Japanese people."
> Tears edged his weathered eyes.
> "We were so proud."

Neatly folded inside my mother's "Treasure Island" photo album were several news clippings from both Japanese and Japanese American newspapers. I imagine my somewhat shy, unassuming mother blushing as she came upon this depiction of herself, since she had, until that time, seen herself merely as a lonely misfit American from Japan: "The Silk Girls became the focus of the visitors' attention. Their appearance with kimono and their graceful manner greatly attracted the young nisei men's hearts. And since they received many letters of proposals of marriage, they were more overwhelmed with this than with their work."

Young kibei bachelors like my father anxiously awaited the opening of the Japan Pavilion at the World's Fair. With his Rolleiflex camera in hand, he intended to get a snapshot of the beautiful Silk Girls arriving from Japan. I wonder if he ever dreamed that he would actually meet one of the "living flowers" brought from Japan wearing the finest of silk kimono.

My father, Itaru Ina, was born in San Francisco on June 10, 1914. His father, Takizō, was the second of three sons born in Wakamiya Village, Yamanashi-ken, Japan. The eldest would inherit the land, leaving the two younger brothers to strike out on their own. Trusting their fate to the toss of a coin, one would go to South America,

Riu Kirino and Shizuko en route to the Golden Gate
International Exposition, San Francisco, 1940

the other to North America. My great-uncle set out for Peru, while my grandfather headed to California.

Takizō found work in San Francisco at the local Japanese American newspaper in Japantown. He eventually decided to stay and make San Francisco his home, but anti-miscegenation laws barred him from marrying outside his race. So, like other issei men, Takizō arranged for his family in Japan to select a bride for him from his home village. Photographs were exchanged between potential mates, and marriage by proxy took place. In time, Itaru's mother, Tokue Iyama, a *shashin hanayome* (picture bride), traveled with other young women to a foreign country to make her home with a husband she had never met.

Foreshadowing the antipathy that was to come, the waiting husbands brought their brides from the ship directly to shops where the women exchanged their Japanese kimono for western-style clothing and shoes to avoid appearing "too foreign" to white neighbors and landlords. And perhaps as assurance against the instability of life as second-class citizens, many Japanese immigrants officially entered their American-born children's names into their village registry in Japan, believing that dual citizenship would provide them an option should that be necessary at some point in their lives.

Ten years after my father died, regretful that I had never asked him about his life growing up in Japan, I finally visited his sister, my auntie Kiyoji Ōkubo, in Kawasaki, Japan. It was Auntie Kiyoji's illness as a child that took her and my father to Japan. Like Itaru, she was born in San Francisco, an American citizen, but she never returned to the US. How strange it was for me to listen to her stories while noticing the crease in her smile, the tilt of her head, as her face seemed to blur into my memory of my father's face and then return to her own again. Sadly, she said her memories of her elder brother were mostly tied to moments of loss. When she became ill, her parents decided that Tokue and the children should go back to Japan to be cared for and supported by Tokue's family. Tokue never mentioned to her husband that she was pregnant with a third child until after they arrived at their destination.

Separated from his wife and children for thirteen years, Takizō

Father Takizō, mother Tokue, and Itaru,
San Francisco, California, 1914

continued working in San Francisco and sent money to his family
in Japan. Young Itaru would receive a Japanese education in an era
of growing modernization and nationalism. Military service and
respect for the "divine emperor" were essential dictates shaping his
formative years. When Itaru turned sixteen, his parents feared that
their bookish and solitary son would be conscripted into Japanese
military service. His father sent for him. His parents believed he
would receive the benefits and protection of his American citizenship by returning to his country of birth.

As Auntie Kiyoji talked about being separated from her elder
brother, tears filled her tired eyes and settled into the creases lining
her cheeks. She and her mother remained in Japan as militarism
increasingly took hold of the country. She shared these stories:

Peeling off his schoolboy uniform,
he would take his dog
to swim in the ocean.
When he left for America
where father waited for him,
his dog swam out alone
and never came back.

* * *

After my brother
returned to America,
I found another dog.
One day,
he didn't come home.
They had come to the village,
gathering up all the dogs.
Food and clothing
for war-weary soldiers.

Two years after Itaru arrived in San Francisco, his father fell ill and decided it would be best to return to Japan. With the continued threat of mandatory conscription, Takizō made the difficult decision to leave Itaru behind in the care of family friends, a childless watchmaker and his wife, who would become Itaru's surrogate parents. Itaru referred to them as Oji-san and Oba-san, Uncle and Auntie. Watchmaker Oji-san, a quiet and cultured man, mentored and encouraged his young ward's passion for traditional Japanese arts and music, accepting him as a son. He taught my father to play the *shakuhachi* (a bamboo flute) and urged him to continue writing the poetry that seemed to emerge from him without effort. Oba-san, a chatty and somewhat overbearing mother-substitute, required Itaru to help her every day after school to develop film in the small darkroom at the back of the watch repair shop. It was here my father would fall in love with the art of photography. Among his lifelong treasured belongings was his Rolleiflex camera.

Itaru attended high school in San Francisco and later found

work as a bookkeeper at the Nonaka Trading and Import Company. Separated from his parents and younger sister, he found solace from his loneliness in playing his shakuhachi, writing haiku poetry, and performing in Japanese theater productions. He pursued his passion for writing haiku and spent a lifetime engaged in studying and teaching this form of traditional poetry. He would earn a great honor as one of the first Japanese Americans to have his poetry published in the prestigious Japanese national haiku journal. When he died, a special issue was dedicated to his work.

It was only when the volumes of my father's poetry were translated into English that I was able to confirm what always resonated in my heart. He had a rich internal life, filled with tender emotions, reverence for nature, and an uncanny intuition about others, but it was a very private life, not one he shared in words with me and my brothers or even my mother. Without a doubt, I felt his love and concern for us, yet my most vivid memories of him are from a distance—studying his books, writing his poetry, working in the basement—always quiet, stoic, and occasionally stern.

Itaru Ina, Buddhist Church of San Francisco Kabuki theater performance, circa 1938

Itaru Ina with Rolleiflex camera, Treasure Island, 1939

I pressed Auntie Kiyoji as she meandered through various life events, until finally I asked with some desperation, "But what was my father like as a boy?" She answered in much the same way I would have answered if someone had asked me what he was like as a father.

> Your father, my brother,
> *Kigamuzukashii*,
> he was difficult to know.
> Our baby sister died
> when she was seven.
> He never said a word.
> Often deep in thought,
> remote and silent.
> I wondered what sufferings
> he kept to himself.
> He wrote his haiku
> as a lover whispers truths
> behind closed doors.

The night after my aunt shared these stories with me, a long-forgotten memory surfaced. I was eleven or twelve years old. Embarrassingly flat-chested compared to my white classmates, I had stuffed cotton balls inside my newly purchased training bra. When I got off the bus after school, I discovered that the cotton balls had fallen out and were stuck to the outside edge of my sweater. Although no one had said anything, I was painfully embarrassed thinking that other kids had noticed and were secretly laughing at me. I ran to my room, threw myself on the bed, and couldn't stop crying. My mother wasn't home, so my father came into the room, looking alarmed, and asked what was wrong. I burst out sobbing, and as he stood over me, I told him what happened. My father seemed to freeze, though I'm sure there were tears in his eyes. He gently patted me on the back, and without a word, turned and left the room, closing the door behind him. I didn't know whether my tears had disgusted, disappointed, or frightened him. All I felt was the oceanic distance between us as the door clicked shut. I buried my face in the pillow, sobbing silently, the fallen cotton balls no longer of consequence. My father's apparent emotional absence often left me with an aching longing I never quite understood, but it served as the driving force to continue my search to learn more about my family story.

Once his father left for Japan, Itaru would never see his parents again. He never spoke of his childhood days in Japan or his life as a de facto orphan in San Francisco. It was only when I heard the deep, melodic sound of his shakuhachi, always played behind closed doors, that I sensed the aching of his heart as it filled the house, and my soul.

Vagaries of life would define both my parents' lives and their identity as kibei nisei. Second-generation American citizens by birthright, they were sent to Japan as children, separated from their families due to poverty and family tragedy; eventually they returned to America. This life trajectory would later be used by the US government, at war with Japan, as a way to quantify their loyalty to America.

The triumphant completion of the San Francisco Bay Bridge and the magnificent Golden Gate Bridge spotlighted the grand opening of the Golden Gate International Exposition in 1939. Trumpeting hope and possibility as America rose out of the Great Depression, the event was staged on the engineering miracle of Treasure Island, constructed in the middle of the San Francisco Bay. The theme, "Pageant of the Pacific," highlighted the goods of nations bordering the Pacific. Embodying this theme were the brilliantly lit Tower of the Sun, the central tower of the exposition ground, rising 392 feet, and an 80-foot statue of Pacifica, goddess of the Pacific Ocean.

The two-year celebration would bring thousands of people willing to stand in line for hours to partake of the exciting exhibits and entertainment representing the participating countries. Among the most popular attractions was the elegant Japan Pavilion, built by classically trained Japanese carpenters and craftsmen, where the Silk Girls, Shizuko Mitsui and Riu Kirino, would demonstrate the reeling of silk thread.

Silk clothing, particularly silk stockings, were in great demand in the US at the time. A Japanese newspaper clipping, carefully saved in my mother's photo album, captured the importance of Japan's participation in this grand event, highlighting US-Japan cooperation and economic trade. The Silk Girls, informal ambassadors to the US, are quoted as saying, "We will do our best to contribute even a little to the Japan-America friendship as well as to help people become more knowledgeable about silk."

Shizuko's wristwatch needed repair, so her chaperone brought her to the watchmaker in Japantown. When she returned to pick up her watch, the watchmaker and his wife kindly invited her to be their guest for dinner. It was at this simple meal in the crowded back room of the watchmaker's storefront that Shizuko and Itaru would meet.

In gathering information for this book, I had the opportunity to interview one of my father's cohort, Tomoye Takahashi, who remembered my father well. She participated with him in the Buddhist church Kabuki theatrical programs. She said, "He was handsome, and one of the most eligible kibei bachelors in our group, so all the girls were heartbroken to hear that he was engaged to a nisei girl from Japan."

The World's Fair ended in 1940. The storybook meeting of the Silk Girl and the poet brought together two young people whose lives had been torn by childhood loss and separation across the Pacific Ocean. As I turned to the task of weaving my parents' writings into our family story, I reflected on the mystery of how synchronicity and silk brought them together, and the words spoken by the Buddhist priest at my mother's funeral service.

> Her tiny watch
> needing repair,
> the chaperone escorts
> the Silk Girl
> to Japantown.
> Watchmaker,

Matchmaker,
Shakuhachi Sensei,
Bamboo flute teacher,
did you know
they would fall in love
to the ticking of the clocks
on every wall?

"Love" was a word rarely spoken in our home, so discovering let-ters filled with romantic optimism and youthful innocence tucked inside my father's stamp and matchbook collections came as a sweet surprise. When my father passed away in 1977, my young nephew inherited these collections. Years later, when he heard I was working on a book about my parents' story, he sent me a small package with a note inquiring whether the letters inside might be of some help. Inside each envelope, addressed in English, were letters exchanged between my parents from the fall of 1940 to early 1941. The letters inside were almost entirely written in Japanese.

By this point, Iko and I had already completed the translation of the prison camp letters, and I felt a familiar ambivalence, a mix of curiosity and anxiety, about what lay within these letters that neither my nephew nor I could decipher. As soon as I received these new-found letters, Iko began working her magic once again, revealing preciously intimate expressions of love between my mother and fa-ther during their courtship and engagement.

Unlike the letters exchanged during their World War II incarcer-ation when censors were privy to their every word, these prewar love letters had been written in free-flowing and expressive Japa-nese. (To distinguish between letters or words written in English or Japanese, I have used italics for what was originally written in Japanese and required translation.)

During my lifetime, my parents were never openly affectionate with each other, nor were they with me or my brothers, Kiyoshi and Michael. Although we never doubted we were loved, I often longed for the parents we saw on television programs like *Leave It to Bea-ver*, in which Beaver Cleaver's mom and dad hugged and kissed, declaring their love for each other multiple times a day. To me, my parents seemed more like business partners, each with their distinct role in the family. Their shared mission was to work hard, meet responsibilities, and do whatever was necessary to make sure we kids had what we needed to be successful in the world. To discover that there was any semblance of romance in their life together was both startling and heartwarming.

In addition to revealing the details of my family's beginnings, these very personal letters also incidentally chronicled the historic events taking place on the world stage. At the beginning of their correspondence, the brutal reality of conflict and combat in both the European and Pacific theaters at the time seem only to trim the edges of Shizuko's and Itaru's awareness as they excitedly made plans for their future.

My parents were formally engaged on October 9, 1940, one year after they met. Shizuko was scheduled to sail to Japan to bring closure to her work and spend precious time with her beloved grandmother. Before her departure, Itaru escorted Shizuko by train from San Francisco to Klamath Falls, Oregon. From there, she traveled on alone to see her parents in Seattle before boarding the ship. As they said their final goodbyes at Klamath Falls, the two young lovers promised never to part again.

In Japan, Shizuko busily tended to family and job obligations, reluctantly anticipating what was likely to be her final farewell to her grandmother Kisa. Itaru waited anxiously, if not impatiently, for her return.

October 17, 1940
My dearly beloved Shizuko-sama,[2]
Yesterday on the night of the 16th, I received your picture postcard from Portland. *I felt sorry for you, a single woman traveling on the train alone. It must have been very lonely. I too felt an indescribable loneliness.*

2. My parents regularly switched between English and Japanese in their letters and diary entries. Where their language is translated from the Japanese, the translated portions are in italics. Where my parents used English, I have preserved their wording and spelling. Some of the letters and diary entries have been edited for length and clarity.

Yesterday the registration for US military draft took place. Next time when you return to America, I may be a soldier. I don't think we have to worry, but in any event, I've prepared myself for the worst, so I ask that you be prepared as well. Please say you won't marry another man. I'm joking so please don't be angry. Please, please, are you still mad? I apologize.

These days, nisei men as well as women have been denied passports, and are prohibited from traveling to Japan for the time being. Please follow the necessary procedures so that you can return to America without any problems. Every day I pray you finish your work successfully and come back to me. Watchmaker Oba-san and I talk about you every night while I help her in the photo darkroom. I put your picture in a frame, and every day I am looking at you.

While you are on the ship, take care of yourself and stay well. You are not alone any longer now that someone is caring about your safety every day. As long as the sun exists, my heart will never change, so do not worry. Please hurry and come back soon.

Bon Voyage!

Itaru

October 18, 1940
Itaru-sama,

I was so relieved to receive your letters and telegram and was able to leave Seattle in good spirits. But I can't fully express the pain of leaving you behind. I will come back to you as soon as possible.

I suppose that you have registered for the draft on the 15th. No matter what happens I will wait for you forever until my death. Even if you stop loving me, I will be waiting for you no matter what. Please do not forget this.

When I arrived in Seattle and told my parents all about you, they were very happy. No matter how I think about it, I can't help feeling that I don't deserve to be so happy. In this moment, I imagine that you are speaking softly with Oba-san in that familiar dark room, processing film. She is truly a gentle oba-san.

The sound of the waves is getting quite loud and the ship is starting to sway.

Please take good care of yourself. I will return to you soon.

Lovingly yours,

Shizuko from the Hie-maru ship

October 24, 1940

Missing you, Shizuko-sama,

Today started with unusually heavy rainfall at dawn. When you return, will you come pick me up sometime with your red umbrella? When I imagine such things, I feel very happy.

You haven't arrived in Japan yet, and I'm already looking forward to seeing you back here. But don't worry, I'll wait patiently.

We won't know when you'll be able to return to Japan again, so please spend New Year's Day with your grandmother and make her happy. Your grandmother is old and once you say goodbye to her, you may not be able to see her again. Since I never had a chance to see my parents before they died, I don't want you to suffer such lonely feelings. We can never fully return our obligation to our parents who raised us. It's getting cold, so take care of yourself and please convey my feelings of parental respect [oyakōkō] to Grandmother Kisa.

Itaru

October 30, 1940

Itaru-sama,

I was seasick, lying down, feeling very discouraged when I received your telegram. I was so happy that I burst into tears. My heart is full, wanting to be with you and take care of you. Always your picture tenderly comforts me.

After the ship left Vancouver, the ocean became very rough and continued that way for ten days. I was in bed almost the entire time. I've crossed the Pacific Ocean many times, but this is the first time it was so rough. All the tables and chairs were upside down. Many times I felt helpless, afraid I was going to die from terrible seasickness with so much in my heart unfinished for us. At

last, in two days Japan will be in sight, arriving in Yokohama port
on November 2nd.

Please take care of yourself. Missing you, Itaru-sama.
Shizuko

November 6, 1940
Itaru-sama,

Fortunately I arrived in Yokohama safely on the morning of
November 2nd, so please do not worry. I went to the American em-
bassy the other day to see about my passport. They said it would
be safer for me to leave for America as soon as possible, so hastily,
I scheduled to board the Heian Maru on December 6th. The ship
will arrive in Seattle on December 18th. I'm very happy because
now I will be able to return much sooner than I expected. Please
take very good care of yourself. I will write to you soon.

Lovingly yours, *Shizuko*

November 11, 1940
Shizuko-san!

Today is Armistice Day. There are wars going on in Europe
and the Pacific, so it seems strange to celebrate a cease-fire anni-
versary, but I'm happy to have a day off from work.

The other day was the US military draft lottery. It turns out
that I don't have to worry about the draft for the next two years.
So when you return we will be able to marry any time. I have
both happy and anxious feelings.

I had finished teaching Sunday school *at the Buddhist church*
and went to Oba-san's. There I found a notice *saying to come*
and pick up a telegram. Let's see, a telegram sent here must be
either from your boss, Mr. Shirai, or you, so without eating my
lunch, I left immediately for Market Street. On my way, I was
thinking, "There is no reason for Mr. Shirai to send me a tele-
gram." So I thought it must be you. "Shizuko started a mischief
because she is bored with too much time." Thinking like this,
I could not contain my joy. I was bothered by the slowness of the
streetcar, but suddenly I worried that the telegram might be tell-
ing me that you are sick. What would I do? So I was very anxious

*until I had the telegram in my hand. I was so overjoyed when
I read it that I forgot all about my hunger. On my way home
I was thinking to myself, "Such a sweet person." Feeling your
love, I was absorbed with thoughts of your sweetness.*

*Since it's getting colder and colder, please make sure to take
care of yourself. Always, always, I pray that you are in good health.*
Itaru

November 18, 1940—11 p.m. in Nagano City
Itaru-sama,

*I am now in Shinshō with my grandmother. Here, rice harvest-
ing is one of the busiest times in the fall. Every day I am raking
leaves. Right now it is persimmon season. Every village I visit,
I see trees bowed down with the weight of brightly colored persimmons. The feast of autumn—dried persimmons [hoshigaki],
newly harvested rice, sautéed grasshoppers [inago], Japanese
pumpkin [kabocha] soup—all indescribably delicious. I wish
I could share them with you. As soon as I saw my grandmother,
I told her about you and showed her your picture. She cried with
joy. I'm sad that I will have a difficult farewell with her when
I leave this time. I enclose a Buddhist amulet [omamori] for
your protection. Please carry it with you.*
Missing you, Shizuko

Within months of Shizuko's return to the States, a sharply changing landscape in the relationship between the US and Japan was
on the horizon. Japan's "Greater East Asia Co-Prosperity Sphere"
mandate to occupy and control all of Asia was becoming increasingly threatening. On September 27, 1940, Japan's ambassador
in Berlin signed the Tripartite Pact with Nazi Germany and Fas-
cist Italy. The pact promised mutual assistance should any of the
three countries be attacked by a nation not already engaged in the
war—a direct warning to the US against joining forces with the Allies. Two weeks later, President Roosevelt invoked economic sanc-
tions against Japan, banning the export of steel and aviation fuel,
and ordering an embargo on scrap steel, thus placing a strangle-
hold on Japan's advancing forces.

Meanwhile, Shizuko stayed at her parents' home in Spokane, Washington, until arrangements could be made for her to travel to San Francisco. Traditional Japanese custom and propriety, still expected of and honored by many kibei at the time, demanded that the couple not be alone together without a chaperone. Born as Americans yet raised in a culture bound by duty, obligation, and emotional restraint, Itaru and Shizuko were much more traditional than their nisei peers. Yet, rather than entering into a traditional arranged marriage between two strangers, Shizuko and Itaru chose to marry someone they loved. The very westernized expressions of love and affection found in these letters stand in striking contrast to the marital communications of my issei grandparents, who were bound not necessarily by love but by duty and obligation. Shaped by two very different cultures heading toward conflict, my parents would have to navigate their relationship not only with each other but also with the world as the ground shifted beneath them.

My parents both gained English language competence during their high school years in the US, where they spent their adolescence in ambivalent immersion in western culture. Unlike their nisei counterparts, who spoke English fluently and aspired to fit into mainstream America, Itaru and Shizuko held close ties to the traditions and values of Japan. They both experienced criticism and ridicule for speaking English as a second language with distinct speech patterns that immediately identified them as "foreign." With each other, they spoke in Japanese, but with my brothers and me, they spoke in what my mother referred to as their "broken English." It made sense that their letters of love were written in the comfort of their first language.

The decades-long bigotry and discrimination led by nativist politicians, newspapers, and industrialists against "Orientals" immigrating to the United States fueled the fear and animosity of the American public toward those of Japanese ancestry on the West Coast. The passage of California's 1913 Alien Land Law made it impossible for issei immigrants, already denied the right to naturalized citizenship, to own land. By 1924, Japanese immigration was halted altogether.

In response to this ongoing exclusion, ethnic enclaves emerged in different areas of the West Coast. San Francisco's Nihon-machi, or Japantown, like similar neighborhoods in other cities, became the center of life for Japanese immigrants and their American-born children. Here, small businesses, shops, restaurants, and churches, along with traditional Japanese organizations, could thrive while meeting the needs of a community pushed to the margins of social and economic life in America.

Racism's icy reach also led to intraethnic fractures. Kibei were often shunned and rejected by their Americanized nisei counterparts. Struggling to become accepted into mainstream American life, many young nisei were embarrassed to be associated with "FOBs" ("fresh off the boat") who spoke with accents and were unfamiliar with contemporary American culture. Consequently, my parents found comfort and acceptance within the microcosm of the kibei community.

Itaru was a Sunday school teacher at the Buddhist temple, an actor in local community Kabuki theater, a leader in the local haiku poetry club, and a member of the Young Kibei Association. He was also a member of the Heimushakai, an organization in San Francisco composed primarily of men who would have been eligible for induction into the Japanese military if they were living in Japan. Encouraged to support Japanese militarism, issei and kibei men were expected to offer financial and material support to Japanese soldiers fighting in China. In addition to his involvement with the organizations steeped in Japanese culture and society, my father was also a member of the San Francisco chapter of the Japanese American Citizens League, a nisei-led civil rights organization, which at the time had a strong Americanization ethos, working to secure citizenship for issei immigrants who were denied the right to naturalization. Membership in these two organizations, one promoting Japanese identity and the other American, reflects the kibei dilemma of straddling both cultures and identities. Having spent his formative years in Japan, Itaru spoke Japanese as his first language, yet America was his home, the place where since his return at sixteen he had always planned to settle down.

With their wedding set for March, Shizuko left behind the comfort of her grandmother's home in Nagano-ken and her issei parents' bustling life with their young children in rural Washington to join Itaru in the culturally rich and busy life of San Francisco's Japantown.

I've read and reread these letters many times, surprised and saddened to see how my parents' youthful romantic love and longing during their separation evoked such deep emotions of unresolved grief from their own childhood losses, while at the same time offering them the promise of companionship and protection they both longed for.

Jan 2, 1941 Seattle
Dearest Itaru-san,

Happy New Year. Although I have had a quiet joyful New Year with my whole family, I missed you terribly. In the morning, I made *sushi* for the first time in my life. I made them all right but half of them have cracked open. So you see, not much success in my cooking. Up here in snowy Skykomish, it was 20 degrees below zero and it's just freezing. Would you be very busy in the beginning of February? I am thinking about coming to see you by then, if possible. Just want to see your healthy face. I can hardly wait till our wedding day. But I must be patient.

With love, yours Shizuko

January 4, 1941
Shizuko-san,

I helped Oba-san with New Year's cooking. Can you guess what I did? I sliced burdock root [kinpira gobo]. *I was sure I did a better job than Oba-san, but on New Year's day when I told my friends about it, they said no wonder the kinpira was so ugly with thick ones and thin ones. After all, they turned out just like your sushi . . . excuse me. Next New Year's Day we may end up serving our friends thick and thin kinpira and collapsed sushi. This is something I look forward to. Let's make an effort so we can make fine dishes to surprise everyone. I will do my best.*

With love, *Itaru*

January 8, 1941
Shizuko-sama,

I'd like to tell you my honest opinion here. These are just my own thoughts, so please understand that it doesn't mean you have to agree. If at all possible, I would like you to come as soon as you can. You can do whatever you like before the wedding to prepare for married life. You and your parents might be worried that if you come to San Francisco alone, people may question your respectability, but I have consulted with Oba-san and she agreed with my idea. She said she is very willing to take care of you, and will be happy to help you with the wedding preparations.

I'm thinking now that I don't want to be apart for a single day. Even if you must come at a later date, please plan to stay for good. If you come and then leave again, it will be a nightmare for me because I hate to be so lonely after you leave. Please talk to your parents about this and give me an answer. Is it possible for you to bring the snow from Skykomish as a gift for me? Snow tempura would be fine.

Until then, Love, Itaru

January 9, 1941
Itaru-sama,

I received your airmail dated the 8th this morning. Immediately I talked with my parents. They said as long as I stay with Oba-san there will be nothing to criticize, so I could go to San Francisco alone next month. I will arrive in San Francisco on Saturday, February 8th. At last I can see you soon. I'm so happy.

I put the pictures along with our memories from Klamath Falls in the album yesterday. It's interesting how we both look sleepy as if in a trance. For the rest of our life, let's live together with that same feeling of harmony.

This time we will never be apart from each other again. After our marriage, no matter how much you dislike me, I will hold on to you, and never, never let go.

With love, yours Shizuko

January 11, 1941
Shizuko-sama,

Soon you will be here, and I am happy thinking about that. The World's Fair Sun Tower has still not been taken down, so I can see it from my office window. The Sun Tower holds many memories for us. We will never forget the World's Fair because I was able to meet you, and now we are together to share the blessings and the struggles of life. The World's Fair is like the temple of the god of marriage and matchmaking [Izumo Taisha] for us, don't you think? I feel sad seeing the fairgrounds being broken down day by day, yet our love will live forever as a remembrance of the World's Fair. I was reminiscing about the day we said goodbye at Klamath Falls. I made this haiku to remind me of that day, so please do not make fun of it.

imoto sakaru	Saying goodbye to
Klamath no o	my sweetheart at Klamath
kari ikeri	wild geese depart

Love, *Itaru*

It was the spring of 1941. The wedding was a splendid affair—the bride in a flowing silk gown, the groom in a tuxedo with a white rose pinned to his lapel. The ceremony took place in front of the gilded altar of the Buddhist church in San Francisco. There were few family members in attendance, but the hall was filled to capacity with members of the local Japanese American community celebrating the fairytale marriage of the young bachelor poet and the beautiful Silk Girl.

As my brothers and I gathered my mother's belongings after she died, I came across a tiny three-by-five-inch red notebook with "1942" embossed on the cover—a diary. Inside, I found my mother speaking to me in ways she never could when she was alive. I read the entries as if I were the trusted friend in whom she was confiding. Written in both English and Japanese in her neat and delicate hand, her first entry was dedicated to her wedding day. The following daily notations gave me a glimpse into her life as a young newly-

Itaru and Shizuko on their wedding
day, March 30, 1941

wed, away from family, new to the city, starting a new life while at
the same time straddling two cultures.

Comfortably ensconced in the tight-knit Japantown community
with many of Itaru's Japanese-speaking kibei friends and associates, the newly married couple lived a somewhat sheltered life
with like-minded neighbors as they worked to merge their previous
lives into something new. My mother was raised in a humble yet
traditional Japanese household. Early on, her duties as a schoolgirl cleaning house and tending to the needs of a white family,
her experience caring for her aged grandmother, and finally, her
work as a Silk Girl at the World's Fair prepared her well for the
next stage of her life. She grew to be a responsible yet deferential
woman highly attuned to others' needs. My father, also from a traditional Japanese household, was the *chōnan*, the privileged eldest
son. More inclined to be self-indulgent, he continued to pursue
the many passions he cultivated as a young bachelor. Good hu-
mored and sociable, he had many hobbies and friends. My mother
writes about his pastimes studying and writing poetry, rehearsing
for Japanese theatrical performances, hiking, and fishing, while

she immersed herself dutifully in the traditional *hanayome shugyō*, cultural training for the Japanese bride's married life. Japanese embroidery, *koto* (a Japanese stringed musical instrument), flower arrangement, and sewing lessons filled her early married days.

It was through their jobs that Shizuko and Itaru had contact with the outside world. Discriminatory hiring practices limited job opportunities for most Japanese Americans. Itaru was fortunate to have found work as a bookkeeper for the Nonaka Trading and Import Company, an issei-owned import/export firm. Here, Itaru's bilingual ability served as an essential asset for a rapidly growing international trade company. Shizuko seemed to seamlessly shift from enjoying the quasi-celebrity status afforded to her by her role at the World's Fair to working once again as a servant doing "day work," cleaning houses for wealthy Caucasian families in the Pacific Heights area of San Francisco. This was often the only work that kibei and issei in the city could find.

In the joyful flush of new beginnings, my mother's diary entries describe visiting friends, furnishing their apartment, watching "talkies" to improve her English language skills, and attending Japanese community events. This time period was also marked with difficult marital adjustments and the loneliness she had hoped would end when she married. She would soon learn the painful limits of her place in the relationship demanded by the traditional Japanese hierarchy of husband and wife. Shizuko and Itaru would struggle to find the balance in their relationship that honored both the traditional Japanese male privilege and Shizuko's more westernized expectation of equity and mutual respect for each other's needs. Growing up, I never witnessed any open conflict about this gender hierarchy. We always knew my mother would defer to my father. It was the role she accepted, yet she often spoke up on our behalf and sometimes found ways to work around my father's decisions without challenging his position in the family.

One Japanese word for "wife" is *oku-san*. My mother sometimes joked that the word was actually a derivative of the word *oku*, which means "to leave behind." I realize now that she had likely been reflecting on her own experience adjusting to life in an unfamiliar city with few friends and only her husband to rely on, in some ways "left behind" while Itaru was able to continue the life he led before he married.

Immersed in a tight-knit male kibei community, Itaru was often oblivious to Shizuko's feelings of loneliness and abandonment. As a psychotherapist I understand that the period of "falling in love" often invites uncharacteristic openness and emotional expressiveness that is profoundly liberating, since we long to know and be known by our loved one. But this honeymoon period does not last forever. It's often the case that over time, familiar ways of defending against one's vulnerability—particularly if there has been early and profound family separation—resurface, and self-protective behaviors and responses, set in place at the time of the original injury or loss, prevail.

I see my father's difficulty with intimacy, his obliviousness to my mother's suffering, as an outcome of his childhood losses. Turning inward to comfort himself in the absence of parents, he learned to be outwardly stoic, uncomfortable with emotional closeness. Japanese cultural upbringing and youthful self-absorption no doubt also contributed to the contours of his personality. Since he never spoke to us about his mother or father, there were no stories about his childhood, only an empty space in our intergenerational connection. Left behind by his father, Itaru was diligently cared for by his surrogate parents, Oji-san and Oba-san, but I don't know that he ever felt the same deep and boundless nurturing that Shizuko received from her grandmother Kisa.

Reading my mother's diary evoked memories of my own longing to know my father. As I was growing up, my mother unknowingly complemented my father's avoidant pattern. She was the one who would deliver to my brothers and me my father's decisions and messages of disapproval or even praise. Although I felt my father's love expressed through his hard work, his ability to fix things that were broken, and his presence at important events, he was like the man in a lighthouse, guiding us through storms and turbulence, always present but never close.

I so wanted him to show his love and affection not only to me but to my mother as well. As I read her diary, I remembered sitting on the stairs on Christmas Day as a child, my eyes fixed on the door, wishing, waiting, and hoping that a surprise present would arrive from my father for my mother. She always had a gift for him under the tree, but a present for her never arrived. At some point, I made it my job to make sure she received gifts. I was still in elementary school when I began saving my allowance to ensure that she would always have a present for her birthday, Mother's Day, and Christmas. See's chocolate nuts and chews were her favorite. Doing this somehow brought me comfort.

It was difficult reading my mother's self-chastising comments when she was distressed over my father's frequent absences. She struggled to be the perfect Japanese wife whose needs were subordinate to her husband's, yet her early years of self-sufficiency and independence made it difficult for her to yield completely. For me, growing up, her disappointment and loneliness were palpable.

In the background, the war in Europe continued. When Germany, Japan's ally, instigated a massive invasion of Russia on June 22, 1941, a sense of foreboding loomed over US-Japan relations. Like millions of other Americans, my parents bought war bonds to support the US prewar effort in Europe. Itaru signed up as a civilian defense volunteer, trained to direct citizens to safety in the event of enemy attack. There was no doubt in their minds that they had to do what was needed to protect their country from threat.

Sunday, March 30, 1941 *Rainy*
Our marriage ceremony took place at the San Francisco Buddhist church at 4:00 p.m.

Vows: I promise to devote myself and fulfill my duty as a wife all my life following these Buddhist teachings, "If you wish true love for a husband and enduring ties, you should love, honor, and trust your husband, and create lasting harmony in your home as you honor the truth." Namukiebutsu, Namukiehou, Namukiesou

Friday, May 23, 1941 *Cloudy*
It has been about two months since we were married. It has passed as if in a dream.

Got up at 7:15. "Oh dear, you are waking up in the morning with a yawn even though you just slept." Poor man, he looked very sleepy. He dressed, washed his face, and shaved *in 10 minutes, gobbled tea over rice* [ochazuke] *in 5 minutes, and left in such a rush. I was going to see him off, but he moves so quickly.*

Tuesday, May 27, 1941 *Sunny*
What a mood I am in today! Just because he might go fishing this weekend. I think I am too selfish. What I need is patience.

6:30 p.m. President Roosevelt fireside chat. He has firmly spoken to the world that he will continue to give material aid to the Allies and use force if necessary to preserve democracy.

Thursday, May 29, 1941 *Cloudy*
Tomorrow is Memorial Day. *We will have a three-day holiday. Right away I asked him, "Are you going to leave tonight for fishing?" "No, I won't." Oh! I was so happy. I realize how much I have been upset about his going fishing.*

Friday, May 30, 1941 *Sunny*—**Memorial Day**
Beep. Beep. Heard car horn in front of our house. It was 7:00 a.m. We were still in bed. Husband rushed to the window with his pajama on and yelled, "Are you going? I can be ready right away." Of course, as I expected, he was going fishing. Without having breakfast he went out in a rush saying, "I will be home soon." I waited and waited all day long, and worried and worried. And finally at 10:30 at night, he came home very tired. I cannot describe how worried I was.

Sunday, June 1, 1941 *Sunny*
We took our lunch and went to Mill Valley for hiking. Enjoyed every minute under the sunny sky. Walking, talking, sun bathing, we have had such a grand day.

Saturday, June 7, 1941 *Sunny*
After dinner we went to Kinmon Hall to see a Japanese movie. When he told me he was going to go fishing tomorrow again, all of a sudden I felt very lonely and cried. Though I tried hard to hold back my tears, I couldn't.

Sunday, June 8, 1941 *Sunny*
He went fishing *with Kuwada-san and Ono-san at 4:30 a.m.*
Since I cried so much last night, today I felt refreshed and could
do a lot of house chores all day. He came home with two bass *at*
7 p.m. Prepared sashimi and ate. Very delicious.

Tuesday, June 10, 1941 *Sunny*
Itaru-san's birthday. Borrowed a cake pan *from Chiye-chan,*
and made my first attempt at baking a chocolate cake *for our*
celebration. It turned out better than I expected.

Wednesday, June 11, 1941 *Sunny*
Start working cleaning house for Mr. Hoffman and Mr. Hall.
I'm looking forward to start working two hours every day begin-
ning today. Husband took me to a movie after supper to cele-
brate the first day of my work.

Sunday, June 22, 1941 *Cloudy*
He went to fishing 3:30 in the morning. Back at 9:30 but no
fish. Instead, he brought the news of German war started
against Russia.

Sunday, June 29, 1941 *Sunny*
Went to Fleishacker Park *with Oba-san in the afternoon for*
fun. Husband came home around 6:00 p.m. I don't know what
made him so dissatisfied after fishing *all day. Again he seemed*
to act selfishly as usual. We cannot make the happy *family that*
we hope for if we both act selfishly. I have a great responsibility.
Must carry it out. And remember, *mugon jikko,* actions speak
louder than words.

Friday, July 4, 1941 *Sunny*
How quiet the 4th of July *was. There were no people or cars*
on the street. *It was a very quiet holiday. I was home by myself*
feeling lonely.

Sunday, July 13, 1941 *Sunny*
German diplomats are being expelled from the US.

The comings and goings of the Japanese transatlantic ships were of great importance to the US government and to the Japanese-speaking community on the West Coast. US-Japan relations were carried out through the travel exchange of dignitaries and business-people. Large passenger ships had also transported Japanese immigrants and later their picture brides to America. Kibei nisei children like Shizuko and Itaru took long ocean voyages, leaving their birthplace in America to live with Japanese relatives they had never met. Years later, the same ships brought them back to the US.

The Japanese-speaking community on the West Coast relied on these ships to carry the mail to and from Japan, enabling families to stay connected across the Pacific Ocean. Itaru's letters to Shizuko during their first separation were often written hurriedly to make the delivery to the ship before its departure. This was also the only way Shizuko could stay in touch with her grandmother Kisa, and Itaru with his sister, Kiyoji.

These great ocean liners also carried goods, including the silk from Japan that was to be made into fine clothing and silk stockings in American mills. As unofficial emissaries from Japan, the Silk Girls had, just a year earlier, crossed the ocean to San Francisco on the *Tatsuta Maru*, a magnificent luxury passenger liner, with the hope of strengthening US-Japan relations.

But as Japan continued its unrelenting military incursions through the Pacific, by midsummer the mounting tension between the two countries could no longer be ignored by the American public. A convoy of fifteen Japanese naval ships and forty thousand troops had arrived in Saigon to occupy air bases and garrison posts, all within easy bombing range of British and American territories. Japanese air patrols closely surveilled the shipping routes of the China Sea, threatening the security of the American base in Cavite in the Philippines, British bases in Hong Kong and Singapore, and the coast of the Dutch East Indies.

Roosevelt struck back, tightening control on all economic exchange with Japan, freezing Japanese cash, oil, ships, silk, and other assets. These actions shut Japan off from vital sources of oil, gasoline, and other necessary military supplies. It was July 25, 1941, when the *Tatsuta Maru* and forty-five other Japanese ships were ordered by Japanese authorities to alter their intended course, forcing world events into Shizuko's and Itaru's lives. This international showdown, while severing the possibility of economic partnership between Japan and the US, was also cutting the umbilical cord connecting my parents to Japan. In her diary, Shizuko intently followed the news of the silk cargo crisis.

Thursday, July 24, 1941 *Sunny*
According to the news, Tatsuta Maru was supposed to have arrived in port this morning. However, nothing more has been heard of since the day before yesterday. The office sent a telegram to the ship, but no answer was returned, and the ship's whereabouts are unknown. All the Japanese people are talking about it, and everyone is very worried.

Saturday, July 26, 1941 *Cloudy*
Last night, President Roosevelt has passed the law "Freezing All Japanese Assets." Reason is Japanese aggression into French Indo-China. This has caused Tatsuta Maru unable to anchor in American harbor again. Today's news said that the N.Y.K. shipping company is endeavoring to get special permission from U.S.A. government to unload American passengers on the boat.

Who knows, tomorrow? We must face things with a firm mind.

Sunday, July 27, 1941 *Cloudy & Rainy*
Suddenly the relationship between Japan and America is worsening. Heard a lot of Japanese will go back to Japan. But being worried too much doesn't help anything.

Wednesday, July 30, 1941 *Sunny*
Tatsuta Maru finally arrived at the San Francisco port at 3:00
p.m. It will only let passengers off, then the cargo of "precious
raw silk" *will be returned to Japan because of the possibility that
the* US government *might seize it.* Today's newspaper is head-
lined with Tatsuta Maru arrival.

Saturday, August 2, 1941 *Sunny*
Troubled silk cargo on the Tatsuta is finally unloading here
because of lawsuit declared by American silk manufacturing
company. Now the U.S.A. has embargo against Japan for everything (silk, oil, food stuff, etc.), which means no more silk
for U.S.A., no more luxury silk stockings for American ladies.
U.S. government ordered silk factories all over U.S.A. to be
closed today.

Monday, August 4, 1941 *Sunny*
According to the radio news, Tatsuta Maru *departed for Japan
early this morning.*

Saturday, August 9, 1941 *Sunny*
Terribly home-sick. *Lately I am feeling very gloomy.* Want to go
home so badly.

Saturday, August 23, 1941 *Sunny*
After dinner Husband was busy with his matchbook collection.
*I watched him as he intently organized them, then with excite-
ment he said, "Someday, my children will be so delighted with
such a large collection of matchbooks." As I watched him and
heard his words, I loved him very much.*

Saturday, August 30, 1941 *Sunny*
Oba-san and I went to see the final movie sponsored by *Heimushakai.* It was a benefit to raise funds to buy shoes for Japanese soldiers fighting in China. Husband was busy helping.

Friday, September 26, 1941 *Cloudy*
On vacation to Los Angeles!
  We had the Fukushima family over for sukiyaki dinner. I bought two chickens, but thought it might not be enough, so I asked Husband to go get more. That was the first time for me to ask such a thing of him.

Wednesday, October 1, 1941 *Sunny*
Went to Fillmore Street again after dinner to look for icebox, but didn't find anything.
  America *seems to be more and more in an emergency situation as* stoves, iceboxes *and other appliances are no longer produced. It is said to be because of* Defense Work.

Wednesday, October 8, 1941 *Sunny*
For the last three days I have had a lonely feeling, which I can't describe. Although I tried very hard not to show my gloomy face to my husband, my heart is feeling dark. I felt sorry for my husband. Times like this, I wish I had a mother to be here close to me.

Thursday, October 9, 1941 *Sunny*
Remembering our engagement a year ago today. I should not forget how I felt at that time and should serve my husband cheerfully and pleasantly.

Wednesday, October 15, 1941 *Sunny*
Went to see Mrs. Sanada. Her daughter, little Michiko-chan, wanted to go to outside, so I took her to work with me and got back 5:30 p.m. She seemed to be so happy to be with me. Surely I like to have my own daughter! I want to have my own baby as soon as I can.

Thursday, November 13, 1941 *Sunny*
Made waffles for him this morning. He complained, "I don't want sweet food in the morning. I feel upset to think that I have to eat this for breakfast." He reluctantly ate one waffle and left.

Monday, December 1, 1941 *Cloudy*

The relationship between Japan and America is worsening. According to the newspaper and the current situation, it seems possible war could start tomorrow.

2.

Non-Aliens

During the COVID-19 pandemic, between March 2020 and June 2022, the organization Stop AAPI Hate received more than 11,500 reports of incidents of anti-Asian harassment and violence. Many thousands more have likely gone unreported as the pandemic continues to take its devastating toll. People of Asian descent, blamed by the former president of the US for causing what he callously referred to as the "China Flu," are once again targets of hate and fear.

Twenty years earlier, in 2001, the catastrophic 9/11 attack shook the country's soul. Like millions of others, I watched the news, seeing images my brain couldn't process as real. Destruction beyond imagination. In a disbelieving haze, I went to work to meet my first patient of the day—a Japanese American man who, the evening before, had shared with me his plan to take his own life with his handgun. By the end of the session, he had agreed to meet me in the morning and bring his gun to me for safekeeping until these self-destructive thoughts abated. On September 11, he was waiting at the door. Still shaken by the image of the plane crashing into the Twin Towers, I managed to ask him for the gun. His emphatic response has stayed with me for years: "Are you kidding? I wouldn't drive here with a gun in my car. Cops could pull me over, find a gun, and throw me in jail because they would think I was a terrorist!"

The first attack on US soil by a foreign power had occurred sixty years earlier on December 7, 1941, when the Imperial Japanese Navy bombed Pearl Harbor in Hawaii. The consequences for Japanese Americans, including this patient's family, were long lasting. I knew right away that he was referring to a prevailing lifelong fear in our community that as "forever foreigners," we could once again easily become the target of hate and fear during a time of intense social and political unrest.

Today, taunting screams of "Go back where you came from!" echo the racism trauma inflicted on Japanese Americans in the aftermath of Pearl Harbor. My mother had mentioned to me once that a woman had spit on her when she stepped off the bus in downtown San Francisco. I didn't ask for any details about when or why, and naively dismissed the incident as random, even innocuous. I realize now that race hatred is a bogeyman that is always lurking, waiting for the perfect moment to rear its ugly head.

I have certainly witnessed acts of racism and have also been the target of both explicit and implicit racism, but today more than ever, in this climate of anti-Asian violence, I can feel the gut-churning fear my mother must have felt then, as I step outside my house with my Asian face.

Nine months after my parents were married, their dreams of blissful family life came to a shocking end. At 7:55 a.m., in a surprise attack, Japanese imperial forces bombed American ships in Pearl Harbor, as well as air stations at Hickam, Wheeler, Ford Island, Ewa Field, and Kaneohe in Hawaii. The attack continued for two hours and twenty minutes, killing 2,395 Americans and wounding 1,178 more. More than three hundred aircraft and eighteen ships were destroyed or damaged. It was a devastating blow to the sense of safety and well-being that America had always taken for granted.

The onslaught began. Government surveillance of the Japanese American community had been ongoing for years prior to the outbreak of war. Within hours of the attack, all of San Francisco

Japantown was blocked off and placed under heavy guard. Police and FBI agents descended on Japanese businesses thought to be affiliated with Japan and arrested an undisclosed number of what news reports described as "suspicious aliens."

Japanese immigrants, many of whom had been living in the US for decades, were now subject to the Alien Enemies Act of 1798. This act allowed the president to imprison and deport noncitizens who were deemed dangerous or citizens of a "hostile nation" at risk of waging war against the US. Most of the issei men who were apprehended were prominent businessmen, community leaders, Buddhist priests, members of Japanese social organizations, fishermen, and farmers. Their property could lawfully be confiscated, and they could be interned without the need for any justification beyond their status as noncitizens. The FBI raided their homes, detained them for varying lengths of time, and then unpredictably either released them or held them in Department of Justice internment camps. Despite false claims that Japanese living in the US were working to actively support the enemy through espionage and sabotage, no evidence of such "fifth-column activity" was ever found. The quick removal and incarceration of Japanese living on the West Coast only served to confirm the American public's suspicion of their disloyalty.

Shizuko and Itaru witnessed their immigrant issei friends and neighbors being torn from their families, arrested, and removed to unknown places of detention. Incredulously, they saw that even decades after making America their home, issei, who by law were never permitted to become citizens, had no claim to protection from arbitrary removal. The declaration of war with Japan had now officially designated them as "enemy aliens," subject to arrest and internment. As disturbing as these arrests and removals were, my parents maintained their belief that as American citizens, they would not have to face the same catastrophic fate.

The *San Francisco Examiner*'s December 8 report on the roundup of suspected enemy aliens foreshadowed the mass incarceration to follow: "There was no immediate disclosure as to the location of the concentration camps which will be used in this area, although one such camp was reported ready on Angel Island."

On December 8, 1941, Congress formally declared a state of war between the US and the Empire of Japan. This declaration compounded the racism and war hysteria already spreading across the country, and Japanese Americans were scapegoated without consideration of nationality. The simmering fear of the "yellow peril" threatening the dominance of the white power structure was now in full force.

As politicians and economic competitors of the Japanese farmers and fishermen began to call for the removal of all people of Japanese ancestry from the West Coast, people in San Francisco Japantown gathered at meetings seeking guidance and support. In the absence of elder issei leaders, who had been arrested and removed, the community turned to the Japanese American Citizens League (JACL) for guidance.

By the time the war ended, my father would regret ever having been a member of the JACL, ostensibly a civil rights organization led by young nisei men whose priorities were to promote citizenship, loyalty, and patriotism to the US. Over time, however, it became evident that the JACL leadership, rather than representing Japanese Americans and fighting for their constitutional rights, served as mediators on behalf of the government. They urged their members and the broader Japanese American community not to resist but to comply with whatever mandates the government imposed. Essentially staunching any possibility of protest, the leaders claimed that such compliance would serve as the community's contribution to the war effort and proof of their loyalty to America.

My parents witnessed the traumatic siege of their neighborhood, believing that their rights as American citizens would protect them from the indiscriminate removal suffered by their immigrant Japanese friends, neighbors, and business associates. As I read my mother's journal from that time, I felt that she was tenaciously holding on to her identity as an American whose country was under attack, yet she dared not say what she truly feared.

Sunday, December 7, 1941 Sunny

While I was waiting for Husband to return home, I looked after Michiko-chan and baked a chocolate cake. It was about 1:40 p.m. when I heard, "Japan, Japan" repeatedly on the radio. I turned the volume up to listen. It was announcing that Japan had dropped bombs on Pearl Harbor and the Philippines at about 8:00 a.m. this morning. After all! The war between Japan and America has begun.

All of a sudden I started feeling uneasy. I managed to calm myself down and got ready to take Michiko-chan home. Then Husband came home. I was relieved to see him. He was very upset saying, "The war has started . . . this means trouble."

Husband went to a special kibei meeting at 7:30 p.m. I felt uneasy at home without him, so went to Oba-san's place until he came to pick me up. He told me that Fujii-san and Kataoka-san were taken by the FBI. There were many policemen and FBI all around watching Japantown from about 3:00 p.m. this afternoon.

Monday, December 8, 1941 *Sunny*—U.S. declared war on Japan

I haven't felt calm at all, so I spent this morning doing embroidery by the fireplace, but after lunch I went to visit Aizawa-san. Aizawa-san's Goshado bookstore was closed under orders of the FBI, and most stores on Post Street were closed. Many Japanese were taken by the FBI.

On the way home, I walked along Post Street and felt very nervous. There was a huge watching-man *from the FBI standing in front of a store. Husband came home at about 2:30 p.m. saying that his office was closed by the FBI. He went to a meeting of Kibei-Shimin Kai and the* Japanese American Citizens League *again at 7:30 p.m. I waited for him while in bed listening to the radio.* Suddenly the radio stopped and all the street lights went off. First blackout. Later I learned that enemy planes had been sighted off Golden Gate. 9 p.m. All clear. *Went to bed feeling uneasy.*

Tuesday, December 9, 1941 *Sunny*
Went to Mrs. Burnick's place to work. Finished at 3:00 p.m. and got paid $2 cash. Since I heard yesterday that it may not be possible to cash any checks, I asked Mrs. Burnick to pay me cash. Husband came home after the JACL meeting. Heard only depressing stories. He was told that yesterday's blackout was because Japanese planes were seen.

Wednesday, December 10, 1941 *Sunny*
News: British Battleship, "Prince of Wales" and its sister ship have been sunk by Japanese.
I felt sorry for my husband because of my disturbed mind and because I cried in bed last night. Yes, my husband is right. This is not the time to think just about ourselves. There is nothing we have to be afraid of as long as we are determined to live with a strong will. After lunch he went to the American Trust Bank *to withdraw money. Nisei are allowed to withdraw cash with a birth certificate. Poor issei, their stores were closed down and they cannot access their bank accounts. They are so disheartened.*

Thursday, December 11, 1941 *Cloudy*
U.S.A. officially declared war against Germany & Italy.
According to the news on the radio, a Japanese cruiser and the destroyer Haruna *were sunk by the US. Husband went to community meeting at the YWCA.*

Friday, December 12, 1941 *Rainy & Cloudy*
I heard that Japanese day-work people were being fired, so I called Mrs. Sokolov. As I feared, I was fired. Being fired is not pleasant at all. Husband has gone to Social Security office. 7:25–10 p.m.—Black out.

Wednesday, December 17, 1941 *Sunny*
The news said that Japanese people who had been taken by the FBI *were sent to* concentration camps *in Montana or Arizona. They might not be able to come back until the war is over. Fervently wishing peaceful days would come as soon as possible.*

Thursday, December 25, 1941 *Cloudy*—Christmas
Got up at 11:00 a.m. What a quiet Christmas. No sound of trains or cars going by. It felt strange. Prepared Christmas dinner: roast lamb, baked potatoes, boiled broccoli, avocado salad, and Jell-o with whipping cream. Invited Tekawa-san and Oji-san for dinner. Oba-san could not come because she had to work.

Monday, December 29, 1941 Clear
All aliens have surrendered their shortwave radios and cameras to the police department today. We American citizens are so fortunate that we don't have to. Husband received his $150 in defense savings bonds from Mr. Nonaka.

Wednesday, December 31, 1941
From 12 noon to 9 p.m., cooking New Year's feast. Roasting chicken, one for Oba-san and one for ourselves. We had *kintoki* [red kidney beans for wealth], *kazunoko* [herring roe for fertility], and *kinpira* [slivered burdock root for abundance]. Mr. Ina helped me cut the *gobo* [burdock]. To ring in the New Year, Oji-san and Oba-san came over and we all had a *toshikoshi soba* [buckwheat noodles for long life].

There was no noise when the clock struck 12 midnight, instead, stillness. We are at war now!

Shizuko innocently believed that military guards in Japantown were there to protect the Japanese community from the threat of enraged Filipinos seeking revenge for Japan's attack in the Philippines. In fact, the presence of military guards was the precursor to the shutting down of the shops and businesses in Japantown.

The declaration of war fueled long-standing racism. Facing the shock and humiliation of a surprise attack, the military and government leadership sought to distract the American public from the failure of those responsible for protecting the country. Immediately, the press joined efforts to demonize anyone who looked like the enemy. Blatantly racist war propaganda in the form of political cartoons and posters cast Japanese people as "yellow devils," inferior, ape-like subhumans, treacherous and morally corrupt.

Shizuko and Itaru wholeheartedly joined their white neighbors in doing their part to support their nation in time of war. But over and over, hate speech and inflammatory images tragically failed to distinguish Japanese Americans from the enemy attackers.

In this climate of antipathy, Shizuko's early childhood losses and fears of abandonment were triggered when Itaru left town for a business trip amid the chaos. Like most Americans across the country, Shizuko followed the war headlines every day. She had been writing in her diary in Japanese, expressing herself with ease and confidence, but, by the start of 1942, her daily entries were almost entirely written in English. Whether a conscious decision or not, it seems in some small way to have enabled her to claim her standing as an American citizen.

Thursday, January 1, 1942
Resolution: 1. Be Cheerful
                    2. Correct the warped mind.
                    3. Do not put off things.
Double guards around Japantown from last night because dangerous attack by Filipinos might happen on account of war.

Friday, January 2, 1942
News: "Manila Falls! U.S. Forces Hold Corregidor: Cavite Evacuated by Navy."

Saturday, January 3, 1942
7:30 p.m. Blackout. We got in bed until all-clear signal was sounded.

Sunday, January 4, 1942
I should not be lazy just because it's so freezing in the morning. Think about men at the battlefield. We had a quarrel about little things, but it is not time to think of ourselves. We are at war!

Saturday, January 10, 1942
Today I heard sugar rationing over the radio, so after coming back from work I went to store and bought 60 pounds of sugar. I think I was so excited to buy sugar, or full of sugar in my mind, when crossing the street I was almost run over by a car. When that incident was over, I felt so thankful to be still alive.

Monday, January 12, 1942 Cloudy
News, *S.F. Chronicle*: "Japanese strike at Dutch Indies! U.S. Navy station in Samoa shelled!"

Mr. Ina has gone to Japanese American Citizens League meeting at 7:30 p.m. Although he was just one block away at the YWCA, it made me worry. He came home quite late 10:45.

Sunday, January 18, 1942 Clear
After teaching Sunday school, Mr. Ina went to JACL's Red Cross Drive. I went to Buddhist Church for service and Buddhist Women's Auxiliary meeting. They decided to buy $200.00 defense bond and donated $25.00 to Red Cross.

Friday, January 23, 1942 Rain
Mr. Ina to Red Cross Drive. When he came home, he heard some news about a blackout tonight, so he rushed to prepare the bedroom by putting blankets on the window. After dinner, we got in bed and waited for the siren but it seems no blackout!

Tuesday, January 27, 1942 Rain
How ashamed of myself! Just because Mr. Ina is going to Fresno for business trip, I sobbed in bed. Why? I felt very lonesome already. What will become of me if he has to join the army?

Wednesday, January 28, 1942 Cloudy
Mr. Ina left for Fresno with Mr. Ono on a business trip for several days. First time ever separated since we got married. I think it will do us good. Idleness makes for loneliness. Be busy!

Shizuko witnessed San Francisco's Japantown disassembling. Military proclamations subjecting all people of Japanese ancestry to an 8 p.m. curfew and confining them to a five-mile radius from their homes became the order of the day. Intermittent blackouts were announced, requiring lights off on the streets and indoors. These drastic measures further spread fear of imminent enemy attack, heightening indiscriminate animosity toward anyone with a Japanese face. People were fired from their jobs, companies owned by anyone of Japanese ancestry were forced to close, and shops and restaurants were shuttered. The Japanese-language press was shut down. Bank accounts of Japanese aliens were frozen, and the FBI began a series of warrantless raids on Japanese American households, searching for contraband.

By the end of January 1942, West Coast politicians, California newspapers, the Joint Immigration Committee, and prominent civic figures began to actively lobby for the removal of all people of Japanese ancestry. Congressman Leland Ford of California called on the secretaries of war and the navy, as well as the director of the FBI, to have "all Japanese, whether citizens or not, be placed in inland concentration camps." General John L. DeWitt, head of the Western Defense Command, fed the clamor with public statements decrying Japanese immigrants and citizens as members of an "enemy race." He would further assert the necessity for the removal of Japanese Americans from the West Coast based on their "undiluted racial strains" that made them innately Japanese and therefore a risk to national security. California governor Culbert Olson and Attorney General Earl Warren concurred.

Shizuko and Itaru's bicultural, binational identity as kibei was quickly becoming a liability. Their foundering contact with Shizuko's beloved grandmother Kisa and Itaru's sister Kiyoji in Japan was a source of anxiety and deep sorrow. As the days went by, full of disturbing stories of the "yellow peril" claiming victory across the Pacific, their future looked bleak.

Thursday, January 29, 1942 Cloudy
News: For several days, voices heard from many politicians requesting the federal government to transfer all alien Japanese inland.

Thursday, February 5, 1942 Rain
It is my 25th birthday today so I wrote this to my deceased mother and brother.

Dearest Mother and Nii-san, Elder Brother, Isamu,
   Although today we live in a war-torn world and we hear sadness and discouragement, you have brought my happy birthday. Oh, Mother, I wish you were alive now! See our happy home. I am so thankful to have most kindest husband. How can I live without him? Please mother and Elder Brother, watch over us wherever we are. Together always. On this day, I want to express my gratitude to you, Mother, for bringing me into this world.
   Your loving daughter,
   Shizuko

Received special delivery mail from Itaru-san. Stating his safe arrival to Salinas. Oba-san has kindly made me birthday cake and invited me to dinner. She is so sweet and considerate. I am very thankful.

Sunday, February 8, 1942
It was a year ago today when I came to San Francisco. That's right. It's been a year. Remembering when Itaru-san came to Oakland to pick me up. When I saw him, I felt embarrassed that I couldn't come up with any words of greeting. I was flustered and my heart was pounding.

Monday, February 16, 1942 Clear
After dinner we went over to Oba-san's for couple hours. Conversation about evacuation from San Francisco. What is our future? Everything seems dark.

Three days after Shizuko's last entry, any cloud of uncertainty about her future was precipitously swept away. On February 19, 1942, President Roosevelt signed Executive Order 9066, setting in motion what would later be considered one of the darkest moments in US civil rights history. Immediately, General DeWitt designated military exclusion zones along the West Coast, ultimately sanctioning the mass removal of all persons of Japanese ancestry from California, Washington, Oregon, and southern Arizona. There were no hearings or trials, no due process of the law. Guilt by reason of race was the only determining factor that distinguished those who would be removed from their homes. Public cries for mass removal were falsely based on the rationale that 125,000 people of Japanese ancestry presented a "risk to national security."

Shizuko and Itaru now found themselves numbed by anxiety as they slowly realized that their American citizenship offered no protection from the viral race hatred spreading throughout the nation. Official announcements quickly posted everywhere in San Francisco Japantown left no doubt that anyone with Japanese blood, "alien" or "non-alien," would soon be taken into custody and imprisoned. In shock and disbelief, Shizuko and Itaru could barely grasp that they would be incarcerated in concentration camps in remote inland areas of the US for an unknown period of time.

Friday, February 20, 1942 Clear
According to paper, mass evacuation of Japanese is possible soon. Don't feel like writing today. My heart is heavy with dark future.

Saturday, February 21, 1942 Clear
Today many alien Japanese have been rounded up in San Francisco. Among them, Mr. Nonaka, Itaru-san's boss. All we hear is the sad news of families left behind.

Tuesday, February 24, 1942 Clear
Many Japanese must move out from forbidden areas (Terminal Island, etc.) by midnight tonight.

Friday, February 27, 1942 Clear
Made roast leg of lamb and invited Oji-san & Oba-san for dinner. We are in position of future uncertainty so having dinner together while we can.

Sunday, March 1, 1942 Clear
Expecting evacuation notice from Army any day now. My mind is unsettled and cannot do anything. Mr. Ina did some packing in the afternoon while I did washing twice today. No dirty clothes when we move away.

Monday, March 2, 1942 Cloudy
Oji-san & Oba-san invited us to dinner so we went to Post Street Chinese place. Kept eye on clock all the time so that we will be at home by 9 p.m. curfew. Expecting official announcement of our evacuation tomorrow. Now we know we have to evacuate. But where?

Tuesday, March 3, 1942 Clear
After sent husband to work, I kept listening to radio news. I was nervous all day and did not go to work. Doing nothing but thinking uselessly. Oji-san went to shop for trunks. We did some packing until 12 o'clock midnight.

Thursday, March 5, 1942 Clear
Yesterday's news was that we will be moved by Army within 60 days. Many stores and groceries are having sales. Trying to get rid of merchandise. I saw a sign at the Aoki Taisedo bookstore: *Eviction* sale.

Monday, March 9, 1942 *Sunny*
Due to evacuation problem, haven't felt calm and couldn't pay attention to work for a while, but since Husband started calmly sorting his stamp collection, I've gathered my courage quite a lot. At midnight, suffered pain in stomach. Did not sleep very well.

Saturday, March 21, 1942 Clear
News: 50 skilled Japanese from Los Angeles left for Manzanar
Camp in Owens Valley to work on buildings at the camp.

*Busy helping at Goshado bookstore. We got home around
9:30 p.m., feeling very exhausted. Too tired to feel like talking.
But we should help each other in times like this. I will try to be
as helpful as possible.*

Tuesday, March 24, 1942 Clear
Many Japanese stores have closed. It is very lonely along Sutter & Post streets.

News: *Nisei Curfew Is Ordered. New Contraband, Travel
Rules by Army Affect all Enemy Aliens, US-Born Japanese. Curfew law to be effective March 27. From 8 p.m.–6 a.m., must be
at home. No Japs on street.*

In 1989, several of my mother's friends called saying they recognized a photo of her "before camp" in a calendar published by the
National Japanese American Historical Society of San Francisco.
My brothers and I discovered that photographer Dorothea Lange
had captured a stark, pivotal moment in our mother's life. Com-
missioned to document what was referred to as the "evacuation
and relocation" of Japanese Americans in the early months of 1942,
Lange had photographed our mother standing in line, in front
of Kinmon Hall, a Japanese community center in San Francisco
Japantown. Her face lined with uncertainty, Shizuko waits to be
"registered." It was here that she, along with others of Japanese
ancestry, was issued paper tags hanging from strings on which she
was to write her assigned family number. These tags were to be
worn the day she and my father were forced to leave their home
under armed guard. Family 14911 would serve as their identity for
the duration of the war.
   In the background of the Lange photo are two poster-size documents that had been hung in prominent places throughout San
Francisco where Japanese Americans were known to reside. The
first poster, titled "Instructions to all Persons of Japanese Ancestry," designated the date and time that all people living in a

Shizuko Ina, San Francisco, April 26, 1942. Photo by Dorothea Lange, titled "Eviction Order." Courtesy of the National Archives and Records Administration.

specified neighborhood were to appear at assigned "Civil Control Stations," where government officials registered each family member and checked for contraband. They were to bring with them only what they could carry, including bedding and linens, toilet articles, extra clothing, dishes and eating utensils, and essential personal effects for each member of the family. From the assigned stations, they would be transported by armed military guards to temporary detention facilities.

The second poster, "Civilian Exclusion Order No. 41," named the specific locations in different neighborhoods where people were to arrive with their belongings. For Shizuko and Itaru, these instructions offered no doubt about what was to take place:

It is hereby ordered that from and after 12 o'clock
noon, P.W.T., of Monday, May 11, 1942, all persons of
Japanese ancestry, both alien and non-alien, be excluded from that portion of Military Area No. 1 described as follows . . .

These notices represent government efforts to cloak in euphemistic language the mass imprisonment of innocent people. A kind
of doublespeak began here as the perpetrator's prerogative was
confounded and obscured by the language of the powerful defining
the experience of the powerless. The "exclusion order" was, in fact,
an arrest warrant, clearly stating that anyone who did not comply
would be subject to criminal penalties. Dehumanized as numbers,
referred to as non-aliens, my parents, American citizens, slowly
became invisible to the rest of world. Racist stereotypes obscured
their identities as individuals, making it possible for bystanders to
turn away from the violence taking place right before their eyes.

Decades later, it would be proven that government officials, in
justifying the mass incarceration to the US Supreme Court, altered and suppressed evidence collected by the Office of Naval
Intelligence and the FBI confirming that the Japanese on the West
Coast actually posed no threat to the safety and well-being of the
American people. The rule of law and basic principles of human
decency seemed to have collapsed in the government-fueled fire of
hate.

As they prepared for the incarceration, people were forced to sell
off their personal belongings, furniture, treasured heirlooms, and
business merchandise for pennies. Beloved pets were left behind,
and the numbers of empty seats in school classrooms, offices,
shops, churches, homes, and farms gradually grew. The perni-
cious racism behind the executive order was difficult to mask when
babies and children with any fraction of Japanese blood living in
orphanages and foster care were also removed to be housed in a
prison orphanage in the Manzanar concentration camp.

By the end of March, Shizuko's war headline entries shifted to
events closer to home. On March 23, she read an Associated Press
report in the *San Francisco Chronicle* about events taking place in
Southern California.

America's first war-time evacuation will start here tomorrow when 1000 Japanese men, some aliens and some citizens, by virtue of their birth in this country, start the 240-mile trek to the new reception center in the Owens Valley. By special train and private automobile the Japanese, all volunteers, will move to their new home at Manzanar. They will find things in readiness for them, preparations having been made by an advance group of 86 Japanese who arrived at the reception center yesterday.

Even if not official, collusion between the press and government authorities continued to disguise the truth of the injustice at play. Words like "war-time evacuation" imply that people are being rescued from harm. Reference to "citizens, by virtue of their birth" creates the impression that birthright is insignificant, and other words such as "reception center," "volunteers," and "new home" further make light of the inhumane miscarriage of justice taking place.

The signing of Executive Order 9066, in reality, marked the perpetration of a profoundly damaging psychological trauma, which would go unacknowledged by both victim and perpetrator for decades. To be victims of mass incarceration is, by definition, traumatic. To be deemed guilty by reason of race, over which one has no control, is, by definition, racism. What Japanese Americans suffered was government-perpetrated racism trauma. The betrayal by a trusted source—in this case, their own government—complicated the response of the victims. Not unlike a helpless child being abused or abandoned by a parent, the victim often clings to the belief that the perpetrator somehow cares about the victim. In the case of the mass incarceration, the perpetrator is the government, an all-powerful, inaccessible, generalized authority, issuing orders being carried out by faceless military authority and bureaucrats, rather than an identifiable individual at whom the anger and outrage could be directed. Such conditions make it difficult for victims to find resolution for the trauma inflicted.

Aside from the courageous personal resistance of a few individuals, there was little organized outrage and protest from within the Japanese American community at the time of their removal. There are likely many complicating factors contributing to the absence of resistance, including traditional Japanese cultural values requiring respect for and subordination to authority, particularly commands issued by those in the highest positions of authority, such as the president of the United States. The absence of political leverage and power was also an important factor, since adult heads of household at the time were primarily immigrants who were denied citizenship and land ownership. And socially, as people of color surviving systemic racism, Japanese Americans tried to remain under the radar, turning the other cheek and avoiding any trouble that would bring shame to the family.

Disempowered and absent strong leadership within and outside the community, Japanese Americans had little capacity for organized resistance. Eventually, more than 125,000 persons of Japanese ancestry were quietly removed and disappeared, away from the West Coast to interior regions of the US.

From a psychological perspective, the absence of protest during this stage of the government assault on the Japanese American community was a survival response to an overwhelming threat of annihilation. Human beings are wired for self-preservation, and threats to well-being and safety automatically elicit a fight, flight, or freeze response. The freeze response in mammals occurs when the animal under attack with no possibility of escape will "play dead." With all other options removed, people and whole communities too will freeze, dissociate, and repress emotions to increase the possibility of survival. The immediate and swift removal of male community leaders in Japantown left the women, younger men, elders, and children without a voice, without legal representation, without the wherewithal to fight or flee. Japanese Americans, under siege and abandoned by their own country, reacted with the survival response of last resort—to freeze.

A numbing dissociation spread through the Japantown community. People anticipated the looming incarceration, for the most part, with both fear and compliance. Race hatred and violence against Japanese Americans surged with war hysteria. Some believed the government officials and spokespersons for the Japanese American Citizens League, who claimed that their mass removal would protect them from the hate and vitriol. There was, in fact, no government-sanctioned plan to protect targeted victims, scapegoats of a fear-ridden American public. Instead, the forced removal and imprisonment of thousands of innocent victims of racism simply served to allay the mounting societal anxiety infecting the American public.

Lacking any frame of reference for the enormity of what was happening, Shizuko internalized the government's perpetrator narrative of "evacuation" and "relocation" as circumstances that could not be avoided and must be endured. Along with other Japanese Americans on the West Coast, she seemed to be operating from a general state of shock as she continued to record the devastation being wrought in the Pacific by the enemy "Japs."

A victim caught up in such a human-perpetrated trauma will naturally look to others for help. There were certainly individual acts of kindness and support by non-Japanese friends, neighbors, and some religious organizations, but there was no real organized effort from bystanders to stop what was being done to a whole community of people. I wonder: During this trying period, where was the voice of dissent? Where were the eyes to see beneath the propaganda presented to the public? There must have been hundreds of thousands of bystanders witnessing the mass removal, yet there was no organized protest, no allies standing up for fellow workers, students, farmers, neighborhood shopkeepers. Through their silence and inaction, the American people abandoned not only their neighbors and friends but also their own humanity. The forever foreigner was othered into invisibility.

Shizuko began to reckon with what lay ahead for her. Blanketed in the dark by citywide blackouts, her world shrank under the oppressive curfew and restrictive orders targeting her community. In her diary, it seems that fear and anxiety are held in her every breath. Abandonment was a fear my mother had lived with since childhood, and I have spent a lifetime trying to make sense of that very same fear living in me for as long as I can remember. Over time I learned that trauma, particularly sustained and chronic trauma, can be transmitted across generations. As I read her diary entries for the first time, discomfort knotted in me, a sharp contrast to the absolute absence of anger and protest written in my mother's hand.

If there was outrage, if there was a cry of unfairness, she didn't commit them to writing, but somehow they were etched deeply into my being.

Wednesday, April 1, 1942 Cloudy
What a disturbing day at the Goshado store today. Fighting with people wanting to buy some merchandise cheap.

News: First San Francisco evacuation order is passed as following: "Under a new order to be signed today by Lieutenant General J. L. De Witt of the Western Defense Command, no Japanese aliens or citizens will be permitted to leave Military Area No. 1 except under Army supervision."

The Examiner also reported: "Under terms of General De-Witt's third proclamation, subjecting all Japanese and enemy aliens to an 8 p.m. curfew and confining them to a five-mile radius from their homes."

Monday, April 6, 1942 Clear
It is last day for Mr. Ina to work at Nonaka & Co. His permit expires tomorrow. Now Nonaka & Co. office has been classified as a Prohibited zone. Mr. Ina must feel lost after today because he has been working there for nearly 4 years.

News: First 660 San Francisco evacuees left this evening for Santa Anita Camp near Los Angeles. God Bless them all!

Friday, April 10, 1942 *Cloudy*
I didn't have a monthly, and since a week ago I've been feeling very dull and my breasts have been swollen and I've been having trouble breathing. So I somehow feel that I may be pregnant.

Saturday, April 11, 1942 *Cloudy*
This morning when I explained to Dr. Togasaki about my physical condition, she told me that she was almost sure of my pregnancy. I believe so, too. I have to take better care of myself for the sake of my child. Oba-san was as happy as if it were her own. Husband was very happy.

Tuesday, April 21, 1942 Clear
Army announced another order of evacuation today, which will be effective from this Friday. The Japanese people who live between California Street and Sutter must evacuate end of this month to Tanforan Race Track. It means us!

Wednesday, April 22, 1942 Clear—hip 32½", breast 30"
We got up early in the morning and did most packing. Oji-san & Oba-san came over and helped us. Most things including stove, icebox, etc. were sent to Pierce Rudolph Storage Co.

In the afternoon, I went downtown with Oba-san and bought baby clothes.

Friday, April 24, 1942 Clear—Received letter from Mother
12 noon today our evacuation order is effective. Every corner of block has a "Notice" on it.

Sunday, April 26, 1942 Clear
At 12:35 noon Oji-san and I went to Kinmon Hall. We registered together as one family. Our Family number is 14911. We shall leave San Francisco either Thursday or Friday. For dinner we were invited to Mrs. Aizawa's. What a delicious sushi! May be the last time that we taste such a good *osushi*.

Tuesday, April 28, 1942 Clear—Wrote to Mother
Mr. & Mrs. Yoshida left for Tanforan Assembly Center at 1:30 p.m.

How calm were the Japanese evacuees! No tears! But they seem very firm minded when they left. God bless them all! We will be following within a couple days. Our departure will be this Thursday 2 p.m.

Wednesday, April 29, 1942 Clear—chest 30½" hip 33.2"
Tomorrow to Tanforan!

3.
Disloyals

It was May 2016, right around my seventy-second birthday, when I joined a group of interfaith volunteers—a Catholic priest, several Presbyterian ministers, and lay members of various churches in the San Antonio, Texas, area. Traveling south by van, I was too busy gathering information from my fellow travelers about what to expect at our destination to notice the terrain. The air was hot and dry. Someone asked if I had ever been to Texas before. Without giving it much thought, I answered that the last time I had been in Texas was when my family and I were held prisoners in the Department of Justice (DOJ) internment camp in Crystal City in 1946. The friendly chatter stopped. Quiet settled in the crowded van as people turned their attention to me, but at the time, I didn't have more to say.

During their weekly trek to the Karnes County Family Residential Center in South Texas, these compassionate witnesses brought hope and spiritual caring to hundreds of women and children seeking asylum in the US. Escaping violence in their home countries in Central America, they were now criminalized and held under indefinite detention. US immigration policy at the time focused on "detention as deterrence" in an attempt to stem the tide of a humanitarian crisis. Outside professionals were not permitted to enter the facility, and the lack of transparency regarding the welfare of the children in particular raised grave concerns for social justice groups.

I was contacted by Carl Takei, a Japanese American attorney with the American Civil Liberties Union. His grandfather had been held in the Tule Lake concentration camp during World War II. He explained to me that the new Karnes facility was run by a private prison corporation, contracted by the Department of Homeland Security to house hundreds of women and children from El Salvador, Honduras, and Nicaragua. Carl, along with members of the press, had visited the newly built facility before "residents" were admitted. Disturbed by the egregiousness of the pending mass incarceration, he described to me, in halting speech overwhelmed by emotion, the freshly stocked supply cabinets, proudly shown to him, filled with "rows and rows of little shoes." As attorney for the ACLU National Prisons Project, he asked if I would, as a child therapist specializing in trauma, be willing to enter the facility, ostensibly as a religious visitor, to observe and report my observations regarding the welfare of the children. Flushed with emotion myself, I agreed to head to San Antonio, Texas, as soon as I could get a flight.

I brought my portable play therapy kit, thinking I would be able to engage the children through play. As my coconspirators and I entered the facility, we were met by uniformed guards armed with stun guns in holsters and instructed to place everything inside lockers. In went my therapy supplies—miniature superheroes, brown family figurines, paper and colored pencils, small stuffed animals, my belt, watch, ring, and purse. We passed through full-body scanners and metal doors to the visiting room, a spacious, sterile room with fixed tables and chairs. A large glass window separated us from a crowded room where women and children pressed their hands and faces, hoping to be allowed the precious sixty minutes with a religious visitor.

In one corner, a shelf of toys sat on a brightly colored carpet. But as mothers with children were counted and directed to the table and chairs where we waited, not one child went to play with the toys. Instead, they clung to their mothers. In hushed voices, the multilingual visitors offered solace and comfort. Not allowed to bring in paper or pencils, they also memorized phone numbers given to them by the mothers to send messages to family outside. One of the priests served as my interpreter, but because visitors were all supposed to be bilingual religious volunteers, he had to position himself so the guard couldn't see that he was translating for me.

The stories the mothers told me were heart-wrenching. As they spoke, they broke down in tears, their toddlers and nursing babies watching them. They had traveled miles in treacherous heat and darkness seeking safety and protection, only to find themselves handcuffed and imprisoned without food or blankets in a concrete holding cell waiting to be transported to the detention facility.

I've been a child therapist for more than twenty years; I knew it would be difficult listening to stories of such despair, but as we left the facility and got back in the van, I felt shaken in a way I'd never experienced before. I could barely imagine speaking of my own childhood incarceration experience so matter-of-factly just a few hours earlier. The so-called family residential center was, in fact, a family prison. Barbed-wire fences, armed guards, the faces of children frozen in fear, staring blankly and seemingly numb—I felt myself sinking into deep sorrow. I cried for the children. I cried for myself.

In an eerie parade of resignation, thousands of people of Japanese ancestry put on their Sunday best, stored or rid themselves of any material affiliation with Japan, packed their bags as directed, and waited in line, all with their paper tag numbers hanging from the buttons on their coats. Soldiers armed with rifles stood guard as families arrived at points of departure.

Facing hostility and hatred at every turn, my mother told me about the woman who stepped in front of her as she carried her precious few belongings and spit in her face. She saw armed guards standing in front of shuttered shops and businesses that had been a part of her everyday life. She was hurt and embarrassed to be fired by the rich white ladies whose houses she had proudly and meticulously cleaned. She had swept the floors carefully, and taught me to do the same—"from corner to corner." My mother, once embraced as beautiful, exotic, and endearing, was now despised, transformed through hateful eyes into a monstrous "Jap."

Like the trees in the great bamboo forests of Japan, my parents and others learned to bend. Heads bowed in the wind, they endured the pain of abandonment by their own country. Deeply rooted in their ability to face adversity, Shizuko and Itaru drew on their cultural and familial values with determined fortitude to face what awaited them.

Archival photos of "evacuees" lined up to board the buses show people with hats and high-heeled shoes, suits, and ties, smiling automatically in response to the camera lens aimed their way. They look as if they might be going away on vacation. *But wait. Where are we going? How long will we stay? What will it be like? Why do we have to go? How will we manage?* These unanswered questions seem to fall to the ground as people are pressed into the crowded bus heading to a destination they've been told will be their "home away from home."

Surrender begins. Their world shrinks as the bus pulls away and the psychological and emotional freeze sets in. For most, there were no tears, no cries for help, no opposition or outrage. How could a person begin to wrap their mind around what was happening to them? This was America, after all. There were no answers.

Tucked inside my mother's 1942 diary was a news clipping from the April 28 *San Francisco News Call Bulletin* marking the day of arrival at the San Bruno, California, Tanforan Assembly Center:

Tanforan "Opener"
for S.F.'s Jap Evacuees

Tanforan, California's historic racing plant at San Bruno, experienced a totally different type of "Opening Day" today—an event unique in its colorful history. Closed to horse racing for the duration under military dictum, the famed turf plant's clubhouse and pit echoed today to the chatter and cries of a new type of crowd—a throng of Japanese adults and children, the first evacuees to pioneer this wartime assembly center.

... Doll-like babies, a small boy with a big orange matching his face in color and contour, young girls with knitting, youngsters with plane models, grandparents bent over canes—a colony picked up in toto—all smiling and cheerful as families on a holiday outing.

Lunch was their first meal in this high fenced hive, and on the luncheon menu for these Japanese were onion soup and sauerkraut! ...

In contrast to this mocking report, my father wrote the following haiku:

harusame no	cold early spring
kaeru hi shira-nu	I prepare for the journey
tabijitaku	not knowing when I will return

After just forty-five minutes by bus, Shizuko and Itaru arrived at their first "home away from home" to find what my mother described as a "small, smelly, windowless horse stable." Much like the demeaning newspaper report of their arrival, the manure-stained wooden horse stalls had been whitewashed over. My parents began their life here, not as evacuees rescued from danger, but as prisoners held in a barbed-wire enclosure guarded by armed soldiers in gun towers.

Once Shizuko and Itaru were assigned to their "apartment," a large truck drove through, dumping canvas bags. Piles of hay were to be used to stuff the bags for mattresses. One Japanese American army veteran who became a medic later in the war told me he recognized those same canvas bags while serving in Europe. They were standard-issue body bags used to remove soldiers killed in action.

Toilet facilities were appalling. My mother described the humiliation of sitting on toilets that were nothing but holes placed along a wooden board. Women had to sit side by side without privacy, exposed to others. All she could do to preserve some sense of dignity was to hold a towel over her face.

From the end of March until May 20, eight thousand people would eventually be forced to live at the Tanforan site, and most of them, like Shizuko and Itaru, were just a few miles from the homes they had left behind. From their side of the fence, they watched people chatting and strolling along the sidewalks, cars filled with families driving by on a Sunday afternoon. On their side of the fence, life was about curfews, roll call, communal toilets, mess-hall dining, the stench of horse manure, and repeated invasions of privacy—a life of day-to-day uncertainty.

Tanforan's close proximity to the city made it possible for neighbors and friends to visit and bring fresh produce and needed supplies that were not available within the temporary prison camp. A room at the top of the racetrack grandstand was used for visits during certain hours. Visits were tightly controlled. Many of those who brought gifts had to watch as guards opened the packages; even melons, cakes, and pies were cut in half in search of weapons or contraband.

The kindness of friends and neighbors was important for both the physical and emotional sustenance of the prisoners. But it was the unexpected kindness of a stranger that sustained my mother for years after her incarceration. She told me about the "church ladies" from the American Friends Service Committee (Quakers) who would come to the fence to toss fresh fruits and vegetables over to prisoners every week. One day, a woman, possibly noticing that my mother was pregnant, called to her to come closer. Then, with enormous strength, the woman heaved a beautiful handmade quilt over the fence. When my mother picked it up, the woman smiled and said, "I hope this helps."

A lifetime later, when my mother was ill and failing, the familiar blanket, now worn and ratty, lay on her bed. I suggested we replace it with a new blanket, but she refused. I knew the story about how it had come to belong to her, but I was surprised by the intensity of her refusal. When I asked her what the blanket meant to her, she said softly, clutching it in her hand, "This blanket helped me to remember that someone outside cared." I realized, in that moment, the healing power of the compassionate witness, someone whose presence countered the dehumanizing narrative imposed on a victim of trauma. Someone cared.

Adjusting to life at Tanforan was a difficult transition for my parents. As newlyweds, they had worked hard and gradually acquired the basic comforts for their modest rented apartment in San Francisco Japantown. Hastily, they had left behind all their belongings, including their treasured wedding gifts. In Tanforan, although no prisoner was required to work, most operations were to be carried out principally by the prisoners. Itaru's bookkeeping skills enabled him to find work in the prison administration office. The wage schedule for unskilled work was $8.00 per month; skilled, $12.00 per month; professional and technical, $16.00 per month. For those whose bank accounts had been frozen, even this small amount would help supplement the subsistence living in these temporary holding facilities.

A prisoner in her own country, Shizuko sought solace in her friendships and pleasure in nurturing the baby growing in her womb. Meanwhile, Itaru wrote haiku poetry in witness of their slowly dissipating contact with the outside world.

nagaki hi yoa,	Long spring day,
mui no inochi no,	a do-nothing life,
oshimaruru	fills me with sadness

Thursday, April 30, 1942 Rain
We left San Francisco on Greyhound bus about 4:15 p.m. Made me miserable leaving in the pouring rain! I could not describe my feeling in words. It took us about 45 minutes to reach Tanforan.

Friday, May 1, 1942 Beautiful day
When we reached Tanforan yesterday, first baggage inspection, physical examination and assignment to Barrack 14, apartment 88. Oba-san is next door. Around 5 o'clock, everybody was getting up. We did too. I did unpacking for couple hours but not feeling well so I got back in bed.

Monday, May 4, 1942 Clear
First time I went to dinner. Menu: bread (no butter), hash, boiled potato, several pieces of sausage. Holding their own dish and lining up for food made me think we are all prisoners. It is a sad picture of war!

Tuesday, May 5, 1942 Clear
We have been eating canned foods for days now.

Thursday, May 7, 1942 Clear—Weight 105 lb.
Both of us spent almost whole day in bed suffering from typhoid injection.
    Many Oakland people have come in today.

Saturday, May 9, 1942 Clear
I am apt to get lazy from body condition, so will try not to be lazy. First time we had roast pork for dinner. I had a second helping secretly. It is against the rule but I am hungry. Today Oba-san's friend came in from San Mateo and brought some butter and bacon. Before we got in bed, we had good coffee with toast, and good old butter!

Tuesday, May 12, 1942 Clear
First time I had a shower today. I feel very light. Received letter from Mrs. Fukushima. She informed me about many important things about pregnancy.

Saturday, May 16, 1942 Clear
Received food stuffs from Mother. It was so good to taste homemade canned pear. Still there is no store so I crave for fresh vegetables and fruits so badly.

Monday, May 18, 1942 *Clear*
Have had morning sickness for past month, but from two days ago feeling much better when I get up in the morning. I must not be lazy, and make sure to go to breakfast. The Japanese potatoes I brought from home have put out buds. They were almost dried up, so I planted them in the yard. Picked wild flowers and made them into pressed flowers.

Wednesday, May 20, 1942 Beautiful day
Terribly hot today. Over 80 degrees. Still vomiting so spent all day in bed.
    Called Dr. Togasaki and she said something that I ate caused illness. Over 50 people were vomiting from food poisoning.

Monday, May 25, 1942
It rained like dog and cats. Somebody stole my precious Japanese potatoes from garden.

Thursday, June 4, 1942 *Cloudy*
Patience is the foundation for long-lasting love. Negligence is an enemy. Lately, I am too careless toward my husband. I should be more careful about my words.
    Since Alaska was bombed yesterday, all San Francisco radio stations were shut down after 9 o'clock in the evening.

Friday, June 5, 1942 Sunny—107 lb.
Today I had my first examination with Dr. Togasaki. I was relieved to hear that my physical condition is normal, and that my baby is now as big as four eggs.

Sunday, June 7, 1942 Clear
All day terribly windy so spent most of the day inside. Heard that letters we wrote to Japan have been taken away by the Army. It's great shock for us.

Wednesday, June 10, 1942 Clear
Mr. Ina's 29th Birthday. Happy birthday to him! Next birthday he will be a proud father!

Wednesday, June 17, 1942 Clear
Maybe it's because of pregnancy that I'm getting irritable and feeling sad and tearful today without knowing why. Even though I know I shouldn't be like this, I can't do anything about it.

Friday, June 19, 1942 Clear
Mr. Winston Churchill is here in the U.S.A. again. Having conference with Mr. Roosevelt.

So happy to hear from sister Kimiko today. Parents are at Tule Lake Relocation Center in Northern California. I'm very sorry that I said so much stubborn things to my husband. I have to reconsider and put my words into action.

Tuesday, June 23, 1942 Clear
Again Mr. & Mrs. Ramos visited us today and brought beautiful flowers. But unfortunately we had a contraband inspection so they [the guards] did not let them in to see us. Official inspection is done all over the barrack and they seized lots of Japanese literature and carpenter tools.

Tuesday, June 30, 1942 Fair
Received letter from mother. Finished baby's pants with pink yarn. I wonder what is it going to be? Today is two months since we came to Tanforan. I am pretty tired of camp life now.

Saturday, July 4, 1942 Clear
Today is Fourth of July but not much meaning for us in Camp.

Friday, July 10, 1942 Clear
Husband got notice to report to the office right away. When he got there, he was told he could work there so he began the job right away. It's better for me that he goes to work so I won't be so selfish and become lazy.

Thursday, July 16, 1942 *Sunny*
Since July, it seems that my stomach has swollen a lot, and every movement feels difficult. I have made it a routine to walk around with Oba-san. Mr. Ramos sent us a box of apricots. He does it so often. I can't help feeling sorry.

Sunday, July 19, 1942 Clear
At the grandstand we celebrated *Obon* [Buddhist festival honoring the spirits of the dead] today.

Wednesday, July 22, 1942 Clear
Fukushima-san's family arrived here 4:30 p.m. They entered Barrack 25, stable #18. Also Mrs. Peterson visited us and brought me the baby clothes, 6 pkgs. tea, baby bottle sterilizer, dozen cucumbers, and dozen green apples and 35 yards of cotton goods.

Friday, July 24, 1942 Clear
Mrs. Fukushima gave me a maternity dress. I made a *iwata obi* [waistband] to support my back and protect the baby. Tried it on but it's very hard to keep tightly on. I'm not sure, but I think I felt my baby move.

Sunday, August 2, 1942 Clear
Since yesterday, I've felt my baby moving. It seems the baby has been growing and doing a lot of exercise. Every time I sense the movement, I feel it very dear.

Tuesday, August 4, 1942 Sunny
Mr. Ina received first pay check of $6.37. It seems everything is getting more restricted these days. Today we must hand in all the sugar we have. Also Japanese phonograph records too.

Friday, August 7, 1942 Cloudy
Received another package of fresh prunes, green apples, and peaches from Mr. Ramos. From tomorrow our visitors are only allowed from 1–4 p.m. in afternoon. Also no perishable foods are allowed in camp anymore.

Friday, August 14, 1942 Clear
Unexpectedly Mr. & Mrs. Peterson visited us around 3 p.m. They gave us baby's gift (sweater set). It's pink so I hope it is going to be Girl!

As stark as life was in the Tanforan Assembly Center, my parents were not far from what had been their home, and the climate was familiar to them. The so-called assembly centers were temporary prison camps, hurriedly filled by thousands of people from nearby communities, while the more permanent "relocation centers," or, more accurately, concentration camps, were being constructed. For the time being, proximity to the city and the presence of visitors provided a sense of civility and contact with the outside world. Visitors also likely served as an informal check on the living conditions and treatment of the prisoners. The love and support of their non-Japanese neighbors and friends brought my parents great comfort. It was something my mother spoke about from time to time, and it was a lesson in life I would never forget. In the face of hate and deprivation, the presence of a compassionate witness was sustenance for the soul.

Saturday, August 22, 1942 Clear
Today it was officially announced that Tanforan people will begin moving from Sept. 15 to Relocation Center. Place is not known yet.

Saturday, September 5, 1942 Clear
No visitors on account of inspection. One F.B.I. and one soldier came and inspected our apt. They took one Japanese book called "How to Play Cards."

Tuesday, September 8, 1942 Rain
Mrs. Peterson visited us for last time.

Wednesday, September 9, 1942 Fair
Feel very tired. First 250 volunteers left for Utah relocation camp at 6:30 p.m. Mr. & Mrs. Ramos visited us for last time. My legs are very stiff these days. Body is very heavy.

Tuesday, September 15, 1942 Clear
First 500 families left today. I think we will go to Utah on Sept. 20th with Fukushima-san's family. Started Mr. Ina's sweater.

Wednesday, September 16, 1942 Clear
Second 500 left today for War Relocation Authority camp in Utah.

Thursday, September 17, 1942 Clear
We received official order to leave here on this coming Sunday (Sept. 20th). Mr. Fukushima came over in the evening and helped us packing.

Sunday, September 20, 1942 Clear
2:30 p.m.—Finished inspection.
4:30—We gathered at gate by 5 p.m.
6:45—Left Tanforan.

My mother watched the armed guards cautiously as she stepped off the crowded, suffocating train during a stop en route to the prison camp in Utah. Struck by the desolation of the desert landscape, she told me later, "I wondered if today was the day they were going to line us up and shoot us. If they did, nobody would have ever known." At the time, she kept such thoughts to herself, as the noose around her freedom tightened. Seven months pregnant now, she had no idea what lay ahead. Held in captivity, prisoners were not entitled to know where they were going, how they would be treated, or how long they would be held.

After my mother's passing, I discovered an amazing collection of prison camp "newspapers" saved from every day of my parents' incarceration. Censored and controlled to varying degrees by the administration, these publications served as a means for camp authorities to dictate information and shape perceptions for the prisoners. They also served as the only means for prisoners to share news about camp activities and events. Although my parents didn't arrive at the Topaz concentration camp in Utah until September 22, 1942, included in the neatly organized box was an earlier issue of the *Topaz Times* dated September 17, 1942, likely reissued to welcome new arrivals. The very nature of an American concentration camp was captured in the surreal messaging that denied and distorted the truth of what was actually taking place. It was the message of the "benevolent oppressor":

GREETINGS

You will be shown every respect as befits the dignity and importance which belongs to every human being. You will in turn be expected to join your best efforts to those of your fellow residents in the common objective of developing our community to the greatest degree possible. The adjustments will be many and difficult. With God's help and blessing we can have faith and hope for the future.

WORDS

You are now in Topaz, Utah. Here we say Dining Hall and not Mess Hall; Safety Council, not Internal Police; Residents, not Evacuees; and last but not least, Mental Climate, not Morale.

Much change was in store for Shizuko and Itaru. When they arrived at the remote, military-style prison camp built on dry desert land, they would find the fine-grain sand, like the indignity of their present lives, a constant intrusion. Insinuating itself through the cracks between wooden wall boards and windows, the grit imposed its presence without reprieve. They slept with dampened cloths to keep from inhaling the dust that would settle on their faces at night.

Choking dust storms and severe extremes of weather took their toll on Shizuko's determined optimism. Full medical services, supplies, and staff were not yet available in the hurriedly built, still-unfinished prison camp. Baby boy Kiyoshi was born on December 3, 1942. With no anesthesia available, it was a difficult delivery. What my mother described to me as "natural childbirth" was, in fact, a medical procedure under harsh and primitive conditions. Despite the cruel circumstances of their lives, Itaru and Shizuko joyfully celebrated the arrival of their firstborn child with great excitement. And with quiet resignation, they settled into a routine, adjusting to life circumscribed by barbed-wire fencing and armed soldiers.

Tuesday, September 22, 1942
Arrived at Delta, Utah at 8:30 a.m. Mountain time. Already many buses were waiting to take us to Topaz War Relocation Camp. It took ½ hour by bus. When we were about to arrive, brass bands played and many people were welcoming us by happy smiles. What a dust! It looks like smoke. So this is going to be our duration home. Block 22, Building 10, Apt. A.

Wednesday, September 23, 1942
What a climate! In the morning it is freezing. But in day time hot as 120 degrees. Dust! Hot! Freezing! We could do nothing except somehow get through the day.

Thursday, September 24, 1942
I asked Caucasian workers about scorpion and they said there are some here, so be careful about babies playing on the sand. Also keep out of sage brush!

Sunday, September 27, 1942
Wind storm began. It was just terrible. So dusty that we could hardly breathe in the house.
What a place! It's just like Hell! Too dusty to do anything!

Tuesday, September 29, 1942
Dust storm again! Spent most of time in latrine. This is the only place to breathe cool air.

Wednesday, September 30, 1942
Thank goodness, no storm today. Felt glad I am still alive.

Friday, October 2, 1942
Wind storm all night and it was too dusty in the room so I couldn't sleep very well. Not feeling so well. Very tired and no appetite.

Monday, October 5, 1942
It was too cold this morning so we turned on the pot belly stove for the first time. Some children in our neighborhood came to warm themselves. They were very happy. There was no merciless wind and the day ended calmly.

Saturday, October 10, 1942
Must have gotten food poisoning yesterday. Felt sick and got up to go to the latrine six times last night. Stayed in bed all day today.

Sunday, October 25, 1942
After I put up the curtains, the room looked brighter and felt more like a home for human beings.

Wednesday, October 28, 1942
First snowfall in Topaz. Lack of coal these days. After dinner, did some cleaning. Preparing for going to hospital any day.

Sunday, November 15, 1942 Snow and Rain and Wind.
Dust storm swept over Topaz from last night until now. Then rain and finally snowfall.

Thursday, November 26, 1942 Thanksgiving Day
Cloudy. We had a good turkey dinner. We took our food over to Fukushima-san's and ate together.

Sunday, November 29, 1942 Cloudy
I wonder if my baby will be born around tomorrow. Ina is devoting himself to making a table for the baby all day today. Is the baby going to be born first? Or is the table going to be finished first? Received baby's nightgowns, shoes, blanket, underwear and sweater from Mother.

Wednesday, December 2, 1942
Since around 7:30 a.m. my stomach started to ache every 30 minutes, and I thought that it was because I had gotten a chill. I went to bed and rested and warmed myself with a hot water bottle. I asked Ina to bring my dinner home and I ate a little. He heated some chicken broth that Fukushima-san sent for me. I enjoyed it and went to bed around 11:30 p.m. Ina was tired and began to fall asleep, but suddenly I felt the pain every 15 minutes so I woke him up thinking that the baby is finally about to be born. He called an ambulance and we went to the hospital.

Thursday, December 3, 1942
It was 1:30 a.m. when we arrived at the hospital. Soon after that I felt the pain every 5 minutes, and then 3 minutes, and I suffered until 7:30 a.m. Finally I couldn't stand the pain and was taken to the delivery room. Baby boy was born at 8:10 a.m.

Baby Boy Ina—Weight: 6 lb. 10¾ oz. Length: 18¾ inches. Delivered by Dr. Teshima.

Wednesday, December 9, 1942
Kiyoshi's cord has come off.

Thursday, December 10, 1942 Clear
Kiyoshi's Weight—7 lbs. He had first tub bath this morning. His hair is very fluffy and his complexion is very clear & smooth.

Tuesday, December 15, 1942
Back home with new member of family! Kiyoshi! Daddy has fixed the house so nicely and welcome us!

Wednesday, December 23, 1942
Mrs. Yoshida prematurely gave birth to a boy at six month pregnancy at 11 a.m. this morning. He lived for two hours and died. I feel sorry for her. We were looking forward to Kiyoshi's friend being born in March. I don't know what caused this. Feel so sorry. Yoshida-san must be heartbroken.

My mother did her best to make the most of what seemed an un-fathomable situation, a surreal quality of life that barely simulated normality. She opened the New Year with her annual resolutions:

Friday, January 1, 1943
Resolutions: 1. Never speak ill of people.
2. Never worry too much.
3. Always keep home in good spirits.
4. Serve husband well.

She cared for her infant son, a new mother marveling at the wonders of her month-old baby. Itaru was tasked with washing diapers in the latrine and went to "work" while she made curtains for their new "home" and sent holiday greetings to friends. Yet Shizuko's apparent cheerfulness and resolute effort to maintain a positive attitude slowly give way in her diary as her entries begin to focus on activities outside the immediate household.

Initially stunned by the trauma of their forced removal, nine months later the prisoners held at the Topaz concentration camp began to awaken from their somnambulant existence and see the reality of what was happening to them. Like the dust storms that continued day after day, the erosion of their hopes and dreams finally became too much to bear, and they made the leap from surrendering victims to outraged resisters. The catalyst was the loyalty questionnaire, the single most destructive mandate given during the entire period of the incarceration. Prisoners were forced to respond under the threat of twenty years in prison and a $10,000 fine.

This questionnaire and subsequent iterations of it, devised jointly by the army and the War Relocation Authority (WRA), were purportedly intended to solve several emerging problems. Most pressing for the army was to meet the need for more soldiers to fill the ranks on the battlefield by first recruiting, then eventually drafting, young Japanese American prisoners into military service. Also, with the increasing exigencies of war, the cost of administering a massive prison program incarcerating hundreds of thousands of people was becoming untenable. Lastly, the ACLU of Northern California was raising questions about the constitutionality of the entire program. In the end, the solution for both the army and the civilian administration required them to separate the proverbial goats from the sheep.

Since the government had declared the mass incarceration necessary for national security, it now had to justify the release of prisoners back into the community. Deeming people of Japanese ancestry "a threat to the peace and safety of the American public" had allowed the government to move forward with race-based removal and mass incarceration, bypassing all due process. If you had one-sixteenth Japanese blood, you were guilty as charged. A large-scale release of prisoners, who had now been incarcerated for almost a year, would be difficult to explain. For this reason, the government needed some way to determine who should be detained or released. A false moral standard was constructed, and the question of loyalty became a powerful tool for manipulation.

The government's solution was to impose a mandatory registration questionnaire to be completed by all inmates sixteen years of age and older. It was a combined strategy to, first, qualify military-age men to register for what was initially voluntary enlistment and later a mandatory draft to serve in a racially segregated combat unit. Second, the questionnaire served as a perfunctory determination of loyalty to quell any fears that the American public might have about former prisoners returning to their neighborhoods while the war with Japan continued. The registration form my parents eventually signed was titled "Statement of United States Citizen of Japanese Ancestry." It was a four-page document with a total of twenty-eight questions requiring background information regarding former employment, location of family members, education level, religion, and so on. The questions that raised the ire and the fear of prisoners were the last two, numbers 27 and 28:

> 27. Are you willing to serve in the armed forces of the United States on combat duty, wherever ordered?

> 28. Will you swear unqualified allegiance to the United States of America and faithfully defend the United States from any or all attack by foreign or domestic forces, and forswear any form of allegiance or obedience to the Japanese emperor, or any other foreign government or organization?

Poorly worded and administered, the questionnaire sparked fear among prisoners that their responses could result in unforeseen consequences. The absence of transparency on the part of the administration led to rampant rumors and anxiety about the potential outcomes of answering yes or no. In meetings with camp administrators and army personnel, prisoners were given inadequate answers to their questions about what exactly they were being asked to register for.

People began to organize, holding mass meetings to galvanize a collective resistance to yet another assault by the perpetrator authorities. I hear my father's voice—"Be strong, don't cry"—words I now understand that he likely said to himself. After months of making the best of a bad situation, my mother, too, uncovered a strength of spirit that could not be crushed.

Tuesday, February 9, 1943
Block 23 meeting was held on *nisei & issei* registration matter. Whether we are loyal or disloyal to America.

Wednesday, February 10, 1943
Ina went to Mass Meeting on "Registration." My mind is made up.

Thursday, February 11, 1943
Today we were supposed to register at Mess 8, but people are out on strike so no one went there. If we are Japanese, it is a matter of course not to go. Kibei meeting was held. Their answer is No.

When registration was initially implemented, organized resistance led Topaz to be the only camp out of the ten WRA camps where every prisoner refused to register. To put a stop to the resistance, in a show of force, military police began patrolling the perimeters, monitoring entries and exits. Internal police were responsible for security inside the camps and conducted roll calls on an unpredictable schedule. The administration took control of camp-wide meetings and claimed that all citizens who refused to register would be in violation of the Espionage Act of 1917, whereby obstruction in the government's effort to raise an army would lead to imprisonment and fine. In fact, there was no such law in existence that penalized people for refusing to complete a questionnaire.

Undeterred, ordinary people, such as my parents, denied their civil liberties and held indefinitely without ever having committed a crime, took a stand.

Saturday, February 13, 1943
Block 23 meeting was held and nominated 4 persons to go to tomorrow's meeting: Ina, Mr. Fukushima, Dr. Ochikubo, Mr. Utsumi. We decided to fight for our civil rights and then register. We were told that any person who breaks the law of registration will get 20 year imprisonment and $10,000 in fine.

Sunday, February 14, 1943
Block representatives' meeting was held at Mess 32 from 2:30 to 10 p.m. Majority of the people made up their minds to fight for civil rights and then register if necessary. They wrote up the resolutions and sent them to Washington, D.C. by telegraph.

Protest through acts of noncooperation, petitions, strikes, and walkouts from work assignments ensued. Outraged that they would be required to respond to such questions while held unjustly behind barbed-wire fences, my parents joined a group of prisoners who refused to register, sending a signed resolution via teletype to Secretary of War Harry Stimson and the national director of the WRA, Dillon Meyer, stating that they would willingly respond to the questionnaire in the affirmative once their civil rights were restored.

The resolution was submitted February 15 by a group called the Committee of 33, representing the various wards in the Topaz concentration camp. In reading this document, I was struck by the articulate rationale, steeped in knowledge of the rule of law. I have included here excerpts that specifically outline the violations of civil rights perpetrated by the US government, while also countering the government portrayal of prisoners as a threat to national security. It clearly reflects the voices of outraged American citizens protesting their unjust, race-based incarceration and demanding that government authorities be held accountable to the principles of the US Constitution.

We, the citizens of the United States of America, residents of the Central Utah Relocation Project, Topaz, Utah, in order to perform our duties as loyal citizens of the United States and in order to uphold the principles of democracy as established in the Constitution of the United States do hereby state that:
[. . .]
Whereas, we have temporarily surrendered many of the rights and privileges of citizenship which we have heretofore enjoyed.

Whereas, we suffered losses of homes, properties, work, freedom of movement, separation from friends, and all things we felt dear to us without protest.

Whereas, we wish to prevent in the future, the mass evacuation or confining of citizens without trial.

Whereas, we feel that there is only one class of citizenship in this country and a loyal citizen of one race should not be treated any different from another.

[. . .]

Therefore, be it resolved:

[. . .]

That we request President Roosevelt to give us assurance that he will use his good office in an endeavor to secure all constitutional and civil rights as American citizens.

[. . .]

That we have the Government note the advantages of the good publicity to be gained by disbursing nisei soldiers into the Army at large rather than by forming a separate combat team.

That we believe that if satisfactory answers can be given by a Government spokesman, preferably the President of the United States, to these questions we can go and fight for this our country without fear or qualms concerning the security of our future rights.

I imagine my parents, drained by insult and humiliation, feeling empowered by the clarity and strength of their formal demands, this earnest effort likely their last hope for freedom and safety in their country of birth. Shizuko notes, after having sent the resolution, "Everyone was encouraged to proceed with registration." Certainly fearful of the penalties threatened by the authorities, but with more resolve and conviction, she seems to have been transformed as she and Itaru proceeded to register, taking baby Kiyoshi with them.

Monday, February 15, 1943
Block 23 meeting was held again. Dr. Ochikubo was chairman. He suggested that we should register now because resolutions have been sent to Washington D.C. Fight has been started! Now it is the only way! Each person must decide his own mind on questions 27 & 28.

Wednesday, February 17, 1943
Kiyoshi's weight is 13 lbs. 6 oz. Ina caught a cold and stayed in bed all day.

    11 p.m. to 1 a.m. special meeting was held for tomorrow's registration.

Three days after the resolution was sent, and on the day of the scheduled registration, the *Topaz Times* published the government's response to the Committee of 33 Resolution:

> It is only by mutual confidence and cooperation that the loyal Japanese Americans can be restored to their civil rights. . . . The United States government has evidenced its faith in the loyal Japanese American by giving them the opportunity to serve their country. This is their opportunity to demonstrate to the American people that they have faith in America.

The dismissive doublespeak response asserts that the only way loyal Americans could have their rights returned was if they volunteered for military service. Ignoring every issue addressed in the resolution, officials insisted that everyone answer the loyalty questionnaire.

My parents, along with thousands of others, responded with anger and despair when the registration was forcefully resumed. Shizuko's and Itaru's answers would, for years, be used to define their loyalty to America. It would take me decades of studying, interviewing, and researching to understand that my parents never suffered a "crisis of loyalty." Their No-No responses more accurately reflected a crisis of faith in their own country, faith that their government would protect them and afford them the rights and privileges guaranteed to all US citizens.

Thursday, February 18, 1943
We registered today. Took Kiyoshi with us too.

There were many complicated reasons for prisoners to respond in the negative to questions 27 and 28. Issei, never allowed citizenship, feared that they would be deported as enemy aliens and separated from their American-born children unless their children, too, answered No. Others, regardless of generation, were incensed at the injustice of sending incarcerated Japanese American men to the front lines in racially segregated combat units. Furthermore, reported incidents of violence against Japanese Americans who were released and returned to their homes and farms convinced prisoners that life in America for people with the "face of the enemy" did not hold much promise. The prospect of forced resettlement to the outside during wartime, without jobs or resources or assurance of government assistance or protection, offered only bleak possibilities. Some realized that if their only hope for a life of freedom and dignity was to go to Japan, even if they had never been there before, they had to state their loyalty to Japan or be held suspect upon arrival.

With little information about the consequences of the answers given, the Topaz prison camp grew rife with fear and conflict. Officials characterized those answering No as troublemakers and actively pursued efforts to create factions within the prison population, identifying any dissident as disloyal and anti-American. Internalizing the perspective of the perpetrator, those answering Yes blamed these "agitators" for delaying the release of all prisoners. Families were divided. Fathers argued with sons; brothers argued with brothers; neighbors became suspicious of one another. Rumors spread, labeling people as anti-American on one side and as fence-sitters and *inu* (dogs), meaning collaborators and informants, on the other.

This characterization of the "disloyal bad boys" was internalized by many of the prisoners themselves, and those who aligned their "loyalty" with the victor-oppressor would carry their animosity toward the dissidents beyond the years of captivity to the present day. With America's eventual victory over Japan, the dissidents would be cast in the shadow of the vanquished enemy, instead of being recognized as defenders of the US Constitution.

Were there truly violent individuals in the camps? Yes, there were bullies, thugs, and gangs, whose behavior, fueled by the smoldering discontent throughout the prison camp, threatened the administration as well as other prisoners. There was also growing belief among those who had lost faith in America that their words and actions in opposition to the authorities would help give credence to their intent to claim Japan as their homeland as they prepared themselves for deportation. Some were considered "fanatical pro-Japan loyalists," known to threaten and assault individuals viewed as fence-sitters or traitors to the fatherland. Most had become disillusioned and outraged at being unjustly vilified, displaced, and imprisoned. Authorities did little to temper the growing internal conflict.

Shortly after the registration was complete and those deemed disloyal were identified, further steps were taken to rid the authorities of the so-called troublemakers. FBI agents entered the Topaz camp, authorized to conduct investigations of individuals who spoke against the registration. Fomenting even more discord, agents sought informants to point out individuals to be interrogated. My father was called in and questioned about the statement he made at a kibei meeting on February 11.

Tuesday, March 30, 1943
Today is my second wedding anniversary. We are just as happy with each other as two years ago. Now we are proud parents! Keep it up!

Thursday, April 1, 1943
Ina has been called by the FBI and questioned by them. *I honestly declared that I'm not able to pledge my loyalty to the United States. From now on, I must be determined to follow my beliefs no matter what happens.*

One of the most corrosive psychological effects of captivity is being forced to relinquish one's own moral principles and betray friends and family in service of approval from the oppressor. In my research, I discovered a report made by one of my father's good friends, another kibei from San Francisco. He had taken notes of the speeches and turned in the names of the speakers at various kibei meetings discussing the registration. On April 1, Itaru was called in by the FBI for questioning. During the interrogation, he was required to confirm the exact words he had spoken in Japanese at the meeting; his speech was then translated into English. Here is an excerpt from his statement to the FBI:

> *At the Kibei meeting held Thursday February 11, 1943, I made a speech generally as follows: The registration is a very important problem to us. My own personal opinion is this: We should be treated equal to the free people. We should ask to the War Relocation Authority to trust us equal to the free people. On account of this problem our parents are worried very much. We citizens have to take some steps to solve the problem. I have taken my stand for Japan because of evacuation.*

This so-called admission of guilt would lead to charges of sedition —a federal crime of advocating uprising against the government or support for an enemy nation during time of war, through speech, publication, or organization.

On the heels of the loyalty questionnaire, another event occurred that heightened tension between prisoners and the administration. Hatsuaki Wakasa, a sixty-three-year-old issei bachelor, was shot and killed by a military guard. Reports claiming the victim was attempting to escape were contradicted by prisoners who discovered a large bloodstain five feet inside the fence. It was later confirmed that the victim was, in fact, facing the MP when he was shot. If he had been escaping through the fence, the bullet would have struck him from behind.

On April 28, at Fort Douglas, Utah, court-martial proceedings found the soldier who had killed Wakasa not guilty. Prisoners protested, demanding an open investigation of Wakasa's death. The army, fearful of a violent backlash, responded with a general alert, and guards armed themselves with machine guns, gas masks, and tear gas. Grief and fear spread through the prison camp. The first known killing of a prisoner represented the unspoken terror prisoners had been living with every day. It had become evident that beneath the superficially benign demeanor of the authorities lay a deadly hatred that could easily be provoked.

A camp-wide committee of prisoners was formed. When the administration refused to conduct a funeral at the site where Wakasa was killed, inmates refused to work until a compromise was made. Finally, when an agreement was reached, Shizuko and others gathered to mourn the tragic passing of one of their own. In the desolate prison camp confines, only paper flowers adorned Wakasa's casket.

After the Wakasa shooting, armed guards were to be on outside perimeter duty only, so when a military police officer was posted inside at a checkpoint entrance to the motor pool area, nisei truck drivers working at the garage refused to pass. Ordered back to work by the Caucasian garage superintendent, workers refused, and the motor pool was closed down. Farm workers joined the dispute, halting work on the camp crops and leading to a camp-wide work stoppage.

The mounting discontent among the prisoners and wariness among the prison staff created a heated and unpredictable environment. With the unresolved mystery of how Wakasa met his death, inmates grew increasingly distrustful and insecure about their own safety within the prison camp confines. Authorities pressed forward, taking measures to get rid of dissident leaders who were gaining support and authority inside the community. Without due process, men were accused of acts of disloyalty, separated from their families, and removed to other incarceration sites managed by the DOJ.

The goal was to work toward closing down the ill-conceived prison camps by first isolating "troublemakers," including those who did not respond with an unequivocal Yes to the loyalty questionnaire. These prisoners could then be segregated into one concentration camp and eventually deported to Japan. Young men deemed loyal were being drafted into racially segregated military units to fight in Europe and the Pacific Islands. Others were informed that they could begin the process of applying for what was euphemistically referred to as "leave clearance," a military term obfuscating the fact that people were actually being released from prison confinement.

Still having no idea about the future consequences of their answers to the questionnaire, Shizuko, along with others, continued to hope for their freedom. She followed the prescribed steps to apply for leave clearance, writing desperate letters to Caucasian friends and teachers, asking them to vouch for her good standing. After finding the letters from her Caucasian teachers, neighbors, and friends in the National Archives, I never had the heart to share with my mother the mixed responses submitted by people she looked to for support. She never knew that her beloved schoolteacher with whom she continued her communication long after the war had written, "Remembering the deep injustice and treachery which we are suffering at the hands of the Japanese, I hesitate very much to suggest she be released."

In the end, even the positive and supportive letters written on Shizuko's behalf were of no benefit. Her answers to the loyalty questionnaire, and an FBI report about her job representing Japan during the 1939–40 World's Fair, had already precluded her from being considered for release.

As for my father, results following the FBI investigation of people who protested during the loyalty questionnaire fiasco culminated in a DOJ memorandum on June 4, 1943, to James M. McInerney, chief of the National Defense Section, regarding sedition charges against the twenty-two men who made speeches at the kibei meetings in February. Vague and unspecified degrees of misconduct were reported, characterizing the men as either "violent," "positive," or "passive." Itaru was placed in the violent category. An excerpt from the report here describes the details and, interestingly, unintentionally lists the true and actual circumstances suffered by the protesters:

The pattern of the <u>violent</u> subjects' activities was very much
the same in that many false arguments were made to enlist the
sympathies of the audience, incur resentment toward the authorities because of the evacuation, and to otherwise inflame
a love for the fatherland. Much of the appeal to the arguments
advanced was because of the alleged hardships suffered by the
evacuees in being uprooted from their fixed home life on the
West Coast and relocation in the Middle West, and much was
said of the economic losses, deprivations, curtailed liberties,
infringement of civil rights, and hardships imposed upon the
Japanese elders in their midsts.

In the meantime, my parents had no knowledge of the case being
made against their release. While they continued to hope, Shizuko
and Itaru found comfort in celebrating traditional Japanese holidays. For Kiyoshi's auspicious first Boy's Day (*tango no sekku*) in
May, prisoners used scrap cloth to make windsocks shaped as carp
to symbolize the strength and determination needed to swim up-
stream against the flow of the water, an apt metaphor for the struggle to maintain one's dignity in the face of overwhelming adversity.

In her diary, Shizuko describes a growing sense of camaraderie
and unity among prisoners who answered No. Even as they prepared to be segregated, they continued to organize ways to protest
the degrading conditions in the prison camp.

Monday, July 12, 1943
There was a meeting about segregation of 'No' people and repatriation group.
    About time to move along!

Friday, July 16, 1943
Every person is thinking hard about segregation, whether it is
better to repatriate or not.

Monday, August 2, 1943
Block 23 meeting from 7:30 p.m. concerning foods. We get too
much liver & heart so we are going to strike.

Tuesday, August 3, 1943
Kiyoshi's weight 16½ lb. From extreme heat, he has lost weight.

In researching my parents' WRA and FBI records, I saw clearly the way that limited, inaccurate, and prejudicial information was compiled to confirm their involvement in suspect activities. These documents claimed that Itaru, rather than Shizuko, was employed at the World's Fair on Treasure Island, and they cited Itaru's membership in kibei social organizations, even though he participated in these groups years before the US was at war with Japan. My parents were never informed of the supposed evidence used to determine their guilt and eventual sentencing to the Tule Lake Segregation Center.

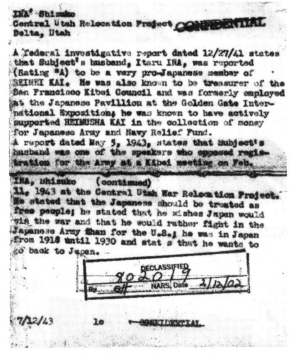

A note from Shizuko's FBI file reveals that an intelligence report on Itaru was made twenty days after the attack on Pearl Harbor.

On August 4, 1943, Shizuko and Itaru were questioned by the US Army Office of the Provost Marshal General's Japanese American Joint Board to determine whether they qualified for "indefinite leave." That day, Shizuko wrote: "Ina and I got a hearing today. We clarified our loyalty to Japan in front of hearing board." After confirming their negative answers to the loyalty questionnaire, my parents were officially denied their freedom. Others notified of their so-called leave clearance were released to attend schools and take jobs, away from the West Coast. Those who answered No would be sent to the Tule Lake Segregation Center, a maximum-security prison camp in Northern California.

In offering a rationale for segregation, national director of the WRA Dillon Meyer explained in a foreword to "The Segregation Program of WRA," a booklet distributed to prisoners, "All relocation center residents found not to be loyal or sympathetic to the United States will be moved to the Tule Lake Center, and those Tule Lake residents found to be American in their loyalties or sympathies will be moved to other centers or, preferably, given permission to relocate outside."

With the denial of leave clearance, Itaru and Shizuko gave up their last shred of hope that their confinement would be recognized as a violation of their civil rights or that their friends outside would help prove that they were worthy American citizens. With no hope for escape or vindication, my parents, like other captivity trauma victims, shifted their perspective, internalizing the perpetrator's definition of who they were. Convinced there was no escape, Shizuko and Itaru were forced to accept the designation of being disloyal. My mother gave up trying to prove her right to justice. In her diary, her voice shifts as she takes on the mantle of the "disloyal enemy." Relieved from the uncertainty of hope, she gathered her righteous indignation, coming to terms with the fact that the America she believed in had completely abandoned her. Japan was now her mother country. Radicalization had solidified. On August 22, she wrote, "It was decided that those of us in Block 23 will be going to Tule Lake on September 13."

In the continuing effort to be rid of the "forever foreigners," authorities sought to increase the number of prisoners deported from the US to Japan, using them as commodities of trade—ultimately, American citizens of Japanese ancestry and their immigrant parents would be exchanged for American civilians held in Japan. The first ship had departed from the West Coast six months after the outbreak of the war, carrying approximately 1,097 people, mostly Japanese officials and businessmen and their families, to a designated neutral location, in exchange for 1,554 American officials and their families. A second ship would carry hostages—Americans held in captivity in Japanese territories to be exchanged for issei and nisei held in WRA prison camps who requested repatriation or expatriation to Japan. The ship was scheduled to depart sometime late in 1943.

Uncertainty about what lay ahead weighed heavily on the prisoners who were being transferred to Tule Lake. As was often the case in the absence of information from the authorities, rumors were the only source that informed people's decisions. Issei leaders who had been removed immediately after the bombing of Pearl Harbor continued to be separated from their families in federal internment camps in New Mexico and North Dakota. Young male prisoners were now subject to military draft to be sent to fight in Europe and the Pacific Islands. Some prisoners—particularly issei parents, many now elderly, who had been denied citizenship despite years of building their lives in America and raising their American-born children—saw repatriation as the only way to reunite or keep their families together.

Repatriation held the promise of a life of freedom, but many families were torn apart under these circumstances. Most nisei, young adults born in the US, had never been to Japan and did not speak the language, yet they were forced to choose between remaining in the country of their birth to be incarcerated or drafted, and staying with their families by expatriating to a foreign land. Also by this time, fueled by rumors and wishful thinking, many elders hoped they would be returning to a victorious homeland.

In the end, 1,513 hostages boarded the Swedish exchange ship, the *Gripsholm*, including more than 100 expatriated Japanese Americans;

737 Japanese Latin Americans who had been kidnapped and transported to the US were used to fulfill the matching exchange quota of US hostages.

With great resolve, Itaru and Shizuko turned their hearts and hopes toward Japan and prepared for transfer to the Tule Lake Segregation Center, committed to taking whatever steps were necessary to eventually board the third prisoner exchange ship to Japan.

Monday, August 23, 1943
From four days ago, Kiyoshi is able to stand by himself. He will be walking soon.

Thursday, September 2, 1943
Second exchange voyage, via the Gripsholm, sailed today from New York. Heard that Aizawa family was on the ship. Wrote short letter (25 words) to be carried on this ship for delivery in Japan to Itaru's sister Kiyoji-san and Grandmother Kisa.

Sunday, September 19, 1943
9 A.M.—gathered at Mess 23
10:30 A.M.—Left Topaz
11 A.M.—Arrived at Delta
12:15 P.M.—Left Delta for Tule Lake

4.

Renunciants

I was a student at UC Berkeley in 1964 when I first learned that my American-born parents had lived without US citizenship status from 1945 until 1959. It was during a time of upheaval on campus. Thousands of students were participating in the Free Speech Movement, protesting the university's ban on campus political speeches. This campus protest would emerge as a beacon of light for the civil rights movement being mounted across the country in the 1960s. The turmoil on campus was at once exciting and disturbing for a third-generation Japanese American college student. I was raised to be a quiet, conforming, and diligent student by parents who had lived on the edge of anxiety since their release in 1946 from over four years of captivity.

Television broadcasts captured images of limp student protesters being dragged onto paddy wagons and driven away to the local county jail as hundreds of other students and faculty members cheered them on. My parents began making urgent calls to me every night, reminding me that my purpose at the university was to get an education. They did not want to see my face in the newspapers. They had made many sacrifices for me to go to college, so I was expected to go to class and absolutely not participate in any form of protest or civil disobedience.

Any thoughts I might have had of even observing the campus sit-ins or protest rallies were quickly redirected. Resolutely, I walked against the tide of excited, noisy students rushing to Sproul Hall to hear the speakers. I arrived at my class to find only three other students seated and waiting for the professor to arrive. So vivid remains the moment when suddenly, the professor, long hair trailing, came running down the center aisle and jumped on top of the desk, his face red with emotion. He pointed his finger at each of us and screamed, "Goddammit! If you come to class again, I will flunk every single one of you!" I left campus in a daze, caught in a double bind, unable to process all the emotions rising up in me.

My mother called that night. Her voice was calm, almost resigned. She told me to come home. She and my father had something they wanted to talk to me about. What followed was a moment that seared itself forever into my memory. My father saw me approaching the house, opened the door, and greeted me with barely a hint of a smile, then quietly went to another room and closed the door. I could see the anxiety in my mother's face as we sat down in the living room of the aging Victorian flat my parents rented in San Francisco's Richmond District. As was often the case when there was trouble in the air, she began speaking for both of them. Her voice subdued, she got right to the point as if she might not speak if the words didn't come out immediately: "We never told you this before, but your father and I renounced our American citizenship when we were in camp. They said we were disloyal, but we believed there was no other way to keep you and your brother safe."

Stunned, I struggled to wrap my mind around what she had just said. Of course I knew that my brother and I had been born in a "relocation center," but conversations about "camp" never took place with my father and only rarely with my mother. Finally, I asked her why they hadn't talked to me and my brothers about what happened. She dropped her head and, speaking softly, said, "We thought you would be ashamed of us." I don't remember if we even cried, but so painful was the realization of something I had always felt but couldn't name—fear, so deeply woven into our being that there were almost no words. It had been a secret my parents couldn't, until that day, ever find the right moment to share with me and my brothers. Finally, my mother gently put her hand on mine. When she spoke, I was surprised at the sternness in her voice. "Do not protest. Bad things will happen."

The Tule Lake concentration camp in Northern California was designated the segregated prison for those found "not to be loyal or sympathetic to the US." Dillon S. Myer, director of the WRA, announced in the *Topaz Times* on July 23, 1943, "The program of segregation is not being undertaken in any sense as a measure of punishment or penalty for those who will be moved." Whether my parents and others believed this to be true or not, they resigned themselves to prepare for yet another forced removal to a prison camp just south of the California-Oregon border, where winter temperatures dropped below freezing and summer temperatures climbed above 100 degrees.

The Tule Lake Segregation Center, one of the ten WRA prison camps, had been retrofitted as a high-security prison. An eight-foot-high double "man-proof" fence was constructed with additional barbed wire. Where there had been six guard towers, there were now twenty-eight, along with a thousand military police officers with cars and armored tanks brought in for heightened security.

Upon entrance to Tule Lake, Itaru and Shizuko found surprising amenities made possible by previous incarcerees, referred to as "old Tuleans." Shizuko was delighted to find "noodle and fish shops" flourishing within the prison confines. But the multiple prisoner mug shots she and Itaru were forced to submit to portended the reality of a slowly tightening surveillance that left no doubt in her mind that Tule Lake was nothing more than a concentration camp.

Monday, September 20, 1943
Arrived at Tule Lake 6:15 p.m. Our hand baggage was inspected by MP's very carefully. Everything passed O.K. Then assigned to 68-16-B as our home.

Tuesday, September 21, 1943
9 a.m., we were photographed and finger-printed 14 times.

 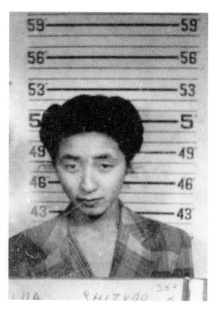

My parents soon found themselves in an even more nightmarish life, with tanks patrolling the perimeter and a guard contingent of fully armed troops at full battalion strength. The 18,526 prisoners segregated from the ten different prison camps were now forced to live in a space meant for 15,000 people. The overcrowded, military-style barracks failed to protect prisoners from extreme weather and choking dust storms. Unsanitary shower rooms and toilets were cause for rampant infectious diseases. There was insufficient milk for children and babies, and significant deficiencies in the diet. And there was no work for the "new Tuleans."

Resentment between the two groups intensified. Old Tuleans who had answered Yes to the loyalty questionnaire, but who for various reasons chose to stay, were considered "loyals" by the administration. They held the best jobs, as well as the favor and ear of the authorities. Meanwhile, the administration ignored complaints about the degrading living conditions from those who arrived later. There was no doubt, contrary to statements made by the administration, that life in Tule Lake was going to be more punishing for the new arrivals stigmatized as disloyal.

There was, however, momentary joy when Shizuko arrived at Tule Lake and reunited with her family. Old Tuleans, her mother, father, and sister, Kimiko, had been arrested and removed from their home in Spokane, Washington, and incarcerated at Tule Lake since the spring of 1942. Having answered Yes to the loyalty questionnaire, Shizuko's issei father, Minoru Mitsui, who had been a section laborer for the Great Northern Railway, received an offer of renewed employment with the railway and was granted leave clearance. After a few short weeks together, Shizuko's parents and siblings were freed to return home. Shizuko was left bereft and despondent, fearful for her parents' safety in a hostile outside world as the war raged on.

Wednesday, September 22, 1943
Mama came over to see us.

Thursday, September 23, 1943
We bought chicken noodle from the noodle shop. Ate a lot with Mama and the family. I couldn't even imagine that there would be a noodle shop and a tofu shop in such a place.

Friday, September 24, 1943
Father came back to camp and the whole family is going out to Spokane on Oct. 4.

Wednesday, September 29, 1943
When we went to Mama's, Mr. Yamazaki, father's friend, was visiting and repeatedly recommended that Mama and Papa stay in camp because of news of violence against Japanese who were being released. But father didn't listen to him at all. It is too late!

Monday, October 4, 1943
Mama, Papa, and Kimiko, left here for Espanola, Washington this morning 11 a.m.

Tuesday, October 5, 1943
I feel awfully lonesome for my family.

Thursday, October 7, 1943
Rain and hailing! Ina went to Placement Office but there is no suitable job for him.

Not feeling well from indigestion. May be pregnant! No monthly since August.

One month after arriving at Tule Lake, on Friday, October 15, Tatsuto Kashima, a fifty-three-year-old prison farm laborer, died from chest injuries sustained in a farm truck accident. Twelve others were hospitalized in critical condition and seventeen others treated for cuts and abrasions. Kashima's accidental death, the result of an inadequately maintained farm truck, brought the simmering complaints about deteriorating camp conditions to a boil. Tule Lake project director Raymond R. Best was confronted by a protest committee with demands for decent compensation for Kashima's widow and safeguards against future accidents. When Best refused to allow a public ceremony in Kashima's honor, tension increased, and prisoners called a general work stoppage. A funeral was held in defiance of Best's mandate.

Monday, October 18, 1943 First snow
First block meeting was held tonight. Ina was supposed to go to farm today, but farmers are on strike so he did not go. It is caused by accident that happened last Friday in which farm truck overturned and 29 farmers got hurt. One man, Mr. Kashima, died today. Four others are seriously injured.

Wednesday, October 20, 1943 1 inch snow
For the funeral of Mr. Kashima on Saturday our Block 68 decided to make an artificial flower wreath. Went to help in the afternoon. Around 9 p.m. the rain turned to snow.

Friday, October 22, 1943
These days there are no vegetables in meals because of farmers' strike.

Saturday, October 23, 1943
2 p.m.—Mr. Kashima's funeral was held outside, near *Sumo* playground.

Sunday, October 24, 1943
So far Kiyoshi has learned to say, *chodai* [please may I have] and *inai-inai* [peek-a-boo].

Tuesday, October 26, 1943
Looks like I'm starting to have morning sickness. When I get up, I feel nausea and don't feel good in my stomach.

My parents witnessed the emergence of a strident, articulate leadership. Having answered No to the loyalty questionnaire, the prisoners segregated to Tule Lake were ripe for resistance. Like many people under circumstances of collective oppression, protesters found solidarity among one another. For some, resistance ignited radicalization. Demonstrating a classic perpetrator strategy to weaken resistance, the administration sought to further divide and conquer the prison community. Individuals among the "loyal" were recruited to infiltrate dissident organizations to report on their activities, and as various groups sought to organize resistance, power struggles ensued.

The issue of loyalty, relentlessly imposed on the prisoners, was now turned on its head. Having been cast out, imprisoned, and designated as disloyal, some issei, kibei, and nisei were now strengthened by the conviction that returning to their ancestral home in Japan was a matter of pride and true loyalty. They formed groups reflecting these values, often collectively referred to as the Hoshidan. Some members of these organizations were bent on a campaign to pressure "fence-sitters" to declare their loyalty to Japan. Extremist elements sought out "stool pigeons," whom they blamed for colluding with the administration to undermine protests, and beat them. Eager to prove their loyalty to Japan, they used threats and violence in an effort to increase their numbers. However, most Tuleans were like my parents—ordinary, nonviolent people, so diminished and humiliated by the abuses of prison life that they found strength, dignity, and solidarity in claiming their Japanese identity and joining others in acts of "noncooperation."

Having segregated the "disloyal" Japanese, politicians continued their efforts to deport them, aliens and citizens alike. On October 28, 1943, the camp newspaper, the *Tulean Dispatch*, reported on California Republican representative J. L. Johnson's proposal that any treaty made with Japan should provide for the deportation of all alien Japanese and American citizens of Japanese ancestry deemed disloyal. Johnson declared, "I have a practical, constitutional scheme that will do complete justice to the bad ones and will do justice to the good Japanese who have been loyal to America." He introduced legislation to create a deportation commission that would review the files of all Japanese Americans whose records indicated that they had been guilty of disloyalty to America.

Although never passed, this proposal set the stage for a massive denationalization program to come. Answers to the loyalty questionnaire, given by the prisoners themselves, would be used as proof of disloyalty and, therefore, risk to national security. In essence, dissidence became conflated with disloyalty, advancing the racist agenda to be "rid of the Japs" who dared to resist the circumstances of their incarceration. Denationalizing Japanese Americans would essentially legalize deportation of thousands of American citizens, many of whom had never been to Japan nor spoke the language.

Growing discontent and conflict eventually erupted between strident No people and Yes people, and within dissident groups. Again, authorities fueled internal strife in the pressure-cooker environment, offering early release or special privileges to those who would collaborate by naming people involved in any form of resistance.

A storm was gathering. Segregated together into one prison camp, dissidents found strength among others who, like them, had refused to be compliant with the injustice they had suffered. Together, they organized to demand better living conditions. On November 1, 1943, when Dillon S. Myer, the national director of the WRA, visited Tule Lake, a negotiating committee of the Daihyo Sha Kai (representative body), an organization of elected leaders, presented a list of inmate grievances. Five thousand prisoners, including men, women, and children, gathered in support of the committee to impress upon Myer the seriousness of the prison-wide discontent. Young kibei men circled the administration building, preventing Caucasian personnel from leaving. Myer was confronted with charges of widespread neglect, incompetence, and black-market corruption going on at Tule Lake. In her diary, Shizuko reported that the meeting ended peacefully, with Myer agreeing to look into the quality and availability of food, and the demands for the removal of Caucasian staff, including medical personnel, who had been hostile and unresponsive to inmate needs.

A few days later, in an unexpected betrayal of trust, Tule Lake director Raymond Best took retaliatory action to punish those who had participated in the strike. Farm workers were fired, and news shortly followed announcing that "loyal" farm workers had been brought in from the Topaz, Utah, and Poston, Arizona, prison camps. They would be paid $1 per hour in contrast to the $16 per month paid to the Tule Lake farm workers. Young men on strike reacted with anger. When they discovered that food was being removed from the warehouse to feed the strikebreakers, prisoners attempted to stop Caucasian staff from loading the food onto trucks, and a fight broke out. Administrators, fearful for their own safety, responded with military force. Prisoners were picked up and savagely beaten, and imprisoned in a hastily built stockade. In the days that followed, workers were tear-gassed and arrested, and martial law was declared. The army entered, taking over Tule Lake, fully armored with guns and tanks.

Under martial law, the atmosphere was marked by armed chaos and suppression. Shizuko now viewed the ongoing events through the lens of America's enemy. In a clarifying sign of having fully crossed over to embrace her "disloyalty," she unabashedly proclaimed herself Japanese by engaging in what had meant little to her in the past as an American citizen—devotion to the deified emperor of Japan. She also placed herself in opposition to the strikebreakers she referred to as the "loyals."

Unrelenting oppression can break the spirit, demoralizing whole communities. It can degrade self-respect and fuel enmity, but it can also radicalize. My parents had never had a crisis of loyalty, but the US government's repeated betrayal of their trust and charges of disloyalty now pushed them to join others in adopting a stance that gave them some modicum of dignity. Their loyalty to America had been shredded and scattered by the winds of hate and racism. They would be welcomed, cared for by family members in Japan. They would be free.

The Japanese word *akirameru* comes to mind. It means "to abandon hope." Any last hope of belonging to America was finally severed. Hope vanquished, the torment ended. My parents turned their loyalty to Japan with hopes for a better life.

Wednesday, November 3, 1943
Meiji Setsu: A magnificent birthday celebration for the Emperor Meiji was held outside at 10 a.m. Many Japanese people gathered for the ceremony. On the doors of some of the houses, the Japanese flag was hung. These flags were made out of handkerchiefs with the Japanese *hinomaru*, red circle drawn on it. We celebrated from our hearts.

Friday, November 5, 1943
Last night several Caucasians got in the warehouse and tried to get some food for loyal Japanese working on the farm. Several young men saw this and there was a fight. This caused passing of martial law from this morning. Immediately Army started building high fence between camp and hospital, admin buildings and Caucasian residents' area.

Saturday, November 6, 1943
After 9 a.m., this camp is entirely controlled by Army. Length of time is unknown. Every food truck is escorted by jeep, sedan, and machine gun car with number of MP when they deliver food to mess hall.

Sunday, November 7, 1943
It's really a big parade when Army delivers foodstuff to mess hall. I wonder how long it will <u>last</u>! 7 p.m. Ina went to *Haiku-kai* [poetry club]. Kiyoshi walks about 4 feet without support from us.

Tuesday, November 9, 1943
Since control by Army, there is no food at canteen.

The Daihyo Sha Kai attempted to represent prisoners and bring their demands to the administration once again. Army officials refused to recognize the committee as representative of the prison community and moved quickly to implement gestapo-like measures, issuing arrest orders for every member of the committee and instituting a policy of removing any persons suspected of challenging or undermining the administration. Suspected dissidents were detained, held without charges or trial, and imprisoned in the closely guarded stockade.

Members of the Daihyo Sha Kai went into hiding inside the prison camp confines. When the prison community refused to betray them, a camp-wide dragnet was instituted, and squads of military police began random searches of the barracks and grounds.

Amid all this protest and retaliation, my mother's diary entries are remarkably detached as she describes incident after incident of the increased militarization of the prison camp. She was now an observer, waiting out her time, and only briefly mentions that she has submitted an application to "repatriate" to Japan.

Monday, November 15, 1943
The food has been terrible lately. Day after day, beans and spaghetti only.

Received "convict ID card." It has a photo of me and finger print.

Thursday, November 25, 1943 Thanksgiving Day
Thanksgiving dinner: Pot roast, mashed potato, lettuce salad & canned prunes.

Friday, November 26, 1943
Army began searching every apartment in the camp without notice. They took our radio. No one went to work today.

Friday, December 3, 1943
Kiyoshi's First Birthday Weight 20¼ lb. Height 28" He is in good health. He says, *nenne* night-night, bye-bye, *wanwah*, doggie and kitty. He has two upper teeth and two lower teeth.

Saturday, December 4, 1943 Rain & Snow
Invited Fukami's children & Akashi's to celebrate Kiyoshi's birthday.

Saturday, December 11, 1943
From a few days ago, noticed fence being built around Ward 7. There are a lot of rumors and we do not know the truth of it. Sent in Application for repatriation.

Friday, December 17, 1943
We have to move from Ward 7 as Army is making double fence around Ward 7. They built a guardhouse today by the new fence.

Tuesday, December 21, 1943 First Visit to Hospital
My second unborn baby is 3½ mo. old, according to Dr. Nakano who did my physical checkup today. Also I had a blood test. Weight 109½ lb.

Thursday, December 23, 1943
Epidemic of influenza all over the camp.

Saturday, December 25, 1943 Christmas
It snowed about inch in the morning. Kiyoshi received toy blocks from Christian Society of Quakers.

The new year opened under continued martial law. Outraged by the arrest of members of the Daihyo Sha Kai, prisoners protested and made demands for the release of their elected representatives through various forms of passive resistance. For weeks, prisoners maintained some modicum of self-determination, holding to a strategy of noncooperation referred to as *genjō-iji*, "status quo." They refused to betray elected leaders who were in hiding, and continued to stifle efforts to install a more administration-friendly committee to represent the community. Prisoners held in the stockade initiated hunger strikes. Work stoppages continued throughout the camp.

But as each day of the strike dragged on, the futility of their efforts began to wear on the prisoners. Without work, they had no income. Meanwhile, food supplies had been curtailed, and a shortage of coal for heating began to impact families. Further resistance was dampened by the continued dragnet arrest and removal of hundreds of dissident "trouble-makers and potentially disruptive elements." Many began to hope that ending the strike would lead to the release of their fathers, sons, and brothers who had been held for months in the stockade. Finally, the issue was put to a vote, and the majority opted to end status quo. By mid-January, people returned to work, and leaders who were in hiding surrendered themselves to the authorities.

As testimony to the barren reality of prison life, Shizuko began the New Year logging the prison menu and continued to do so from time to time throughout the year. With limited access to medical care, my parents' day-to-day lives were interspersed with colds, migraines, toothaches, and repeated exposure to camp-wide flu epidemics. Itaru continued his participation in the Tule Lake haiku group, other cultural activities, and many unspecified "meetings," while Shizuko tended to their toddler son and prepared for the birth of their second child.

Saturday, January 1, 1944 Snow 3"
breakfast—boiled egg, & toast
lunch—horsemeat *sukiyaki*
dinner—sandwiches
Mess hall closed. Several homemade *mochi* rice cakes from
Mr. Uenaka and couple inches of snow flavored us a feeling of
New Year at Tule Lake disloyal camp.

Wednesday, January 5, 1944 Snow 3"
For the first time felt baby moving! Dr. Loebmann examined
me. Everything is OK. Weight 115½ lbs.

Friday, January 7, 1944 Fair
Kiyoshi knows which side is right side of a book. If I give it to
him upside down then immediately he turns it the right way.
These days he is continuously saying things when he is playing
by himself.

Tuesday, January 11, 1944 Fair
We had a block meeting and each person over 18 years of age is
supposed to vote against or in favor of STATUS QUO.

Wednesday, January 12, 1944 Fair
Noticed shortage of coal these days. We have shower only
once a week.
    Results from voting is Against STATUS QUO.

After sixty days of punitive conditions, martial law was finally lifted.
Outwardly, it appeared that the prison population had regained a
semblance of normality and order, while also understanding the
reality of their powerlessness. Apathy and resignation seemed to
pervade the camp.
    Shizuko and Itaru pressed forward with their decision to go to
Japan, but when they made a second request for the application,
they learned that as American citizens, they could not qualify for
repatriation. Only immigrant issei could repatriate. Expatriation of
an American citizen was not possible while a person was living on

American soil unless they were convicted of treason. WRA officials had not anticipated the groundswell of resistance evidenced by the responses to the loyalty questionnaire, or the resurgence of unrest when young nisei men were being drafted out of the prison camp into racially segregated combat units. By 1944, the number of repatriation and expatriation requests had reached nearly twenty thousand, or 16 percent of the total incarcerated population. Because the government had a vested interest in getting rid of dissidents, it had to find a way to be able to deport American citizens.

Thursday, January 13, 1944 Fair
For the second time we received soap coupon to buy soap at canteen. Got notice that our Repatriation Application was received. Haven't been feeling well.

Friday, January 14, 1944 Cloudy
End of martial law. Back to WRA control from Army.

Monday, January 17, 1944 Cloudy
It was a beautiful warm day so we took Kiyoshi for a walk.

Tuesday, January 18, 1944 Clear
breakfast—hot cakes
lunch—boiled beef
dinner—pork & beans
Because of the vote against Status Quo, many people started working. I see internal security police have started from today.

Tuesday, January 25, 1944 Fair
Mrs. Fukami made me a maternity dress. Tummy is beginning to show so must wear smock.

To reestablish control once martial law ended, WRA authorities instigated further conflict by recruiting forty so-called loyal men, referred to as the Responsible Men, to establish a more compliant and accommodating representation of prisoners in place of the previously arrested leaders of the Representative Committee, who were still being held indefinitely in the stockade.

In the midst of the dreary conditions, prisoners reveled when "comfort goods" arrived from the Japanese Red Cross. Designated for the citizens of Japan held captive in American prison camps, the gifts struck a chord in the hearts of Tule Lake prisoners, citizens and immigrants alike. The simple political gesture was experienced as a mother's warm embrace. The small cup of soy sauce apportioned to Shizuko was medicine for her soul, strengthening her resolve to make Japan home for her family.

Before arriving at Tule Lake, prisoners had limited access to news about the war in the Pacific, but now, contraband shortwave radios made it possible to hear broadcasts directly from Japan. Little did Shizuko know that by the time she learned of Japan's loss of the Marshall Islands more than eighteen months earlier, the American victory at the Battle of Midway had crippled Japan's naval forces. The Marshall Island victory marked the first time the US had penetrated the outer boundaries of the Japanese Pacific sphere.

Thursday, January 27, 1944 Fair
breakfast—egg & toast
lunch—horse meat *sukiyaki*
dinner—salted pork
Comfort goods arrived from the Japanese Red Cross for the people of Tule Lake. It includes as follows: *shoyu*, soy sauce—747 barrels, *miso*, soy bean paste—30 barrels, medicines—5 boxes. Whether we get these goods or not, we are thankful for their thoughtfulness. It's too good to be true!

Wednesday, February 2, 1944 Cloudy
Radio news: Japanese Marshall Islands has been invaded by American forces. It's really a blasting news of American victory.

Friday, February 4, 1944 Cloudy & snowing after dinner.
breakfast—scramble egg
lunch—broiled sardine
dinner—2 fried eggs
For the first time we heard "Voices of Japan" on Japanese radio.
It touched my heart very deeply.

Saturday, February 5, 1944 Fair
Today is my 27th birthday. Ina bought fresh tuna for my birthday.

Sunday, February 6, 1944 Fair
breakfast—2 fried eggs
lunch—roast mutton
dinner—fish
Ina to *haiku* meeting. Kiyoshi started saying "No, no" from a
few days ago.

News spread that young men in other prison camps were receiving
their draft notices. These individuals had to somehow reconcile
putting on a uniform to fight for a country that held their families
behind barbed-wire fences while they risked their lives in Europe
and Asia. And yet with courage and determination, many chose to
prove their loyalty as worthy Americans and to honor the integrity of their parents, hoping their sacrifice would allow their families to be freed from captivity. For these reasons, young Japanese
American men gave their lives to fight for democracy, saying Yes to
America.

Others who had answered Yes to the loyalty questionnaire were
outraged to learn that after three years of wrongful incarceration,
they were being drafted into a racially segregated combat unit. As
each man searched for his truth, families argued, grieved, and endured separation. In the end, some thirty-three thousand Japanese
Americans served in the military during World War II, including
twenty-eight hundred prisoners who were drafted from within the
concentration camps. Nearly three hundred imprisoned men resisted their conscription into the US Army. More recently recognized as heroic "resisters of conscience," most of these men were

sentenced for up to three years in federal prison and suffered a lifetime stigmatized by their own community as cowardly draft dodgers.

Once again, a resurgence of prisoner militancy emerged. Prison camp administrators had earlier contributed to the fomenting of internal conflict within the prison camp by ignoring activities of various factions, including pro-Japan organizations whose initial purpose was to prepare prisoners for life in Japan. Over time, the mission of these organizations became more intensely focused on convincing, and in some cases pressuring, prisoners to give up their hopes for a life in the US and commit their allegiance to Japan.

When military authorities turned control back over to the WRA, it was made clear that all pro-Japan organizing activities were considered subversive and anti-American. Immediately, civilian authorities moved to suppress all such activities. Tension mounted with the continued influx to Tule Lake of No-No prisoners segregated from other WRA prison camps. Many of the new arrivals had engaged in active protest in their respective prison camps. When they found that they would not in fact be physically segregated from prisoners who had answered Yes, some demanded resegregation. Embracing their distinction as pro-Japan loyalists, they demanded separate living quarters where the emphasis of all activities would be to prepare to return to Japan to serve their mother country. The separation of "loyals" from "disloyals" continued to be a malignant, disruptive force. As victims of powerful repression with few options, prisoners internalized and appropriated the roles they had been designated.

Extremist pro-Japan loyalists consolidated their outrage and gained power within the confines of the prison, while the administration neglected to intervene to protect other prisoners. Referred to as "resegregationists," the pro-Japan extremists petitioned to distinguish "true Japanese," prisoners who not only answered No to the loyalty questionnaire but also applied to repatriate to Japan, from people who had not made the same commitment. Rumors spread that those who did not sign the petition demanding resegregation would be ineligible to return to Japan. My parents, determined to return to Japan, joined the effort to petition for resegregation.

In the end, the administration dismissed the resegregation petitions and designated the pro-Japan issei and kibei organizations as violent and dangerous. Now that their increasing influence posed a threat to administrative control, these groups were ordered to shut down, and their activities were officially deemed illegal.

Reading my mother's accounts of the news on radio broadcasts from the Japanese Imperial Headquarters, along with descriptions of the deteriorating living conditions in the prison camp and repeated illnesses within the family, it was clear to me that any ambivalence regarding her loyalty to Japan had been fully dislodged. Her pride and dignity as an American crushed, America was now the enemy, and she found an increasing strength and comfort in her identification with her ancestral home.

Thursday, February 10, 1944 Clear
It was such a nice day so took Kiyoshi to canteen. He walked half way up to canteen.

In all 10 centers there was a sudden announcement about the draft, and everyone is worried and upset.

Friday, February 11, 1944 Fair but very cold—*Kigensetsu* [National Empire Day]
breakfast—hot cake
lunch—squid
dinner—2 fried eggs
At dinner time, mess hall played *AIKOKU-KOSHINKYOKU* patriotic march record to remind us today is *National Empire Day*. There was no hot water in the laundry room for couple a days.

Wednesday, February 23, 1944 Fair
breakfast—biscuit
lunch—mackerel
dinner—macaroni
Each family of Block 68 received *shoyu* [soy sauce], *miso* [soy-bean paste], and tea. Just to look at it, some unknown feeling comes up to my heart. Japanese soy sauce barrels have been decorated at Mess Hall very respectfully, with the flag of the Rising Sun. We sang *Japanese National Anthem* and prayed for VICTORY. Everyone's eyes were full of tears. We are deeply grateful to the people of Japan.

Thursday, February 24, 1944 Windy
Third group of no-no people from Manzanar camp arrived and settled into new place.

Tuesday, February 29, 1944 Snow
breakfast—biscuit
lunch—mutton hash
dinner—wienie
Ina taught Kiyoshi to say his name. He points to his nose and says "Kiyoshi" very clearly.

Sunday, March 5, 1944 Clear
Boiler is broken again and no showers for about 10 days now.

Thursday, March 23, 1944 Cloudy & Windy—Dust storm all day long.
Kiyoshi coughing and not feeling well. Many people are suffering from flu epidemic with high fever.

Tuesday, March 28, 1944 Clear
Kiyoshi is almost recovered from cold but now I got it. Soldier came around to every house and asked about our Identification number, if we had any relatives in the Army, and if we were educated in Japan, etc.

Saturday, April 8, 1944
Not completely well but I got up today. Still Kiyoshi has a fever.

Sunday, April 9, 1944 Fair
Made notices for people to sign the petition for segregation of repatriates.

Saturday, April 29, 1944 Fair but windy in afternoon
Today is Forty-third birthday of Emperor of Japan. We had a special ceremony at mess hall before breakfast. Holiday for all Japanese residents. No work today.

My mother gave birth to her second child in May, and my poet father proudly named me Satsuki—child of the fifth moon. On that same day, May 25, 1944, Shoichi James Okamoto, twenty-nine years old, died from a gunshot fired at close range by an army sentry. While Okamoto was driving a construction truck between the

A pregnant Shizuko carrying Kiyoshi at
Tule Lake Segregation Center, May 1944

camp and the work site, the sentry demanded that he step out of his truck and show his pass. Reportedly, Okamoto stepped out of the cab but refused to show his pass, whereupon the sentry struck him on the shoulder with the butt end of his rifle. The two exchanged words, and the sentry then shot Okamoto. At the court-martial trial, the soldier was acquitted of the homicide, having reportedly "conducted himself in the performance of his duty," and fined $1 for the cost of a bullet fired in an "unauthorized use of government property." Eyewitness testimony, however, reported that the shooting was an unprovoked attack.

The shooting death aggravated the ever-present sense of powerlessness and anger felt by prisoners enduring the torture of indefinite detention and rapidly deteriorating living conditions. A June 1 article in the camp newspaper, the *Newell Star*, described the mood of the gathering at Mr. Okamoto's funeral service:

> Nine thousand people stood bareheaded for hours in a chilly wind and a drizzle of rain Wednesday afternoon to pay lasting tribute to the memory of Shoichi James Okamoto, martyred victim of a shooting which Secretary of Interior Harold L. Ickes termed "completely unwarranted and without provocation on the part of the victim . . ." Thousands came from all parts of the center, in spite of the cold discomfort, to stand with bowed heads in tribute to the deceased. At the same time they were expressing protest against the hate and intolerance engendered by this war. Men and women, young and old, mothers with babies in their arms, thus offered sympathy to the bereaved family. Every person present was moved by sorrow.

Wednesday, May 3, 1944 Fair but a little windy

To prepare for move to Japan we applied for our 13 wooden boxes from P.R. Storage.

Block 68 made petition to army Director Best to release men from the stockade.

8 p.m.—Over 500 disloyals from Jerome camp arrived here.

Sunday, May 14, 1944 Dust storm
What a dust storm! It is the worst dust storm we have ever had. Windy all day long. This morning Rohwer disloyal segregees arrived.

Wednesday, May 24, 1944 Clear—little windy
Heard that Mr. Okamoto, young man who came from Heart Mountain camp has been shot by MP in the afternoon. Rumors are going around but heard that he was arguing with MP concerning work badge.

Thursday, May 25, 1944 Fair—Birth day
From 5 a.m.–8 p.m., pain every 10 minutes. Went to Tule Lake Hospital at 10 a.m. terrible pain. Baby born at 11 p.m. Weight—7 lbs. Delivered by Dr. Nakano.
    Mr. James Okamoto died last night.

Friday, May 26, 1944 First Day
Nurse brought my daughter in and let me see her for first time. She looks so chubby and so different than Kiyoshi. Whole body is in pain from last night's exhaustion.

Sunday, May 28, 1944 Third Day
First time she took 2¼ oz. of my breast milk. Thank God!

Wednesday, May 31, 1944 Sixth Day
Applied for birth certificate for Satsuki. Cost $1.06.
    Heard Mr. James Okamoto's funeral is going to be held today.

In spite of the war and the increasing turmoil inside the barbed-wire fence, Shizuko's focus, like that of any young mother, was the everyday care of her children. The life she dreamed of as a newlywed had been disassembled, and her claim to her rights as a citizen had fallen on deaf ears, but her despair and humiliation were transformed by her determination to return to Japan for the sake of her children.

My parents' firstborn son had been conceived in joy, before

their arrest and incarceration. Kiyoshi's birth was the fulfillment of a long-awaited dream for both of them, a healing of their own childhood losses. I'll always remember the pained expression on my mother's face when I asked off-handedly why she would have another child while living in the squalor and uncertainty of captivity. As if making a confession, she said, "We never knew what was going to happen to us. We lived every day not knowing. There were rumors that families with more children would be kept together. We thought if we had another child, we would not be separated." Her answer stayed with me for years. My brother Kiyoshi had been born of joy and fulfillment; I was born of fear and promise. In the end, it was a promise not to be kept.

Thursday, June 1, 1944 Seventh Day 6 lbs. 12 oz
Getting up day. Baby has lost 4 oz. since her birth. All mothers are feeling well today. We talked about our delivery time and laughed so much. Baby's cord came off this morning at 2.

Sunday, June 4, 1944 Tenth Day
Leaving hospital! Left hospital at 10 a.m. Soon as we got off from the ambulance Kiyoshi looked at me very curiously and just stared at us. But about half hour later he called me Mumy. He has grown so much in 10 days.

Monday, June 5, 1944 Fair—First Day at Home
I did not sleep very well last night. Had a terrible headache. Certainly Ina is very busy with housework. Feel so sorry for him but I can't do any work. Received Brother Masami's graduation pictures. Gave first bath to baby. She is so tiny and very hard to handle even with Ina's help.

Meanwhile, the world war raged on outside the prison. In the first five months after the destruction of Pearl Harbor, Japan had seized Singapore from the British, and Malaya and the Philippines from the Americans, furthering their "Greater East Asia Co-Prosperity Sphere" agenda. Tule Lake prisoners listening to daily broadcasts from Japanese Imperial Headquarters on their contraband radios heard exaggerated reports of the victories of the "invincible Japanese forces," but by this time the tide was turning, and Japan was unquestionably on the defensive. By 1944, American forces had invaded the Marshall Islands and won the Truk Lagoon battle, crippling Japanese defenses.

Shizuko and others who had committed their fate to Japan held out hope for a Japanese victory. In her diary, she continued to keep an accounting of events of the war, not realizing that the reports she heard were obscuring the truth of Japan's and Germany's slow defeats.

Tuesday, June 13, 1944 Fair
breakfast—biscuit
lunch—beef stew
dinner—macaroni & doughnuts
News: Japan's fierce attack of China and India Fronts. Allies second front. Terrible losses on Allies side!

Friday, June 16, 1944 Rain
News: 20 American planes went over to bomb northern Kyushu on June 16th, at 2 a.m. Light damage was inflicted on Japanese side. On the other hand, 7 American planes have been shot down and 3 were damaged.

Tuesday, June 27, 1944 clear
Satsuki smiled when I held her in the early morning. How fast she has grown!

Friday, June 30, 1944 hot day
From last night having 102° fever and waist down is very painful. Called ambulance immediately and went to clinic. Dr. Ikuta looked me over. Sickness unknown so have to go to hospital tomorrow morning. It's big worry for me. Hope nothing serious.

Saturday, July 1, 1944
Went to hospital and examined by doctor Nakano and he said
it's just a infection so nothing to worry about. Thank God!
Today is center-wide carnival. Ina took Kiyoshi to see it. *He
bought a hamburger sandwich and brought it to me. It was unusual for him to do that, so I enjoyed it.*

Internal struggles continued to consume prison camp life. Pro-
Japan loyalists increased in numbers as dissidents from other
camps arrived at Tule Lake. Among the pro-Japan resistance groups
often collectively referred to as the Hoshidan were the Sokuji Ki-
koku Hoshidan (Organization to Return Immediately to Serve the
Homeland), made up of elder issei; the Hokoku Seinen Dan, for
younger nisei and kibei men; and the Sokoku Joshi Seinen Dan,
the women's auxiliary.

Even as the administration attempted to shut down organized
opposition, dissident leaders worked to subvert WRA control,
strengthen morale among those who turned their hopes to Japan,
and continue increasing their groups' numbers. Cast out and be-
trayed by their adopted country, and drawing on their Meiji-era
education emphasizing honor, integrity, and loyalty, the issei and
kibei were now fueled by a righteous passion. Wrongly accused of
being the enemy, they had become radicalized and now openly proclaimed their identity as "true Japanese."

As intensely driven as the leadership may have been, most of
the members of the Hoshidan were like my father: not necessarily leaders, and not extremists, but people seeking to restore their
self-respect and dignity through positive identification with Japan.
There was also a very practical reason for participating in the resistance movement. Prisoners who decided to go to Japan were told
by elders that they would be arrested and confined as potential
spies upon their arrival unless they could prove their loyalty to Japan. Membership in the Hoshidan and verification by fellow members would be evidence that they were above suspicion.

My mother admitted that although she participated in the rituals
honoring the emperor of Japan, she never believed him to be a divine being as others did. She told me a story, one she didn't tell of-

ten because when she had shared it in the past, people responded with disbelief. After being selected as one of the Silk Girls, she was called to the Imperial Palace in Tokyo. There, she was to have an audience with Emperor Hirohito.

"I wore my best kimono, was told not to speak, and instructed to sit on a cushion on the floor. I was told to keep my eyes down," she told me. She pointed her finger skyward as she recalled the encounter. "He was seated way high up so his voice sounded like it was coming from far away. I was nervous and afraid. He had only a few words to say, but I will never forget. He kindly said to me, 'I will expect you to represent Japan well. Take good care of your health.' Then I was led away."

She explained to me that Japanese people believed the emperor to be a god. Called Tennō, "heavenly sovereign," he was believed to be a direct descendant of the sun goddess Amaterasu. As a rule, the emperor did not meet with commoners, and people were never to see his face or hear his voice. But my mother said, "I quickly glanced up, heard his voice clearly, and knew he was just a man, a very kind man."

The belief in the emperor's divinity added to the zeal of many prisoners joining the resistance. In addition to nationalistic songs and rituals of bowing toward the east to honor the emperor, military-style exercises were organized to physically prepare young men for service to Japan. As a show of strength, hundreds marched in step to bugles, with heads shaved, and wearing headbands and shirts marked with the rising-sun emblem of Japan. The focus of the Japanese schools shifted from language education to indoctrinating students with the values of a victorious Japan.

Polarization within the movement was frighteningly punctuated when Yaozo Hitomi, general manager of the Tule Lake Cooperative store, was found murdered with his throat cut on July 3, 1944. Hitomi, an alleged *inu* (dog), a dreaded label given collaborators and snitches, was suspected of giving up names of "troublemakers" to the administration. It was also rumored that he was involved in the mismanagement of funds belonging to the co-op. The murder marked a new level of violence. And though fingers pointed to extremists within the pro-Japan group, no one was ever found guilty of the slaying. Anyone suspected of having collaborated with the administration or associated with Hitomi's activities became a potential target of violence. They were removed by the administration, often under cover of night, and relocated outside the prison camp.

The murder created an atmosphere of frenzied terror. As administrators failed to contain the growing violence, extremists sought out anyone who opposed their tactics. Those still undecided about their loyalty feared for themselves and their families. At the same time, random arrests of "troublemakers" were taking place in draconian fashion. The internal police force was completely ineffective; to mitigate any threats of violence, volunteers, including Itaru, took turns patrolling the blocks where they lived.

Finally, draft notices began to arrive at the Tule Lake Segregation Center. Twenty-seven young Japanese American men chose to resist the draft as a means of protesting their incarceration. They were arrested and taken to the Humboldt County jail to await trial for refusing to appear for their induction examinations. Simultaneously, draft resisters in other concentration camps in Wyoming and Idaho were also being tried, given felony convictions, and sent to federal prison for draft evasion.

On July 17, 1944, some glimmer of acknowledgment of the injustice of the mass incarceration briefly surfaced when federal court judge Louis Goodman found the Tule Lake defendants not guilty. In pronouncing his decision, he concluded that it was "shocking to the conscience that an American citizen who had been confined on the grounds of disloyalty, and then, while so under duress and restraint, be compelled to serve in the Armed Forces, or be prosecuted for not yielding to such compulsion." He dismissed the charges as violations of the defendants' right to due process of law under the Fifth Amendment of the Constitution. The men were then returned to their prison camp barracks. Judge Goodman was the only judge at the time who upheld the rights of men who refused the draft while incarcerated in US concentration camps.

Early on, one voice, if it had been heeded, could have changed the fate of the 125,000 incarcerated people of Japanese ancestry. The American Civil Liberties Union (ACLU), a nonprofit organization of civil rights lawyers founded in 1920, professed a mission of "defend[ing] and preserv[ing] the individual rights and liberties guaranteed to every person in this country by the Constitution and laws of the United States." Although Roger Baldwin, director of the National ACLU, warned President Roosevelt that Executive Order 9066 was "open to grave question on the constitutional grounds of depriving American citizens of their liberty and use of their property without due process of law," history has shown that not only was the warning dismissed but Baldwin, presumably out of loyalty or deference to President Roosevelt, also quashed any subsequent challenges regarding the constitutionality of Executive Order 9066, instructing local ACLU chapters to refuse cases that would challenge the government's constitutional right to carry out the mass removal.

Fortunately, the Northern California branch of the ACLU broke ranks with the central office. Led by Ernest Besig and firebrand attorney Wayne Mortimer Collins, they pursued repeated challenges on behalf of incarcerated Japanese Americans. In 1944, Besig visited the Tule Lake Segregation Center to investigate the reportedly harsh conditions where alleged troublemakers were being held in a stockade for months without charges. He would later send Collins to threaten habeas corpus proceedings, resulting in the release of prisoners and the dismantling of the stockade.

Meanwhile, reports from secret Japanese radio propaganda kept renunciants' hopes alive. Radio Tokyo convincingly presented Japan as victorious in the Pacific, and exhorted the listeners to be "true Japanese." Noboru Shirai, an issei author held at Tule Lake, wrote in his memoir, "The news from Japanese Imperial Headquarters always began with the rousing patriotic 'Naval March.' This was followed by exaggerated praise for the advances of the invincible Japanese forces."

Shirai described the practice of people taking handwritten notes of battle reports to pass from prisoner to prisoner. I found one such battle report tucked inside my mother's diary. Written in my father's hand was a tally of losses for the US and Japan, possibly following the conflict near the Philippine Islands. He noted that 500 US planes were "shot down," while only 126 Japanese planes "failed to return."

Sunday, July 2, 1944 hot
Last night after the carnival, Mr. Hitomi, president of the Co-op, was killed by knife by unidentified attacker.

Wednesday, July 5, 1944 hot
For the last 4 days we have had baloney, baloney!
    Last Sunday night, Mr. A. Takahashi was attacked in the dark and his life was endangered. For safety he and his family were taken out of camp today.

Wednesday, July 12, 1944 Hot
Breakfast—French toast
Lunch—mutton
Dinner—*eggs with vegetables*
Kiyoshi plays with hammer and nails every place he goes, even when he goes to sleep.

Friday, July 14, 1944 Hot
Took Satsuki to hospital for first check up. Weight—9 lbs. 12 oz. Height—22"
    Still not enough breast milk so have to give her SMA formula once a day.

Saturday, July 15, 1944 Hot 92°
On my way to Dr.'s appointment I saw a group of young boys who refused draft being taken away by the army to unknown destination for trial.

Tuesday, July 18, 1944
News: Fall of Saipan to enemy hands. It was a big shock to us. Darkest day since war started.

Friday, July 28, 1944 Cool—rain in evening
9–12 p.m. Ina went with neighborhood young men to guard this block.

Tuesday, August 8, 1944
The Nationalist Chinese Army has fallen into Japanese hands today.

Sunday, August 20, 1944 Hot
News: Northern Kyushu has been bombed again by Flying Fortress. Little damage to our side. Enemy lost 25 planes and 20 prisoners were captured.

Wednesday, August 23, 1944 Hot
Fresh spinach from our own garden helps Kiyoshi very much. Gave some to other mothers too because their children are lacking fresh greens. Mr. & Mrs. Tomine visited us with their baby.

Friday, August 25, 1944 Hot
Today Satsuki is 3 months old. Already she baby talks and laughs aloud. She is getting along fine except not enough breast milk.

The duress of confinement took a toll on my mother's health. The chronic psychological and physical stress of indefinite detention, with inadequate medical care and impoverished living conditions, may well have contributed to the kidney, blood pressure, and dental problems she suffered for the remainder of her life. Medical anthropologist Dr. Gwendolyn Jensen's research examined the physical and psychological health consequences of the World War II mass incarceration of Japanese Americans. She concluded in her doctoral dissertation at the University of Colorado that former incarcerees suffered long-term health consequences that included psychological anguish as well as greater risk for cardiovascular disease and premature death. Jensen also found that the "youngest detainees," less inculcated with cultural coping mechanisms, reported more posttraumatic stress symptoms, such as unexpected and disturbing flashback experiences, than those who were older at the time of incarceration.

From an intergenerational perspective, both my brother and I were in utero, then infancy and early childhood, while both parents, but especially our mother, were physically and emotionally overwhelmed by the trauma of the incarceration. Research has shown that when a pregnant mother experiences high levels of fear or anxiety, her body produces a cascade of stress hormones, which affect both her and her child's immune system, setting the stage for a wide array of trauma-based problems at birth and later. Transmission of trauma from one generation to the next can occur in this biochemical way, but also through conscious and unconscious patterns of behavior and language expressed by the parent that indirectly but consistently communicate to the child the presence of danger.

My mother was disheartened when she couldn't produce enough breast milk to feed me. Given the context in which she was living, it's no wonder that her body was likely to be not just malnourished but also responding to the ongoing stress of captivity. She must have relived many times the fear of that moment when she thought to herself, "I wonder if today is the day they're going to line us up and shoot us."

When I was a child, my parents often jokingly referred to me as a *nakibeso*, "cry baby." They said I cried all the time—whenever strangers approached or my brother Kiyoshi was out of sight. They said I was easily startled and that I cried when left alone. I think back now and recognize signs of the transmission of my mother's anxiety during and after my birth. As an adult, I compensated for my anxiety, usually with a hell-bent drive to prove my worth through accomplishments. My mother would often say to me, "You don't have to go overboard." In the midst of one of my sprints to achieve, her oft-repeated refrain was, "You live like there's no tomorrow." Looking back, I think it was not achievement and accomplishment I was seeking so much as safety and acceptance. I think again of my earliest conscious childhood memory: sitting with my stranger-father, hearing him say to me, "Be strong. Don't cry." He may have hoped that those words could erase the trauma that had been deeply chiseled into my psyche.

Monday, September 18, 1944
Today is 1 year since came here to Tule Lake.

Thursday, October 5, 1944 Clear
Breakfast—French toast
Lunch—wienies
Dinner—mutton stew
Each person donated 5¢ to make a fund and send tobacco, *takuan* pickled radishes, *zori* slippers, and *okoshi* sweet rice crackers to unfortunate Japanese soldiers held prisoners by the U.S.A.

Thursday, October 12, 1944
Over 400 enemy planes bombed TAIWAN twice today.

Friday, October 13, 1944 Rain
Kiyoshi is better today. Not so fussy. It must be caused by new tooth coming out and not completely recovered from prolonged cold. Ina to *haiku meeting*.

Wednesday, October 18, 1944 Fair
Took Kiyoshi to hospital. He had a diphtheria shot for first time. Certainly he hates the sight of the hospital. Cried terribly.

Friday, October 20, 1944 Sewing Class—Fair
Had Block 68 mothers meeting concerning baby food. We requested that children over 1 year of age who desires adult food, it is OK to have it. Under 1 year of age, it is OK for whoever desires to have raw food to take home to cook.

When once they bought war bonds and prided themselves on never missing an opportunity to vote as American citizens, Shizuko and other prisoners now, despite their own impoverished state, gathered goods to send to Japanese soldiers being held as prisoners of war on US soil. Fourth of July celebrations gave way to traditional Japanese celebrations, such as Buddhist holidays, Boy's Day, and Emperor Meiji's birthday.

I wonder what psychological gymnastics my parents, having taken their stand for Japan, had to manage as Japan showed signs of nearing defeat. Following several critical military losses, the Japanese imperial forces deployed pilots from the Special Attack Unit, known as *kamikaze,* "divine wind." As if channeling the typhoons that miraculously saved Japan from two Mongolian invasions in the thirteenth century, young men and boys sacrificed themselves by flying their planes headlong into US battleships, signaling the country's final days of desperation. The successful Allied invasion of Leyte cut Japan off from the Southeast Asian countries it occupied, resulting in the loss of oil and other resources desperately needed to fuel the Japanese Navy. Soldiers were called on to make the ultimate sacrifice according to Bushidō, the traditional samurai code of loyalty and honor. The belief in the nobility and honor of death over defeat, capture, and shame was deeply entrenched in wartime Japanese culture.

Tuesday, October 24, 1944
Have been quite busy making paper *kiku* chrysanthemum flowers for *Emperor Meiji's birthday celebration* with Mrs. Kobayashi.

Wednesday, October 25, 1944 Satsuki—5 mos. old., 14 lb. 1 oz
Took Kiyoshi to hospital and had his first TYPHOID shot. After we came home, he vomited and had high fever. It made him very upset.

Friday, November 3, 1944 Cloudy & rain
Meiji Setsu ceremony held at Block 68 mess hall and also center-wide ceremony was held at the outside theatre. Last night Block 68 group went to mess hall and made *hinomaru omanju* [sweet bean cakes decorated with a Japanese flag] for today's celebration.

Thursday, November 9, 1944 Snow (2 in)
Chilly winter is here now. Surprised to see 2 inches of snow on the ground when we got up in the morning. Busy making Kiyoshi's overall with Block 68 sewing machine. We all need warm clothing for the winter.

After my mother passed away, I discovered a small, rusted metal box with a built-in combination lock on the front. To my surprise, it opened easily. On top was a slip of paper with words in my mother's familiar, delicate hand that read, "Renunciation *[sic]* of U.S. Citizenship." The items inside were carefully placed and clearly meant to be opened in a specific order. She had never mentioned this box or its contents to me or my brothers; it's likely that she had intended to do so, before the dementia slowly crept into her memory. There were two similar envelopes, brown with age, one labeled "Kiyoshi's *hesonō*" and the other, "Satsuki's *hesonō*." I held each up to the light to see inside a small, lumpy mass. Neatly wrapped and sealed were the remains of our umbilical cords. Elders explained to me that it was an old Japanese practice to save these, to be ground up and used as medicine if the child ever became gravely ill.

Next were my parents' birth certificates, a bit ragged and torn, but authenticated with gold-embossed state seals—*Itaru Ina, born June 10, 1913, San Francisco, California* and *Shizuko Mitsui, born February 5, 1917, Seattle, Washington.*

Then a letter from Herbert Wechsler, assistant attorney general in the DOJ War Division, addressed to each of my parents at their barracks in Tule Lake and dated May 3, 1945:

> You are hereby notified that, pursuant to Section 401(i) of the Nationality Act of 1940, as Amended, and the regulations issued pursuant thereto, your renunciation of United States nationality has been approved by the Attorney General as not contrary to the interest of national defense. Accordingly you are no longer a citizen of the United States of America nor are you entitled to any of the rights and privileges of such citizenship.

As I read this document, I flashed back to that moment when my mother, afraid that my brothers and I would be ashamed of our parents for having renounced their American citizenship, finally shared their long-held secret. I recognized also the manipulative use of distorted language by government officials to obscure the true motives behind their actions. With such euphemistic language as "evacuation," "relocation," and "for their own protection," America had been lulled into accepting what was, by all standards of a democratic society, an act of state violence and systemic racism. This document implied that officials were granting approval for a request made of the applicants' own volition, without the context of their status as innocent people held in government captivity because of their race. The document further implied that Shizuko and Itaru were only now officially stripped of their "rights and privileges of such citizenship" in spite of the fact that by this time, as American citizens, they had endured the loss of their rights for three torturous years. I would have to dig deep to understand this part of my parents' story.

In order to deport the so-called disloyal troublemakers, many of whom were American citizens who had never been to Japan, government authorities first had to create legal means to remove their US citizenship. On June 23, Congress passed H.R. 4103, the Renunciation Act of 1944. This law made it possible for persons residing in the US to renounce their citizenship during time of war. As with the letter to my mother, its wording implied that such a decision was made of one's free will, but it was intended to apply specifically to Japanese Americans who were being held against their will in prisons, at this point for nearly three years. In no other country in the world was it possible for an individual to relinquish their citizenship while still residing in their home country. Prior to this legislation, in order to "expatriate," a person had to be living outside the US. President Roosevelt signed the act into law on July 1, 1944, making wartime renunciation of American citizenship a legal means of getting rid of dissidents, thus purportedly assuring the safety of America.

Of the 5,589 people who gave up their US citizenship, 5,461 were from Tule Lake. A year earlier, at the Topaz concentration camp, my parents' petition to have their constitutional rights returned to them before swearing unqualified allegiance to the US had been summarily dismissed. In dissent and in despair, they answered No to the loyalty questionnaire and chose to return to Japan, where they had each spent part of their childhood. To achieve this goal, they had submitted applications for "repatriation" to Japan. What they and, apparently, government officials hadn't realized was that because they were US citizens, the repatriation process would not apply to them. They would have to renounce their US citizenship to make a new life for themselves in Japan. To "renounce" one's citizenship implies self-efficacy, reflecting confidence in the ability to exert control over one's life. It implies freedom of choice, when in fact, the Renunciation Act of 1944 was a forced-choice situation— stay in the US indefinitely imprisoned or released into a hostile and suspicious community, or be deported to Japan.

After three years of confinement, many families were poor, having drained both their material and emotional resources. The idea of starting all over in a hostile community was overwhelming. Many feared that their immigrant parents would be deported to Japan while their nisei children (US citizens) would be left behind or, worse yet, drafted into military service. For some who had never even considered renunciation, it suddenly appeared to be the only way to keep families together. Others believed that if they renounced, they would be able to delay being forced out into a hostile society with no viable means of supporting themselves. And finally, there was no trust that once released, families would be protected from the surge of virulent hatred and violence directed at them from Americans unable to distinguish the enemy from a fellow American. Given the circumstances, with no clear answers in sight, prisoners were essentially coerced into renouncing their citizenship. Some held to the rumors that when the war ended they would be able to withdraw their renunciation request. Renunciation appeared to many as the solution to the crisis created by forced resettlement.

My parents, with no better options, clung to the possibility that renouncing their American citizenship would be the answer to their prayers. On November 13, 1944, Shizuko and Itaru, along with nearly 70 percent of all adult US citizens at Tule Lake, formally submitted papers to surrender their American birthright, transforming them with the stroke of a pen into "enemy aliens." In the years since, the story of the legalized denationalization of American dissidents and their subsequently justified deportation to Japan as enemy aliens has remained suppressed by the US government and hidden in shame by the victims of a draconian attempt to be rid of people who dared to challenge their jailers.

Soon after my parents submitted their renunciation applications, the attorney general's office sent an inquiry to J. Edgar Hoover, director of the Federal Bureau of Investigation (FBI), requesting information concerning both Shizuko and Itaru. Hoover responded within days, reporting that my father had held membership in kibei organizations before the war, "made speeches in opposition to solicitation for volunteers for a Japanese American Army Combat Team," and answered No-No to numbers 27 and 28 on the loyalty questionnaire. My father had been charged with sedition for making his speech, but no action had been taken since his interrogation.

Monday, November 13, 1944 Clear
Sent application of Renunciation of U.S. Citizenship to Washington, D.C. Enclosed birth certificate.

Tuesday, November 14, 1944 Clear
Courageous *KAMIKAZE* activities are continuing at LEYTE.

Saturday, November 25, 1944
Today Satsuki is 6 months old. Her second tooth is coming out any day.

While the renunciation process was taking place, challenges to the mass incarceration were reaching the US Supreme Court. Although attorney Ernest Besig of the ACLU and Wayne Collins lost their case on behalf of Fred Korematsu, a nisei man who resisted incarceration, the case of Mitsuye Endo, a twenty-two-year-old nisei woman incarcerated in the Tule Lake and Topaz concentration camps, culminated in October 1944, when the Supreme Court heard oral arguments challenging the army's right to detain Japanese Americans. While avoiding the issue of the constitutionality of the race-based mass incarceration of American citizens without due process, the US Supreme Court reached a unanimous decision in the case *Ex parte Endo*, ruling that the government had no authority to detain and incarcerate loyal citizens.

Giving credence to the legitimacy of the so-called loyalty questionnaire, the court ruled that "loyal" citizens (as opposed to prisoners who were in fact *innocent* citizens), after three years of imprisonment, were free to leave. The Roosevelt administration, having been alerted to the court's decision, issued Public Proclamation No. 21 on December 17, 1944, the day before the *Endo* and *Korematsu* rulings were made public, rescinding the exclusion orders and declaring that Japanese Americans could begin returning to the West Coast in January 1945.

All ten War Relocation Authority prison camps were slated to be closed within a year. At the same time, it was announced that individuals considered to be "potentially dangerous to military security" would continue to be incarcerated and would be transferred to DOJ internment camps. Results of the Supreme Court decision would eventually reach the prisoners, as in this December 19 item from the *Newell Star Extra*:

> The Commanding General of the Western Defense Command has today issued the necessary orders to terminate mass exclusion of persons of Japanese ancestry from the Pacific coastal area. In the future only these individuals whose records indicate that they are potentially dangerous to military security are to be excluded.

Once again, the government used twisted rhetoric to avoid admission of wrongdoing. Orders to "terminate mass exclusion" failed to state clearly that the people now being released had been wrongly imprisoned merely on the basis of race.

Army teams immediately began to hold hearings at the rate of 400–500 a day, and, as the hearings progressed, anxiety spread among prisoners. Some of the army officers were repeating the infamous questions from the loyalty questionnaire. Reports quickly spread that irrespective of the answers given, almost everybody called for a hearing was issued an "individual exclusion order" allowing for their release, but restricting them to areas outside the previously established exclusion zones. They were not free to return to the West Coast.

By the end of the year, leaders of the men's resistance organizations were removed to a DOJ internment camp in Santa Fe, New Mexico, to await deportation as "undesirable enemy aliens." My parents, along with others who had committed their future to Japan, saw the departure of the leaders as assurance that they would be returned to Japan as courageous and dignified "true Japanese nationals."

Sunday, December 3, 1944 Fair
The wind feels so cold that it pierces my body. Today was Kiyoshi's second birthday. I couldn't give him a special celebration, so we will celebrate his birthday and New Years at the same time! He is cheerful, stubborn and naughty, and often leaves us at our wit's end. He is becoming more and more difficult, but this is good, it is the way it's supposed to be. Last 4, 5 days I haven't felt well. I feel sorry that I have been taking it out on Ina and the children.

Wednesday, December 20, 1944
Since West Coast Exclusion Order has been banned last Sunday, immediately from Monday, Army began interviewing all the residents.

Thursday, December 21, 1944
Ina got interview appointment yesterday so he went after lunch. He came home with a paper of "Exclusion." He is classified as a dangerous person and excluded from military zone. Up to today most of the *nisei* received interviews but today *issei's* interviews started also.

Monday, December 25, 1944 Cloudy—7 months old, 15 lb. 14 oz
War news of Japan and Germany are very bright. The coming New Year is going to be cheerful and joyful.

Tuesday, December 26, 1944
Satsuki is 7 months old as of yesterday. She could sit quite

well and rolls over very freely. She says papa papa and mama mama. Holds and reaches objects very well.

Wednesday, December 27, 1944 Windy
Over 70 important members of *HOSHIDAN* have been taken to unknown destination today by FBI. Residents were in quite a stir about it but it is better for us. Ina is ready to go any time.

Sunday, December 31, 1944
It was most busiest day of the year. Trying to get everything done as much as possible. Cleaning, washing and dusting. Ina cleaned the windows for me. Kiyoshi's condition is O.K. But he is very cross. No fever so he is getting his pep again. Received *mochi* rice cakes from mess hall. Each person— 6 pieces. Ready to welcome New Year. Mentally and physically stable.

In December, when the announcement was made that all "loyal" citizens would be freed while individuals considered to be "potentially dangerous" would continue to be incarcerated and transferred to federal DOJ internment camps, shock waves rippled through the prison camp.

Chaos ensued. Most people had lost everything when they were forced to leave behind their homes, jobs, farms, schools, shops, and businesses. With the war still raging and anti-Japanese sentiment at its peak, stories about people who had received early leave clearance facing threats and violence left prisoners fearful of returning home. Where could they live? Who would hire them? How would they survive? What of the elderly who had lost all hope of ever starting over again?

Lawmakers had swiftly pushed through the racist denationalization legislation, making it legally possible to deport a few thousand Japanese American citizens considered recalcitrants. They never expected that their actions would lead to thousands more dispossessed, incarcerated citizens rushing to give up their birthright in exchange for expatriation to Japan.

On January 11, 1945, the assistant attorney general, John L. Burling, serving as head of the DOJ's renunciation hearing team, arrived at Tule Lake to conduct renunciation hearings. Hoshidan members saw renunciation as an opportunity to increase the number of people declaring loyalty to Japan. They were intent on recruiting as many renunciants as possible, tutoring members to avow unquestionable loyalty to the emperor during their hearings in order to guarantee their welcome upon arrival in Japan. The hearing officers told applicants that signing the renunciation document would forever terminate their American citizenship rights and likely mean removal to Japan at the end of the war. With that end in mind, my parents followed the steps they believed necessary to guarantee their safe return to Japan.

My father, like other Hoshidan members, appeared before the officers with his head shaved, identifying himself as a member of the resistance group, determined to convince interrogators of his unqualified allegiance to Japan. He responded evasively to some questions and avoided admitting he had access to shortwave radio broadcasts from Japan. Pressed to respond to the provocative question of whether he would commit "hari kari," an Anglicized reference to death by ritual suicide, if Japan lost the war, Itaru held to the advice from elders to answer such questions unequivocally.

For my parents, renunciation was the culmination of their long fight for justice and redemption. With a newfound sense of pride and dignity, Shizuko and Itaru pledged themselves to return to what they now considered their mother country. Renouncing their American citizenship was not a crisis of loyalty but rather a crisis of faith in their country of birth. Rendered disloyal in the eyes of America, they turned from living at the mercy of government officials dictating their everyday lives and joined other young nisei kibei with a renewed sense of purpose and meaning. They joined others to engage in various acts of nonviolent resistance against tightening prison repression. And they held fast to their hope for a victorious Japan.

Scholar Donald E. Collins summarizes his study of the renunciation experience of incarcerated Japanese Americans in stating, "Citizenship was a word with increasingly little meaning, and they were well on their way to using it as their last significant protest."

Monday, January 1, 1945—Fair & warm
Japan's Victory! That is all that matters. New Years has come and gone three times since we've been locked up in barbed wire. What difficulties we have and shall face, doesn't matter, as long as our mother country wins the war. Whatever we do, we must think about spirit of *Kamikaze tai*. I have no doubt about Japan's Victory! That is my belief. New Year's ceremony was performed at Block 68 mess hall.

  1. *Bowing ceremony honoring the Emperor*
  2. *Banzai! Exultation for the great empire of Japan*
  3. *Kimigayo*, Japanese National anthem

Tuesday, January 2, 1945—Heavy Frost
Busy sewing children's clothes for winter. Satsuki knows if I scold her. She will cry instantly.

Sunday, January 7, 1945—Fair & warm
We are having food shortage these days especially bread. So we often have *okayu* [rice gruel] in the morning instead of usual toast. Very much lack of flour. Some people say maybe it's one kind of WRA policy to chase us out of camp.

Sunday, January 14, 1945—Cloudy
Ina received hearing appointment. Tomorrow—8 a.m.
  Cut Ina's hair to *KURI KURI BOZU* [shaved head].
  News: Enemy's 60 planes bombed Nagoya today. Purposely bombed sacred Ise Jingu shrine.

Monday, January 15, 1945—Little snow and very windy
Ina went to renunciation hearing this morning. It took over two hours.

HEARING ON RENUNCIATION OF CITIZENSHIP

Applicant: ITARU INA
Hearing Officer: Ollie Collins
Case Number: 208   Date: January 15, 1945

Q. What is your name?
A. ITARU INA
Q. Did you file an application for permission to
   renounce your United States nationality?
A. Yes.
Q. Why did you sign it?
A. I have to go back to Japan.
Q. Why do you have to go back to Japan?
A. We are disloyal to this country.
Q. When did you become disloyal to this country?
A. I am loyal to Japan. I have no special reason to
   this country but I am 100% loyal to Japan.
Q. Where are your parents?
A. In Japan.
Q. Why did you come back here in 1930?
A. My father brought me to this country with
   him, and left me. He died in Japan.
Q. Whom did he leave you with here?
A. My father's friend.
Q. He brought you back here because he wanted you
   to live in the United States rather than Japan?
A. My father wanted me to live with him
   and he went back and I stayed.
Q. Did you like it all right?
A. I should go back to Japan but I did
   not have enough money.
Q. When did you get married?
A. March, 1941.
Q. You had no family or anything to hold
   you here prior to March 1941?
A. I know. I did not have the money.

Q. What did you do before evacuation?

A. I was working in a wholesale store.

Q. How much money did you make?

A. About $80 a month. I had to pay for
my own board and room.

Q. Had you planned on continuing with that store?

A. Yes.

Q. How long had you been with them?

A. About 4 years.

Q. If Japan and the United States had not gone to
war against each other, and if we had gone to war
with say Germany or any other country, would you
have felt it was your duty to serve in the armed
forces of this country if you had been drafted?

A. I understand what you mean. I think I would
have refused to serve because we are educated
just for Japan. I don't think I could serve for
some other country that I am not loyal to.

Q. You were loyal to this country prior
to evacuation, were you not?

A. (no answer)

Q. What was the name of your employer?

A. Nonaka and Co., 214 Front St., San Francisco, Calif.

Q. Where is Nonaka now?

A. I don't know.

Q. Are you a member of Hokoku Seinen Dan?

A. Yes.

Q. Do you hold an office?

A. Not yet.

Q. Do you expect to?

A. Yes.

Q. What office?

A. Block official.

Q. What is your religion?

A. Buddhist.

Q. Have you ever attended any other church?

A. No.

Q. Do you think Japan is going to win the war?
A. Yes.
Q. Do you base that belief upon reports you have
   heard while here, such as shortwave broadcasts?
A. I got the Japanese newspaper and
   just believe Japan will win.
Q. If you thought Japan was not going to win,
   would you still want to go back?
A. Of course, I'll die with Japan.
Q. You mean die in the war?
A. If Japan is destroyed by some other country, I will die.
Q. You mean you want to commit hari kari?
A. Yes.
Q. In other words, if United States wins the
   war against Japan, you fully intend to com-
   mit suicide, regardless of where you are?
A. Yes.
Q. This is a form for renunciation of United States na-
   tionality. If you abandon your United States citizen-
   ship and should return to Japan you will probably
   never be permitted to reenter the United States?
A. That is understood.

APPLICANT SIGNED HERE:

As renunciation hearings were taking place, leaders of the resistance movement were gradually being removed to DOJ internment
camps for enemy aliens. Once Japanese Americans renounced
their citizenship, their new designation as enemy aliens meant that
they too could legally be held in these internment camps for the
duration of the war. The denationalization process further punished and dehumanized the dissidents by immediately separating
family members. Although a handful of women were removed to
internment sites for women, for the most part, fathers, brothers,
and sons were apprehended and transported to all-male camps in
New Mexico or North Dakota while mothers and children were left

behind at Tule Lake. The administration intended for all renunciants to be deported to Japan at the war's end.

As leaders of the resistance were removed, the authorities were
surprised to see the number of people joining the Hoshidan and
applying for renunciation rise exponentially. As leadership positions became vacant, they were immediately filled in order to keep
the organizations intact. The women's auxiliary, Joshi Seinen Dan,
became increasingly active. Both of my parents were called on to
serve in positions as needed. To quell the chaos, the administration
decided to delay the closing of the prison camps for another year.
And yet the renunciation numbers continued to climb.

Although my mother understood the sacrifices she and Itaru
would have to make to reach their ultimate goal, she lived with
the fear of not knowing when he would be picked up, jailed, and
removed to an unknown destination. With two small children to
care for behind barbed wire, she mustered her courage to face
what lay ahead. Thousands of other women, especially elderly issei
women with limited English language skills, were left to fend for
themselves.

The arrest and removal of Hoshidan members continued with
increasing force. Still, resistance continued. While detained in the
stockade, Tatsuo Inouye wrote in his diary that many of the men
who were arrested and placed in the jail were brutally beaten. But
their dignity and purpose remained intact, frustrating prison administrators. On January 26, when the second group of 171 men
was to be transferred to the Santa Fe internment camp in New
Mexico, witnesses reported:

> At five-thirty in the morning, in a spectacular gesture of de-
> fiance, Hōkoku bugles were blown loudly at dawn and the
> young members who were not being interned, drilled and or-
> dered themselves in rows facing the fence. As each truck of
> internees left the gate a farewell shout "Banzai!" arose.

Such departures came to be viewed as the "honor of internment,"
bringing Hoshidan members a step closer to removing what had
become the shackles of their American citizenship. Hundreds of

men were being removed in rapid succession now. These men were seen as making the great sacrifice of leaving their families behind as their impending internment rekindled their personal dignity.

The administration, caught off guard by the continued pro-Japan demonstrations, were outraged. Threats, arrests, and removals were soon followed with Internal Security breaking up meetings and destroying offices of groups it had formerly condoned. Photographs surreptitiously taken give credence to reports of officers beating prisoners with billy clubs and bats.

Meanwhile, an epidemic of dysentery, a bacterial infection of the intestines contracted by both children and adults, spread across the prison camp, causing serious illness and, in some cases, death. Poor sanitation, mass food preparation, public latrines, and crowded living quarters caused repeated waves of communal disease, all exacerbated by medical treatment by some white doctors that was often dismissive, incompetent, even, in my mother's words, "not human."

In the midst of all of this, Shizuko was also notified that her brother, Masami, recently out on early leave clearance, had been drafted into the US Army.

Thursday, January 25, 1945—Clear
Many *HOKOKUDAN*'s leaders are being sent to Santa Fe Internment camp tomorrow. In our Block, 4 people including Mr. Yamakido, Mr. Nishimoto.

After supper, Block 68's *HOKOKU Women's* meeting. They elected me as a one of Block 68's *ward committee members*.

Friday, January 26, 1945—Clear
8:30 a.m. *I took Kiyoshi with me for the sendoff of the men being sent to* internment camps. *Everyone went off in good spirits. They are like soldiers going to the front. The gate was full of people sending them off.*

Sunday, January 28, 1945 Clear
2–4 p.m. to *Joshi Seinen Dan* [women's auxiliary meeting]. 159 members.

Monday, January 29, 1945 Clear
Got up at 5 a.m. Attended the prayer for victory and after that participated in the marching exercise for an hour.

Tuesday, January 30, 1945 Windy—*Prayer for victory.*
Dillon Myer WRA Director Statement: 9 relocation centers will not close until January 1, 1946.

Wednesday, January 31, 1945 Rain and Windy—*Prayer for victory.*
Telegram came to HOSHIDAN's headquarters yesterday. Mr. Yamakido's group safely reached Santa Fe internment camp day before yesterday. Got cold, not feeling so well.

Saturday, February 3, 1945 Fair
It was very warm day so took children out for sun bath. Went around the Block and got the Japan address for every member of Joshi Seinen Dan.

Hoshidan members sending off those being removed to Department of Justice internment camps, January 24, 1945. Photo by Robert Ross, reports officer for the WRA and official WRA photographer. Courtesy of the National Japanese American Historical Society.

Monday, February 5, 1945 Cloudy
Went in evening to Block 68 women's meeting. Today is my 28th birthday.

Thursday, February 8, 1945 Rain
Last night's meeting's announcement has come true after all. Over 500 members and leaders got a notice that they will be sent to Santa Fe internment camp on Saturday. Among them are Mr. Fukami and Mr. Yanari. Now it's time for Ina to realize his intention. He is going to be one of the leaders from tomorrow. In our Block 68, 12 young Nisei are going to Santa Fe.

Friday, February 9, 1945 Fair
Ina was named the Block leader of Ward 7's Hokoku Seinen Dan. He hardly ever eats meals and is busy attending meetings. *"Shaved heads"* [Bōzu] *are busily coming in and out.*

Saturday, February 10, 1945 Clear
Ina has been busy all day. There are so many new *Seinen Dan* members. He is trying to make a list of members to send to the main office, but one after another members are increasing. All 12 young bugle boys came to say farewell. It's going to be lonely without these boys in our Block.

Sunday, February 11, 1945 Fair but windy
"Kigensetsu" [National Empire Day]—Big ceremony performed at 5:30 outside.
    635 young men left for Santa Fe today. Getting nearer to their goal.

Monday, February 12, 1945 Rain
9:30 p.m., we were just about going to bed, when a messenger boy came and told Ina to come to Block 82 immediately. Something has happened. Main *Hoshi Dan* Office has been broken into by Internal Security. They took everything away. Ina came home 10 o'clock in morning, thank god.

Thursday, February 15, 1945
Received loving message from grandmother through Red Cross. She is still in best of health and waiting for us to come back. God Bless her!

Monday, February 19, 1945 Fair
Ina to meeting 9–12 noon. Afternoon meeting has been broken up by Internal Security.

Wednesday, February 21, 1945 Fair
Wrote letters in English for Mrs. Nishimoto. Her two sons have been sent to internment camp and now she is all alone.

Thursday, February 22, 1945 Fair
Wrote letters to mother and sister Kimiko. Sent cheer up message to them after brother Masami has been drafted to Army. Both Kiyoshi and Satsuki are having *diarrhea* from yesterday. Many children are suffering from it these days. It's epidemic of this camp.

   Mr. Gennishi's soldier friend brought his camera and Mr. Gennishi took picture of the children.

Friday, February 23, 1945 Fair
Satsuki is vomiting everything she eats. She is quite weak today. Got some fresh milk from canteen for her. Kiyoshi is getting well. He has a big appetite. I am feeling not so good. Ina is still not recovered.

Thursday, March 1, 1945
In afternoon Mr. Yamazaki rushed to our house saying he had received apprehension paper from Dept. of Justice. We waited for Ina's but it didn't come. Same for Mr. Kobayashi. This time only little over 100 men. No luck for Ina this time!

Kiyoshi (26 months) with Satsuki (9 months), Tule Lake Segregation Center, California, February 1945

Sunday, March 4, 1945 Fair
Big send off of our members to Internment camp. They left 8:30 this morning. Nobody knows whether they are heading for Santa Fe or North Dakota internment camps.

Monday, March 5, 1945 Fair
Sachiko Yamazaki is quite ill. Went over few times and helped her mother. It's awful to watch her suffer from fever. Her mother took her to clinic but doctor won't do much for her. Such unkind doctors. They aren't humans!

Tuesday, March 6, 1945 Snow
Sachiko-san's condition seems very serious so I went over to Dr. Nakamura's residence and asked him to come and see her. He came immediately and kindly examined her. He showed us how to care for her.

Wednesday, March 7, 1945
Sachiko-san is improving. It looks like she has passed critical condition. Thank God!

Saturday, March 10, 1945
Received letter from brother Masami. He has been drafted by
the army and is at Camp Wolters, Texas. Kiyoshi is sick again
and very fussy all day long.

Sunday, March 11, 1945
Ina to *Rengo Taiso*, marching drill, then all the *Seinen Dan* and
Joshi Seinen Dan went to clean up Graveyard of Tule Lake.

Whether through incompetence or deliberate divisive intent,
WRA authorities had allowed extremist elements to gain power
and influence in the Tule Lake prison, ignoring prisoners' complaints about harassment and coercion. When DOJ officials suddenly found themselves inundated with thousands of requests for
renunciation hearings, Assistant Attorney General Burling blamed
the Hoshidan for pressuring American citizens to renounce.

In an attempt to counter the growing resistance, authorities
tightened restrictions. Activities promoting "Japanese nationalistic
and anti-American activities and the disruption of peace and security within the center," previously condoned by the WRA, were
now declared punishable crimes. Marching, parades, bugling,
wearing nationalistic emblems, public ceremonies, participating
in organizational meetings, and speeches were banned.

The administration also threatened severe consequences for
prisoners who continued to violate regulations, imposing what
were called the Special Project Regulations, devised to divide mil-
itants. They were as follows: "1) cease all prohibited activities and
remain at Tule Lake without further family separation, 2) cease violations of the regulations while the WRA arranged an internment
trip for eligible males, 3) continue the pattern of defiance and take
the consequences."

Hoshidan members split over whether to cease all activities or
continue to protest. For some prisoners, demoralized by the insult
of constant repression, the increased restrictions only heightened
dedication to resistance. My parents became increasingly active in
the resistance, choosing civil disobedience to reach their goal of
finding home.

Shizuko continued to record news from the Japanese Imperial Headquarters, but over time, mentions of Japanese victories over the enemy diminished as it became evident that Japan was suffering major losses at the battlefront and from US bombing raids over Tokyo. Although Shizuko followed news of the Japanese army cabinet's changes, along with the undeniable military losses at the front, she either consciously avoided or unconsciously denied the apparent undercurrents driving the disintegrating leadership. In his 2006 book *Racing the Enemy*, Japanese war scholar and historian Tsuyoshi Hasegawa explains that secret plans to seek termination of the war had actually begun in July 1944. However, the resignation and replacement of Japanese army cabinet members was partly a result of disagreement about whether to end the war or continue fighting until the end.

Morning fitness exercises had taken on a militaristic tenor in defiance of the rules set by the authorities. Every day at 5:30 a.m., young boys played the Japanese national anthem on bugles. Three hundred to fifteen hundred members of the Hoshidan gathered to perform ritual bowing toward the east, then march in formation. Shizuko and Itaru continued to participate in the morning drills, ceremonies honoring the emperor, and recitation of Japan's "Prayer for Victory." Such activities, previously ignored by the prison administration, now led to mass roundups. Those arrested were held in the Tule Lake jail, the prison within the prison, then dispatched to federal DOJ internment camps.

Hoshidan leaders demanded that those who refused to comply with the Special Project Regulations be released and referred to as "enemy patriots," acting honorably in defense of Japan. In a letter posted in every mess hall at Tule Lake, Burling shared his enraged response to such demands, which not only revealed the hatred and contempt held by government officials toward the renunciants but also continued to divide the prison community:

> They are not patriots, but traitors. They are, thank God, but a small minority of the young people of Japanese ancestry born in this country, but they are a disgrace and a shame to their brother Japanese-Americans who have proved with their

blood that they understand what it means to be loyal to the country of one's birth.

Once again, those who complied were the "good guys" and those who protested were the "bad guys." The splitting of patriots from traitors would have a profound effect on the prison community, as captive people without control over their lives internalized the binary choices afforded them. The power and control reasserted by camp authorities were best exemplified in this moment as threats of family separation, deportation, and other unknown consequences.

"Pro-administration" prisoners were sent out to urge people like my father to stop participating in the protests; meanwhile, extremists continued to use physical threats and social pressure to keep prisoners from giving in to administration demands. Noboru Shirai referred to the men segregated from the Manzanar prison camp as the "tough fishermen of Terminal Island, California" and the "staunch protesters who had participated in the 'Manzanar Riot.'" This formidable group of men, backed by the black-belted judo and kendo groups, were known to use violence against those viewed as accommodationists.

As Hoshidan leaders were arrested and removed, members mobilized to replace the leadership. Itaru was chosen to be one of the men to fill the leadership gaps in his ward. Meanwhile, J. Edgar Hoover, director of the FBI, responded to an inquiry from the attorney general's office regarding my father:

> In May, 1942, information was received that Itaru Ina was a member of the Reimei Kai and treasurer of the San Francisco Kibei Council. In April, 1943, information was received that at the Central Utah Relocation Center (Topaz) a number of Japanese made speeches in opposition to solicitation for volunteers for a Japanese-American Army Combat Team. Among those in opposition was one Itaru Ina.

An order stamped March 28, 1945, signed by Attorney General Tom C. Clark, deemed my father "an alien enemy dangerous to the public peace and safety of the United States . . . ordered to depart from the United States within thirty days." And if he failed to do so, "the Commissioner of Immigration and Naturalization shall provide for the alien's removal to Japan." None of this information was ever made available to my father.

By the end of March, Japan had been defeated in the bloody battle of Iwo Jima. Within a week, the US launched the largest amphibious assault in the Pacific theater with the invasion of Okinawa. At the same time, the Soviet Union denounced the Soviet–Japanese Neutrality Pact signed in 1942 and joined the war against Japan; days later, the Soviet army entered Berlin. The Japanese empire was collapsing. And yet hope burned eternal as Shizuko's anger about the destruction bound her more closely to the land of her ancestors and to her decision to renounce her citizenship.

Friday, March 16, 1945 Cloudy & windy & snow
Although Mr. Best announced new regulation of this center, none of the members were alarmed about it. Straight to our aims. Putting us in jail or penitentiary doesn't mean a thing to us.

Saturday, March 17, 1945 Windy
Ayabe, who is this Block's warden paid a visit to give Ina a warning. He advised Ina to stop *"Seinen Dan"* activities, but nothing is going to stop us.

Sunday, March 18, 1945 Fair
Ina and I went to *Rengo Taiso* [group marching]. Internal Security were very alert but didn't arrest any of our members.

Tuesday, March 20, 1945 Cloudy & Windy
A few of the Seinendan leaders have had their renunciation hearing.

Wednesday, March 21, 1945 Fair
Loss of Iwo Jima to enemy. Imperial Headquarter announcement: Lieutenant General Kurihara of Iwo Jima commanded

remaining officers and men to last ditch on day of March 17th and made heroic death.

Thursday, March 22, 1945 Windy and Little Snow
Ina went to work as usual, but he didn't seem well. All day long he was sleeping off and on. This illness is terrible and everybody is in trouble with aches all over the body.

Sunday, April 1, 1945 Windy
Today is Easter. *Two eggs were served for each person at breakfast.*
   Announcement of "Imperial Headquarters" in Okinawa: 105 SUNK OR DAMAGED *enemy ships.*

Friday–Wednesday, April 6–11, 1945 HOSHIDAN's CRISIS
Some members have split from Seinendan as a result of difference of opinion on WRA's proposition. Ina hasn't slept a wink for 4 days and hasn't eaten much because of mental exhaustion.

Thursday, April 12, 1945
President Franklin D. Roosevelt died from sudden illness at Warm Springs, Georgia.

Friday, April 13, 1945
Japan is paying respect to death of President Roosevelt and didn't broadcast as usual. Our Seinendan stopped usual activities until after his funeral.

Sunday, April 15, 1945
Roosevelt's burial day. His resting place is Hyde Park, New York. Mourning all over the U.S.A. No commercial broadcast over the radio. Just everything about Roosevelt's life story.

Thursday, April 19, 1945 Beautiful weather
Kiyoshi had very high fever from last night and didn't sleep at all. Fever hasn't gone down today either. Heard it's camp epidemic now.

Sunday, April 22, 1945 Fair
Took children to *Rengo Taiso*. Ward 7's *SEINENDAN's exec-utive officers* have been reestablished. Ina is the *shuyobucho*, Chief Section Head.

Sunday, April 29, 1945 Beautiful Day
44th birthday of Emperor of Japan. Our group had a cere-mony at 6:00 a.m. Took children to *Rengo Taiso* group march exercise.

Monday, April 30, 1945 Beautiful Day
Several of the boys of our *DAN* group have been arrested and their bugles were confiscated.

Tuesday, May 1, 1945 Beautiful Day
American propaganda news states that Hitler has been killed at Berlin fight.

Tuesday, May 8, 1945
President Truman made an official statement of "Uncondi-tional Surrender of Germany." Today is holiday for Americans.

Wednesday, May 9, 1945 Cloudy & little rain
Germany has surrendered to Russia today and Russia is hav-ing national holiday.

Tuesday, May 15, 1945
After supper, Mr. Ono came over and told us one of the men in his Block was killed by fallen wall while working as a carpenter at High School building.[1]

---

1. This is a reference to the tragic death of Mr. Daisaburo Kawano when a forty-three-foot section of a corridor collapsed. Kawano's body was found several hours later, pinned beneath the structure.

Thursday, May 24, 1945
All day long, the weather changed from sunny, to cloudy, to rainy, so unpredictable.

When we got up at 5:30 a.m. and Ina was about to go to work, a car driven by a Caucasian was going around our place and watching us. I worried that he might have come to take Ina away, but nothing happened.

In the afternoon, I sewed. I'm glad to be able to make a new coat for Kiyoshi out of my old coat.

Friday, May 25, 1945
Today is Satsuki's first birthday. I made ice cream, nigiri-sushi, etc. and celebrated the day by inviting Fukami Kiyoko-chan, and Hisako-chan. She is now able to walk freely all over the room.

Received U.S. Citizen Renunciation approval from Washington D.C.

Saturday, May 26, 1945
It's a gloomy day. Such is our enemy's barbarous act that two hundred fifty B29s attacked Tokyo again and burned Miyagi and Ohmiya Imperial Palace. I couldn't help feeling bitter all day long.

Thursday, May 31, 1945 *Clear*
From 4:30 a.m., Kiyoshi continued to suffer from diarrhea. As I checked his stool carefully, I was shocked to find some blood. Right after lunch, Ina and I took him to the clinic and had Dr. Yamaguchi examine him. The doctor simply told us, "Give him skim milk and this medicine for two days."

By summer, 5,461 prisoners in Tule Lake had renounced their US citizenship, and 1,200 renunciants were removed to DOJ internment camps in New Mexico and North Dakota. Like the child ambivalently shrugging off the hand of an abusive parent, those who renounced their birthright had no idea what was to become of them. Shizuko gathered her courage, knowing that Itaru would soon be taken from the family.

Saturday, June 2, 1945 *Rainy*
There is no change for Kiyoshi from yesterday.

Around 7 p.m. in the evening, the Manzanar gang showed up at Kobayashi-san's place, but since he wasn't there, they all waited in the house for him to return. All together about twenty people noisily poured in. Apparently, they came to talk to Kobayashi-san with the intention to do something depending on how the conversation went. They put a guard outside and soon Kobayashi-san returned home and everybody came out and surrounded him. Ina was also called to be there. By the time the discussion ended and nothing bad happened, two Caucasian Internal Security and a couple of Japanese internal security wardens came and took all the Manzanar people away in a car.

Sunday, June 3, 1945 *Clear*
Again, three young men were arrested in the middle of our marching exercise. I heard that INTERNAL SECURITY tore up their group uniforms, punched them, did quite cruel things to them, and took them away. I can't help feeling angry that they were accused of being trouble-makers.

Monday, June 4, 1945 *Clear*
Today Kiyoshi got much better and wanted to eat. It looks like the bleeding stopped.

Friday, June 8, 1945 *Clear*
Today Ina was looking forward to going to HAIKU-KAI meeting in the evening, but these days the Manzanar group has become violent so he decided to cancel. It's not safe to go out in the evening. Ina is disappointed, but for now we must be patient.

Sunday, June 10, 1945
Today is Ina's birthday, but I couldn't do anything special for him. He turned 32.

Tule Lake Segregation Center, circa June 1945. Unlabeled photos by
Robert Ross, WRA photographer, passed on to ACLU attorney Wayne
Collins. Courtesy of the National Japanese American Historical Society.

Thursday, June 14, 1945

I won the photograph lottery in the Block *and took the children
to the studio to have their photo taken, but Kiyoshi got so frightened that we had to stop and come home. I decided we would go
back tomorrow.*

Friday, June 15, 1945

*Today I asked Kiyoshi's favorite uncle, Yamashita-san, to come
with us to have the children's photo taken. Kiyoshi was fine
because he was with his Yamashita Oji-san, but Satsuki kept
crying, and I didn't know what to do with her. When I finally
tricked her and got her to stop crying, they got a photo of her. Because they are children born in the camps, it's understandable
that they are so fearful.*

Sunday, June 17, 1945

*Finished laundry in the early morning and took the children to
watch marching exercise. Ina was in charge of giving the commands. Two of the buglers were arrested.*

Wednesday, June 20, 1945
We all received a notice that 450 people, including almost all of the Manzanar group, will be sent to internment camps this coming Sunday. Twenty or thirty members in our group are included. Kobayashi-san also received a notice this evening.

Friday, June 22, 1945 *Sunny*
Our group members are opposed to going to the internment camp with the Manzanar group. It would be foolish, since our group could be assaulted by them on the way to the camp. Ina and others went to the meeting in the afternoon, but nothing has been decided yet. I didn't go to sewing because I didn't feel settled.

Saturday, June 23, 1945 *Sunny*
Some of our group members were taken to the jail tonight, and it was confirmed that they would leave for Santa Fe internment camp tomorrow.

Sunday, June 24, 1945 *Rainy*
I'm not sure about the exact number, but about 450 people left for the internment camp. I was relieved to hear that 31 members of our group left safely.

Monday, June 25, 1945
Today during the morning assembly, 35 of our members were arrested by Internal Security. Ina was one of them. But he came home around 7 p.m. in the evening. He only had three sandwiches for both breakfast and lunch, and two rice balls [onigiri] for dinner.

Tuesday, June 26, 1945
Again, this morning 306 men wearing Hoshidan emblems were arrested during the morning assembly. Ina hasn't returned home tonight.

The "jail within a jail" at the Tule Lake Segregation Center. The six cells, designed to hold twenty-four prisoners total, were packed with more than a hundred men during the roundup of dissidents. Courtesy of the National Archives and Records Administration.

Wednesday, June 27, 1945

Ina came home around 10 a.m. All 306 men who were arrested yesterday have returned to their families. He told me that they were only given two meals. And all of them had to put a mattress on the floor and each of them were given two blankets. It was very cold yesterday evening. This morning, the rest of the men were taken.

Friday, June 29, 1945 *Clear*

Nothing unusual happened during today's morning assembly. We were very glad to receive a telegram from Kobayashi-san. He arrived safely in Santa Fe. Of course, Auntie Kobayashi was very happy. Ina went to HAIKU-KAI meeting.

Saturday, June 30, 1945

Around 9:30 a.m. Internal Security came with an arrest warrant for Ina, but he wasn't home. I was told that he only gives the arrest warrant to the person himself. He came back around at 1:30 p.m. and gave it to Ina. Departure date is July 2 at 2 p.m. Fifty members of our group received the same warrant. The other fifty people are from the Manzanar group. There is a rumor that they will go to internment camp in Bismarck, North Dakota. Ina must feel strengthened since he will be with his friends, Yamasaki-san, Tani-san, and Mitsui-san.

Sunday, July 1, 1945 *Sunny*

It is such a very hot day. We finished packing for Ina early, and visited our neighbors and friends to say goodbye. Later, Ina and others were taken to jail. Most of our group members left today, saying that they won't go tomorrow with the Manzanar group. Midori Ikejiri had her engagement ceremony early because her father is scheduled to go to internment camp now.

Monday, July 2, 1945 *Sunny*

In the afternoon, Tani-san brought me a note from Ina. The note said that they will be leaving tomorrow and that he slept in the jail last night. I'm sure he couldn't sleep well. I was relieved to get his note.

Tuesday, July 3, 1945 *Sunny*

I woke up at 5:30 a.m. this morning when somebody knocked on the door. I got up right away to see who it was, but the person was gone. I realized that Ina and the others might be leaving, so Auntie Kobayashi and I went out to the fence, but we couldn't see anything. I learned that Ina and others left at 5:30 a.m. this morning by two buses. I missed it.

5.

Enemy Aliens

After I completed a one-year contract teaching in Europe for the Boston University overseas program, my thirteen-year-old son, Adrian, and I stopped in Washington, D.C., en route to our home in Sacramento. My older son, Dylan, had decided to continue traveling for a few more months before returning to college. It was 1988. After years of unstinting grassroots effort by West Coast Japanese American activists, the Civil Liberties Act of 1988 had been passed, acknowledging the injustice of the mass incarceration of Japanese Americans during World War II. To mark this occasion, the Smithsonian Institution was holding an exhibit titled *A More Perfect Union: Japanese Americans and the United States Constitution*.

Housed in the National Museum of American History, the exhibition focused on both the bicentennial of the US Constitution and "a period when racial prejudice and fear upset the balance between the rights of citizens and the power of the state and led to the internment of some 120,000 Japanese Americans for much of World War II." Just before arriving at the exhibition hall, we stopped at the Vietnam War Memorial, where my tears flowed in grief for all the losses wrought by war.

Itaru Ina, foreground right, July 1, 1945. This photo by Robert Ross, WRA photographer, was part of the Smithsonian Institution's 1988 exhibit *A More Perfect Union*.

I had no idea that this brief educational excursion with my unenthused teenage son would bring about a life-changing moment. In the exhibition hall, the lighting was dimmed, making the scene—a replica of a prison camp barrack, with a three-dimensional hologram of an elderly man speaking to a young boy projected inside—look eerily surreal. As we turned the corner to head deeper into the exhibit, I found myself face-to-face with a large black-and-white photo of men in a prison cell. The image was a bit blurred, but as my eyes focused, I recognized the figure in the foreground. It was my father. He was standing with other prisoners crowded inside the "colony jail" in Tule Lake. Stunned, I stared, not quite able to comprehend what I was seeing, yet the tears, unstoppable, streamed down my face.

As if from a distance, I heard Adrian ask softly, "Mom, are we going to have any fun on this trip?" In that moment, as if roused from a dream, I felt myself jolted awake from a dormant knowing that I had no words for. We went on to have fun on our trip, searching for any number of comic book stores where Adrian could add to his

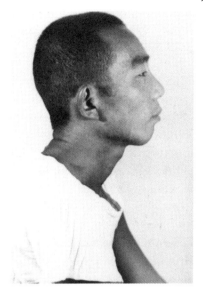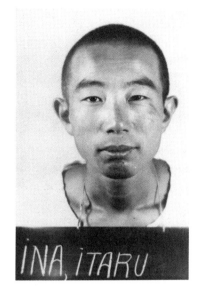

Itaru Ina, Ft. Lincoln Internment Camp (run by the
US Department of Justice), Bismarck, ND, July 1945

growing collection of favorite underground comics. Looking at his
innocent face, so full of curiosity and excitement, I knew, for the
sake of both of my sons, that I had to learn more, to dig deeper to
unearth my parents' World War II story. I had to make conscious
what had happened to my parents and what emotional remnants
had been passed on to me and now to my own children.

I eventually located the official mug shot of my father at the National Archives. It was taken on his arrival at the Ft. Lincoln Internment Camp south of Bismarck, North Dakota. Having read
previous accounts of beatings inside the Tule Lake jail, I was disheartened to see what appear to be bruises on my father's forehead,
nose, and neck. There were signs of cuts and abrasions on his right
cheek, lips, and chin. His name was awkwardly printed on a chalk-
board sign hung from his neck by a strand of wire. He wore the
same white T-shirt, loose around the neck, as in the photograph
from the Tule Lake jail.

Among the attendant documents was the official arrest report
signed by the attorney general, Tom Clark: "Itaru Ina . . . has been

apprehended as being potentially dangerous to the public peace and safety of the United States. . . . It is ordered that said alien enemy be interned."

After my mother passed away in the spring of 2000, I gathered together the 180 letters exchanged between my parents while they were held in separate prison camps during the war, along with my father's prison haiku poetry journals and my mother's diaries. It was as if my parents wanted to make sure that their story would eventually be known to the family. Through these treasured writings, my mother and father have been speaking to me, leaving some gaps, some mystery, much history, and, more than anything, many lessons about how to choose to live my life. Coming upon my father's blurred photograph was what propelled me forward. My need for clarity and understanding finally overrode my fear of knowing, and I found myself on a lifetime journey.

The first communication from Itaru to Shizuko was a postcard.[1] Of all the letters exchanged between my parents during their separation, it is the only letter my father wrote in English. To convey the message of his safe arrival, he strictly followed the rules laid down by authorities regarding written communication by prisoners, while also trying to reassure his wife. The stamp mark identifies my father as a "detained alien enemy"; the censor's secret identity is coded by number, in this case 23-9; and the communication is under the authority of the US Immigration and Naturalization Service.

At one point in my research, I found the name of censor 23-9. Those numbers were written in the corners of several of my parents' letters. He was a kibei who lived not far from my home in Sacramento. He was, in some sense, a voyeur who erased meaning and identities with his razor pen, redacting my parents' and other prisoners' letters in exchange for some unknown benefit. I considered contacting him to ask how he felt about his role reading and

1. As noted earlier in this book, some of the following letters have been edited for length and clarity.

censoring letters of his fellow Japanese Americans, but thought better of it.

In her studies of the psychological consequences of captivity, Dr. Judith Herman found that "prisoners, even those who have successfully resisted, understand that under extreme duress, anyone can be 'broken.'" A victim/prisoner held in a chronic state of uncertainty, like many at Tule Lake, could in time be compelled to relinquish their own inner autonomy, worldview, moral principles, or connection with others for the sake of survival. Serving as a censor for the administration may have been a part of this man's incarceration story never shared with his family. As I reflect back now, my vengeful inclination to "out" him was a perfect illustration of how my own trauma was being activated. I realized that I myself, thankfully, have no idea how I would have coped as an adult under those circumstances.

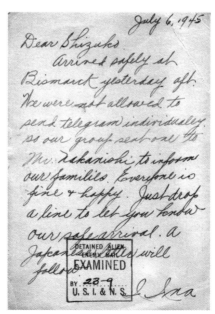

Postcard from Itaru to Shizuko with a censor's stamp

When my father was arrested and taken from us, I was just fourteen months old, and my brother Kiyoshi, two and a half years old. Both of us were born "doing time" in American concentration camps. Even as my parents did their best to shelter and comfort us, their own anxiety and uncertainty likely emanated from the arms that held my brother and me. Kiyoshi and I grew from infancy into early childhood only knowing life in captivity. I was too young to consciously grasp what was going on, but my father's seemingly sudden, inexplicable disappearance was traumatic for my brother. Unable to comprehend our father's absence, Kiyoshi turned to childish imagination and angry outbursts as the only ways to cope with his pain.

July 14, 1945
Dear Itaru Ina,
Received your first letter dated July 6, and for the time being, I felt relieved.
Otō-chan [Daddy], I'm happy to know that you can write many haiku. I know this is what you love to do. You don't have to worry at all about the family, so please write many memorable haiku. Today is Saturday, and Kiyoshi is sleeping peacefully and Satsuki is playing by herself, busily wiping the floor with a rag, so I am able to write to you. Every day I am working hard chasing after the children, and at night, chasing away the mosquitoes, so my life is always busy. Kiyoshi is often asking, "Where is Otō-chan? He's not here!" so I tried to show him your picture, but he wouldn't calm down. He insisted that "Otō-chan is not wearing his shoes! I want to see his feet!" One night while I was busy, he sneaked the picture to his bed and carefully removed the picture from the frame, then he came running to me and said over and over again, "Mommy, Otō-chan's shoes are gone and his feet hurt and are bleeding." Of course, the picture does not show the bottom of his Otō-chan's body and so the shoes don't show. I tried to explain this to him in many different ways, but he doesn't seem to understand. For days he would say over and over again, "His shoes are gone!" In the past few days he has finally stopped. He doesn't seem to understand that his

Otō-chan is gone. Now he looks at the picture and believes that the picture is his Otō-chan. When somebody asks him about his Otō-chan, he answers, "He's sitting at home." Every day he asks the picture, "Otō-chan, I'm being a good boy, so please make me a boat and an airplane." His belief that Otō-chan didn't have his shoes was very difficult for me. Lately, I feel troubled about his bad mouth. Whenever he is angry with anybody, he yells, poop head! [unkotare!] and stupid! [bakatare!].

If you need anything, let me know and I will send it immediately. I will close for now. Please take good care of yourself.

Shizuko

The Immigration and Naturalization Service censored all incoming and outgoing mail between Tule Lake and Bismarck. Internees were on notice that letters mentioning any complaints about mistreatment, reports of incidents, or movement of prisoners would be excised by censors.

The restrictions on written communication and the peering eyes of censors, along with the formality and emotional restraint of Japanese expression and emotions generally, set a tone in my parents' letters that was often inconsistent with the experiences being described. Another tendency, perhaps cultural, perhaps unique to my family, but prominent in our communication has always been to downplay anything distressing or disturbing in order to avoid upsetting others. In fact, I often felt that the more effort made to be upbeat about a negative experience, the more likely that much more pain was being hidden. My parents' initial letters seem to rely on this family pattern.

Camp life for my father in Ft. Lincoln, a former military post built in 1895, offered a sharp contrast to the living conditions in Tule Lake. Unlike the hastily built, civilian-run WRA prison camps, the federal internment camps were operated in accordance with the Geneva Convention, which required that detained civilian foreign nationals be provided humane living conditions during times of war. Itaru, having renounced his American citizenship, suddenly became an "enemy alien internee." Taken more than a thousand miles away from his family, he now had the benefit of

third-party oversight that made it possible for American noncom-
batants to be housed under livable conditions. Japanese nationals and renunciants shared a large dormitory room inside a solidly
built brick building that had previously served as officers' quarters.
Steam heat protected internees from the bitter cold, and a swimming pool, canteen biergarten, and ice skating rink were shared
with German internees.

An important distinction needs to be made in order to fully
understand the changes that were taking place at this time. The
words *internment* and *internee* have, in the past, been used to refer to all Japanese Americans who were incarcerated during World
War II. However, these terms are only accurate in reference to
those prisoners being held in federal Department of Justice internment camps for so-called enemy aliens, such as Ft. Lincoln, where
Itaru was held. Japanese Americans and Japanese immigrants held
in the War Relocation Authority incarceration sites, such as Tule
Lake, were not by definition "internees." They were, in fact, civilian prisoners held without due process in American concentration
camps, and therefore are appropriately referred to as "prisoners" or
"incarcerees."

Letter from Itaru to Shizuko,
July 9, 1945

July 9, 1945
Dear Shizuko,
    Five days have passed since I arrived in Bismarck, and the
weather has been very pleasant. I feel as if I'm on a vacation
from the heat. [XXXXX SEVEN TO EIGHT WORDS CENSORED]
After breakfast and until lunch, I take walks, collect stones,
read, and talk with others. After lunch I take a nap, study, watch
the swimmers and baseball players, and go for a walk. Every
other day I see a movie, and after dinner, I go for walks with my
friend Yanari to get inspiration for haiku. After that, I sometimes
go to have a drink. I feel sorry because my life is so easy here.
[XXXXX FIFTEEN WORDS CENSORED] *I have been told by*
people who haven't seen me for a long time that I have lost a lot
of weight. If Dr. Koike from Minidoka sends you his published
haiku, please send to me. Please give my regards to Mrs. Fu-
kami. Let her know her husband is in good spirits and getting
very dark from the sun. When the picture of Kiyoshi and Satsuki
is developed, please send to me. I am not allowed to write more
than 25 lines, so I will close for now.
    from Bismarck, Ina

Elders had advised the young men at Tule Lake that renunciation
and internment as enemy aliens would give them credibility as a
"true Japanese" and accord them good standing upon their arrival
in Japan. Finally, here in the Ft. Lincoln Internment Camp, reseg-
regated with others who shared the same intention of returning
to Japan, the intracamp strife all but disappeared, and the men
waited out the war in solidarity, hoping to be reunited with their
families and start life anew in Japan.

    My father, an inveterate poet, continued to stay in touch with
other poets held in different WRA prison camps through his correspondence with my mother. In his memoir, *Tule Lake*, Noboru
Shirai describes the activities of what could be considered a widespread underground resistance movement of poets, writers, and
intellectuals who managed to remain under the radar of censors
and camp administrators, determined to express themselves and
record their prison life:

> A group of talented young writers got together to start a lit-
> erary magazine called Tessaku (Iron Fence). Printed on a
> hectograph machine, each issue featured life at Tule Lake as
> described in fiction, essays, literary discussions, social criti-
> cism, tankas and haiku. . . . There were so many good entries;
> each issue was a hundred or more pages long.

Several of my father's poems were included in these publications.

I visited the former internment site near Bismarck in 2001 while
doing research for my documentary film *From a Silk Cocoon*. The
Ft. Lincoln site, now owned and occupied by the United Tribes
Technical College, is a beautifully landscaped residential campus.
In contrast to the way my father arrived, off-loaded from a train
carrying the last one hundred men from Tule Lake by soldiers with
open bayonet rifles, I was warmly welcomed by the tribal faculty
and president Dr. David Gipp. I had not been the first Japanese
American to travel to the site searching for information about
World War II family history. As we toured the campus, my guide,
Dr. Russell Swagger, the dean of students, pointed out where the
now-built-over swimming pool had been and where markings on
walls were made by the Japanese internees. Carved into the front
of the red brick building where my father was held were kanji (Chinese characters) for the resistance group Hokoku Seinen Dan.
Native American students escorted me to a small grove of trees
believed to have been planted by the Japanese American internees.
They said that when the winds blew, the branches rubbing together
sounded like the internees weeping. One student had heard stories about sightings of ghostly figures of Japanese men who had
died there. A medicine woman offered healing chants and rituals
around the trees from time to time. I was comforted knowing that
my father's presence at Ft. Lincoln had not been erased.

I returned two years later in 2003 with my brothers, six former internees, and several scholars and journalists. In collaboration with
the University of North Dakota Museum and the United Tribes
Technical College, I helped organize a photo exhibit capturing life
in the Ft. Lincoln Internment Camp during World War II. Titled
Snow Country Prison, the exhibit featured my father's Bismarck

haiku. The lasting impact of the renunciation debacle surfaced when the former internees, now in their seventies and eighties, were invited to speak about their experience. Each of them struggled with the fear that no one would understand their decision to renounce their citizenship. One man disclosed that he had never told his wife that he had been interned as an enemy alien. All of them asked that their names not be made public. One man said, "Today I'm not proud of the decision I made, but I'm not ashamed either." As a consequence of the government's effort to justify the continued incarceration of "disloyals," men like my father were referred to as traitors, cowards, and draft dodgers. Dissidence was conflated with disloyalty, and shame rained down on them. I wondered, if my father had been alive, what he might have said.

When the thousands of issei and kibei renunciants were sent to federal internment camps, the women left behind at Tule Lake were faced with not only grief and uncertainty about the fate of the men and the future of their families but also the loss of whatever minimal income the men had brought in from their prison jobs. Shizuko, suddenly an "internment widow" and single mom with two toddlers living under prison rule, had to apply for welfare. She struggled alone to care for her children, carrying my brother and me through snow and searing heat to meals at the mess hall three times a day. In their effort to sustain life for themselves and their children, the women left behind turned to each other. Some, including my mother, continued to carry on the resistance work left behind by the men.

By contrast, the atmosphere at the enemy alien internment camp at Bismarck was less chaotic and more like a slow-ticking clock as the men waited to be reunited with their families and return to Japan. They turned their attention to preparing for a new life as free men, engaging in studies and recreational activities. My father was surrounded by fellow Tule Lake dissidents and poets, many of whom had been friends from earlier bachelor days in San Francisco. He occupied his leisure time writing letters to my mother, composing haiku, reading selections from his trunk full of books, playing his shakuhachi, and making toys to send to me and my brother.

Thursday, July 12, 1945 *Sunny*

Since many Hoshidan members have been interned, there are only a few men left, so the Joshi Seinen women's group is taking responsibility for many things, and I am busy every day. Another notice from the "Dan" came today. To continue our efforts together until the end, they want the names of those who are committed to our goals. It is too hot to sleep.

Sunday, July 15, 1945 *Clear*

At 1:30 p.m. attended a meeting for the new leaders of the women's group of Ward 7.

July 17, 1945
Dear Itaru Ina,

I received your second letter yesterday. You seem to be having a very easy life over there, so shall I send you one of our children by separate mail? Our children are in good spirits as usual. There are no friends who are close by anymore, so from morning to evening they go to the other side of the block to play with Takiguchi-san's children.

Today mother sent us clothing and plenty of candy, so please don't worry about sending.

Next, [xxxxx's] address is as follows. [xxxxx ONE LINE CENSORED] I will close now because Kiyoshi is standing beside me whining.
Shizuko

July 17, 1945
Dear Shizuko,

How is everyone doing? How are Kiyoshi and Satsuki? It must be very hot in Tule Lake at this time. Inside here it is very cool, which is different from the barracks in Tule Lake, so I am half naked, wearing only a pair of pants. It is quite pleasant to take a nap under the big tree near the building. Since I arrived and have nothing to worry about, I am able to sleep well and eat well. I might get fat. *Please send me a copy of the new Tessaku poetry journal when a new one is available. I would like to make toys for Kiyoshi and send them to him, but right now I don't have any materials. I think Yanari will be making something for him. That's all for today.*

   Ina

July 21, 1945
Dear Itaru Ina,

   Today is the third day of dust storms. We suffer being inside in the stifling heat. Right now Kiyoshi is playing with water inside the room wearing only his pants. Satsuki is taking a nap, and both of them are full of good spirits. From a few days ago, Satsuki started coming to me whenever she was teased by Kiyoshi, saying, "He took it! He took it!" [Totta! Totta!], and every day she is saying more and more adorable things.

   On this block there have been more cases of chickenpox. I'm afraid our children might get it.

   Since it is so hot, please take care of yourself, and especially be careful about what you eat.

   Shizuko

July 23, 1945
Dear Shizuko,

   I'm glad to hear that Kiyoshi and Satsuki have been in good spirits. As for me, I am doing well each day and recovering from the heat of the past 4 or 5 days. As far as correspondence is concerned, there is a rule that we can send two letters (each letter within 25 lines) and one post card a week. Of course there is no limit on correspondence from you. Next, things I would like you to send to me. You don't have to rush these things, but please send carpenter tools—plane, chisel, square rasp, and hammer in separate four pound parcels over time. Right now I don't have any materials to work with, so you don't have to rush. This is preparation for the winter when I will have nothing to do. The day before yesterday, I finished alien registration. This means

that we are now full-fledged Japanese. Let me know how Kiyoshi
and Satsuki are doing. It is my greatest joy to hear what the chil-
dren are doing as they grow every day. I have reached the limit
(25 lines), so I will write next time.
    Ina

Urgent, sometimes desperate letters between husbands and wives
were chopped by censors, leaving gaping holes of disappeared
meaning. In hopes of evading the censor's razor cuts, my parents
managed to communicate using vague allusions, code words, and
double entendre in their letters. Itaru relied heavily on kanji, which
took up less space than words written in the phonetic hiragana al-
phabet, to stay within the twenty-five-line limit.

My father was, by nature and by Japanese upbringing, a quiet,
reticent man who could more easily express himself through his
poetry than in conversation. Yet in spite of the creature comforts he
describes in his letters, his longing for his wife and family cannot
be contained. The separation requires him to speak more openly
from his heart in his letters. Shizuko struggles between writing
about her difficulties while at the same time telling Itaru not to
worry. She seeks Itaru's comfort, but can't help leaking lighthearted
resentment. It is another familiar communication pattern in my
family to express anger or disappointment indirectly so as to avoid
blaming and being blamed. Shizuko was clearly overwhelmed and
often at her wit's end concerning the children, her health, and the
circumstances of her life without her husband.

July 29, 1945
Ina Itaru-sama,
    The children are finally taking a nap, so this is my chance to
write to you. I will tell you about many things. Kiyoshi and I suf-
fered heat and food poisoning. We had high fever, vomiting, and
lost a lot of weight, but we are much better now, so please do not
worry. I have not allowed Kiyoshi to play outside. It's good that it
was not chicken pox. I wouldn't know what to do, and I would
feel so sorry for him if I had to keep him inside for a month in
this heat. While we were sick, our friends made every effort to

*take care of us. They have been so kind. I felt very lonely while
I was sick.*

*Satsuki is cheerful and healthy every day. I have to make sure
to lock the door because she leaves by herself to go next door
to play.* [XXXXX FOUR LINES CENSORED]. *Letter, clip, clip
please keep in mind mulberry field.*[2]

Today it is burning hot, and the strong smell of "idoo"[3] *is overwhelming. I think it is going to become more full scale and we
are getting more busy. I'd like to have it more easy going like
you, ha ha ha. Absolutely do not worry about 9:10*[4] [XXXXX ONE
LINE CENSORED].

Please take care.

Until next time, Shizuko

Morning, July 31st
Dear Shizuko,

*While living here, the letters from home are truly what make
me the happiest. At 5 p.m. every day Yamazaki-san, the room
representative, goes to the post office to get everyone's mail. And
then he distributes the letters to each person one at a time. Until
the last letter is distributed, each person waits, thinking that the
next one will be his. Although it is not said out loud, when there
is nothing for us, there is disappointment, and happiness when
there is a letter for us. Day after day, we all look forward to 5 p.m.
Those who were disappointed yesterday are happy today. Those
who were happy yesterday are disappointed today. And everyone
waits in the room, patiently looking forward to Yamazaki-san's*

---

2. Code from Shizuko reminding Itaru about Kuwada-san: *Kuwa* = mulberry and
da = field. "Clip, clip" is a reminder that Kuwada was working as a censor.

3. Here Shizuko is writing the Japanese word *idō* in English; it has a double meaning of "water well" and "transfer," as in movement of people. Any communication
regarding movement of people was censored.

4. 9:10 in Japanese is pronounced *kuji no juppun*. In Japanese *kuji* means lottery
or draft. It could be that Shizuko is using a double entendre to avoid censorship to
reassure Itaru that there is no longer the threat of being drafted since renouncing
his US citizenship.

return from the post office at 5 p.m. every day. I wasn't expecting
the letter that I received on the 28th, so I felt especially happy.
This is all for today.
   Ina

July 31, 1945
Dear Itaru Ina,
   Every Monday or Tuesday we look forward to the mail arriving
because Kiyoshi waits to get a letter from his Otō-chan. These
days he seems to understand a little more that his Otō-chan is
gone. He says that his Otō-chan has gone to Tokyo, Japan. For
the past 4 or 5 days while he has been sick and I've had to keep
him inside, he would ask about his Otō-chan, but now when he's
outside busy playing, he doesn't ask as often.
   Please take care of yourself and rest well.
   Shizuko

August 6, 1945
Dear Shizuko,
   You mentioned that you and Kiyoshi were sick with food poisoning and heat. It must have been difficult for you. I'm glad
that you are better now, but please take very good care from now
on. I will write thank you letters to the people who took care of
you, but I am only allowed to write one postcard and two letters every week, so I won't be able to write to them all at once.
So starting from next week, for the next two weeks I will communicate by postcard to you and write thank you letters to the
others, so please understand. Regarding Kuwada, I know about
it because I heard from a friend that he was working as a censor. The letter you sent by airmail had many holes, so I couldn't
make sense of it. But I read that there is nothing for me to worry
about regarding the kuji. I was worrying about it every day, so
I felt relieved. In the near future I will send a package for Kiyoshi. I think it will be more fun if I don't say what it is yet. If
you want pretty pebbles, I will send them to you. The other day
while Yanari and I were taking a walk, we saw a single firefly.

We chased it, but it disappeared somewhere. I have gone back every night to the same place, but it never appeared again. I was happy since it was the first firefly I've seen since I left Japan as a boy. Until next time.

Ina

August 7, 1945
Dear Itaru Ina,

Just like you, I'm always looking forward to your letter every day. Whenever I receive a letter from you I am uplifted and I can work more because I feel my courage is strengthened.

Kiyoshi finally came down with chicken pox. He was very tired starting yesterday evening. I thought it was unusual, so I tried to wash him up early and put him to bed. But when I took off his clothes, I found many bumps on his back. I washed him and put him to bed right away. He had a fever and couldn't go to sleep for a while. He was saying, "I'm hot, I'm hot." When I checked on him this morning, he had rash on his stomach, neck, and face, and I thought for sure it was chicken pox. I called the clinic and took him to the doctor right away.

He does have chicken pox, and now he is not allowed to go out for three weeks. A quarantine sign was hung right away. I'm sure that Satsuki will get it, so I expect we'll have to stay inside for about a month and a half. But I feel most sorry for Kiyoshi. This morning he had a terrible temper tantrum, crying, "I want to go outside!" I felt so upset. No matter what I said, he doesn't understand, so we both cried together.

Since I have to leave the children inside and go out to wash the dishes, I decided to shut the icebox door by hammering a nail. I tied all the chairs to the table with a rope. When Kiyoshi saw this, he looked puzzled and asked, "Mommy, what's wrong?" The other day, when I had to leave the children at home alone so I could wash the dishes for dinner, Kiyoshi opened the icebox and the two of them broke six raw eggs. They were covered with eggs on their face and heads when I returned, and they were so excited while laughing and playing that I was speechless.

Whenever I'm away for a short time, they always do something very naughty, so I have to be on my guard.

Next, brother Masami will go to the South Pacific. He sent me a letter saying that he will come here to say goodbye. I feel sorry for him that he was drafted right after he was released from camp, but there is nothing to be done about it. Sayonara, goodbye, for now.

Shizuko

While my mother struggled to manage with two children quarantined for weeks with chicken pox inside a prison barrack, the world outside was on a collision course of unimaginable destruction. On August 6, 1945, an American B-29 bomber deployed the world's first atomic bomb over the Japanese city of Hiroshima, killing an estimated eighty thousand people. Two days later, Russia, having ended the Neutrality Pact with Japan, declared war on Japan, and within hours launched a surprise invasion of Japanese-occupied Manchuria. On August 8, the US dropped a second atomic bomb on Nagasaki, Japan, killing more than forty thousand people.

Tatsuichiro Akizuki, MD, provided medical treatment to *hibakusha*, victims of the atomic bomb. In his first-person account, he wrote on August 9, 1945:

> It seemed as if the earth itself emitted fire and smoke, flames that writhed up and erupted from underground. The sky was dark, the ground was scarlet, and in between hung clouds of yellowish smoke. Three kinds of color—black, yellow, and scarlet—loomed ominously over the people, who ran about like so many ants seeking to escape. . . . It seemed like the end of the world.

The surrender of the Empire of Japan was announced by Emperor Hirohito on August 15th and formally signed two weeks later, bringing the war's hostilities to a close. With limited access to the news, prisoners remained uninformed, confused, and anxious for weeks following the cease-fire.

Thursday, August 9, 1945 *Sunny*
Couldn't sleep well last night after hearing Russia's declaration of war with Japan. But after hearing the Japanese news this morning, I was able to understand it more clearly, so I felt more reassured. I believe that Japan will certainly win. I wrote to Ina right away.

August 9, 1945
Dear Itaru Ina,
     [XXXXX ONE LINE CENSORED]
Satsuki cried and whined all night, so I'm afraid she will be getting chicken pox *sooner or later.*
     [XXXXX NINE LINES CENSORED⁵]
Today Kiyoshi's chicken pox has improved. He is feeling better and is in strong spirits. He's been throwing a tantrum from this morning, screaming, "Let me out! Let me out!" He is mean to Satsuki, and he hits and kicks me and I cannot bear it. Sometimes Yamashita-san brings different toys he has made to comfort Kiyoshi.
     Well, I will write to you again. You are precious, precious Otō-chan for Kiyoshi and Satsuki, so always take good care of yourself.
     Shizuko

Friday, August 10, 1945 *Clear*
This morning the Japanese news reported that Japan made overtures of peace with four countries, including Britain, US, Russia, and China. There's big confusion all over camp and the United States. I'm not able to eat.

August 13, 1945
Dear Itaru Ina,
     Since last time, our children have been in good spirits, so please don't worry. Ever since I've been keeping them inside,

5. It is possible that Shizuko was conveying news about Russia's declaration of war with Japan.

their mischief has gotten worse. For example, while I quickly went to the latrine laundry room, Kiyoshi got Satsuki out of the bed. And they turned the chamber pot over and made a mess walking all over. Please imagine this. Sometimes they lock me out and I have no choice but to climb through the window.
[XXXXX THREE LINES CENSORED]
Shizuko

August 13, 1945
Dear Shizuko,
    I sent a package to Kiyoshi on the morning of the 7th. I'm thinking that you have received it by now. Yanari-kun took a long time making this toy "duck" for Kiyoshi and Satsuki. Since last time there has been some disturbing news, but I found out that these were entirely rumors, and now I'm feeling relieved and taking sunbaths again. Yesterday was Sunday, and while I was taking a walk near the Germans' flower garden that is now in full bloom, I heard symphony music being played on a record, and suddenly, I felt happy. It was as if I was walking on the fairgrounds with you at the World's Fair in San Francisco.
    Ina

Censored letter from Shizuko to Itaru, August 9, 1945

August 17, 1945
Dear Itaru Ina,

Thank you very much for sending us the unusual toy duck the other day. Kiyoshi and Satsuki are very excited and have been pulling it around all over every day. Now Kiyoshi is almost completely well, but he can't go outside for another ten days.

On August 14, 1945, a peace treaty was settled. Soon we will be able to return to Japan, our dear mother country. [XXXXX ONE LINE CENSORED]

Let us take care of ourselves and have hope for our children's future. We will be together in Japan soon. Sayonara.
Shizuko

Saturday, August 18, 1945 Clear
During this week, I have felt so unsettled that I could not write in my diary. Every day there was no news, and I continue to feel anxious. There is nothing I can do even though I worry a lot. The fact is the fact.

Sunday, August 19, 1945 Cloudy
Japanese broadcast was changed to 8:30 a.m. The radio reception was very clear. All of a sudden I felt stronger. Whatever happens, I want to go back to Japan as soon as possible.

Monday, August 20, 1945 Clear
Received postcard from Ina. It seems that he doesn't know what has happened yet. Apparently he's living in ease and comfort. I wrote to him right away.

While other Americans danced in the confetti-strewn streets in celebration of the end of the war, Japanese American prisoners struggled to grasp the cataclysmic atomic destruction of Japan. As the news of the bombings of Hiroshima and Nagasaki slowly seeped into the mass consciousness, the prison community was left in shock and disbelief. It was as if the wafting dust from the black rain had been scattered over Tule Lake, where thousands had families in the obliterated regions of Japan. Confusion, grief, and denial swirled from barrack to barrack, followed by the realization that the bombings had irrevocably changed the lives of every prisoner. It was perhaps profound grief that kept Itaru and Shizuko dedicated to their plan to take the family to Japan in spite of the destruction that likely awaited them.

To avoid unwanted razor cuts, my parents were forced to write in vague terms in response to the disastrous climax of the war. More emotional transparency is evident in my mother's brief diary entries, which I have interspersed between the letters. My father wrote these two haiku in August 1945 in response to news of the cease-fire:

enten ka   Under the scorching sun
ogore-ru kuni ni   on and on I curse
noroi are   the arrogant country

  * * *

chiroro aware   Crawling out of the fire
karikusa no hi ni   onto the mowed grass—
hai-izuru   poor crickets!

August 20, 1945
Dear Itaru Ina,

 Our life in camp *won't be much longer. The war is over, and people are preoccupied with what their future will hold. According to the statement by Director* Best, *we are to wait until the announcement of future policies from* Washington.
 [XXXXX THREE LINES CENSORED]
 Brother Masami should be coming home soon because there is no longer a need for soldiers.
 Our hope from now on is for our children's future. I will write to you again. Sayonara.
 Shizuko

August 21, 1945
Dear Shizuko,

   Kiyoshi has chicken pox and I feel sorry for him. I think that the toy duck has arrived, so it might give him some comfort. It must be very difficult for you to take care of the two children and take care of the home. I am sorry for you. It shouldn't be too long, so please make sure to take very good care of yourself. Almost half of your last letter was cut out. I felt relieved to hear that Kiyoshi is getting a little better. However, I suppose Satsuki will also get it, so it will be hard on you again. Because of the change of circumstances, there are many different rumors, but rather than being distressed, we are all trying to live calmly and peacefully. Until next time.
   Ina

August 23, 1945
Ina Itaru-sama,

   Have you been well? Kiyoshi is much better now and is very mischievous. From yesterday, Satsuki has gotten chicken pox. *Every morning, every morning, my feelings don't lift, so it's just as well to have to stay inside with my children.*
   [xxxxx TWO LINES CENSORED]
   My heart is full of longing to return to Japan as soon as possible. I want to let you know that my family in Fuji-mura, whom we had hoped to rely on, has suffered and fallen into poverty due to the current circumstances.
   I will be looking forward to your next letter. These days nothing gives me more strength than your letters. Take care of yourself. Sayonara.
   Shizuko

Saturday, August 25, 1945 Clear
The radio news from Japan has been terrible. Every day I'm feeling gloomy.

August 25, 1945
Dear Itaru Ina,

   Last night Satsuki had a high fever and cried all night long and didn't sleep at all. As I look at her this morning, the chicken pox is all over, from her face to her body, and her eyes are almost closed. Hers is much worse than Kiyoshi's. Today she is not feeling well, and she is drowsy from the fever.

   Next, I'm sure you've already heard that Japan became a defeated nation. It took so long until now for it to become clear. We have to come to the full realization that we have been defeated. The only word I heard the Emperor say on the radio was "surrender."

   We need to think seriously about our future from this point on. Please take very good care of yourself.
   Shizuko

Sunday, August 26, 1945 Clear
Kiyoshi went to Sunday school at the Buddhist church for the first time. When he came home, he was truly sweet, showing me how he joins his hands together in gratitude [gassho] and repeating "num num" for Namu Amida Butsu.

August 28, 1945
Dear Shizuko,

   It's good that Kiyoshi and Satsuki have been in good spirits and have been mischievous. By the time you receive this letter, I think the quarantine will be over. The photo came out very nicely. Right away I put it on my desk, and at this moment I am writing this letter in front of it. Since the war is over and the day will come soon when we will return to Japan, we must be prepared whenever we get the order. I don't know for sure how much we can take on board with us on the ship to Japan [xxxxx]. I heard we could take $50.00 and 75 pounds of baggage. For the baggage it will be especially important to prepare plenty of clothing for the children.
   [XXXXX THREE LINES CENSORED]
   Now I'm making a toy tank for Kiyoshi. I am worried about

the children getting hurt since I didn't have a chance to make a fence around the coal stove before I left, so will you ask someone to make a fence using the window screens? Please give my best regards to Kobayashi, Yamashita, etc.

Ina

August 29, 1945
Dear Itaru Ina,

I've been very worried listening to many rumors. I'm sure that you have heard on the radio and in the newspapers, but I'm going to tell you the true facts. Korea became independent, Manchuria became China, and Taiwan became China, and I think there will be more changes by formal agreement on September 2nd. It was decided that the Manchurian Railroad would be run as a partnership between Russia and China. Ten million casualties and missing persons as a result of the bombing, 9,200,000 people have lost their homes, over 30 percent of each of the 37 cities out of all 44 cities bombed were reduced to ashes. Now the greatest problems are the shortage of food and housing. This is beyond our imagination. There are no words to describe this misery. I will stop for now about this news. It is endless.

Next, I was shocked to see Mrs. Fukami so completely changed. She came to talk to me and she was crying. Haruo wrote saying he does not want to go back to Japan. The only thing I could say to her was that, if I were her, I would be determined to do whatever my husband decides. I will write again.

Shizuko

Now that the war was over, and no justification remained for continuing the incarceration of innocent people, authorities began closing the last WRA prisons and DOJ internment camps at a rapid pace. The Tule Lake Segregation Center was emptied of so-called loyal prisoners, but remained open for DOJ "mitigation hearings" for renunciants requesting a reversal of their coerced decision to go to Japan. It would be the last American concentration camp to close.

Now, as people were forced to leave Tule Lake, many to resettle in areas of the country where they had never lived before, they faced uncertainty about where to find housing and jobs. They feared that they would have no protection from the racism and violence that had already followed some prisoners who had been released earlier.

What had been a united brotherhood of mostly young kibei friends from San Francisco who in despair and protest had renounced their American citizenship was now slowly splintering from its collective commitment. Some refused to believe the truth of Japan's defeat. Others began to have second thoughts. Friends such as Haruo Fukami and Yoshida-san in Bismarck chose to cancel their repatriation requests in order to remain in the US, some in opposition to the wishes of their wives in Tule Lake. Others, such as Ono-san and Yamashita-san, who chose not to renounce and were now free, began considering whether to return to San Francisco or make their way to the Midwest, where they were told they would face less hostility. The band of men who left Tule Lake together had been determined to start anew in their reclaimed mother country. Loyalty to one another fortified them in Bismarck. Those who began to waver in their commitment to repatriate, including some of the elder leaders of the Hoshidan, were ridiculed and shunned for "taking the easy way out."

Japanese Americans such as my parents who had renounced their citizenship and were unwittingly deemed enemy aliens had no idea what their future held. At Tule Lake, rumors abounded. Internment widows feared that their husbands would be deported to Japan without them. Others believed that repatriation was now optional for those who had renounced. Some, particularly elders without family, who lost everything when imprisoned, were daunted when contemplating leaving the prison confines. Financially bereft, with nowhere to go and no possibility of starting over again, suicide seemed to be the only solution for some issei men. Demands for a more measured release process were ignored by WRA director Dillon S. Meyer, who pressed for swift prison camp closure. Under his direction, over the course of 1945, the WRA cut off all but the most essential services within the camps.

Shizuko and Itaru exchanged letters, determined to stay the course. In their minds, the only honorable thing to do, whether

Japan won or lost the war, was to hold to their commitment, no matter the sacrifice it required. My parents believed that they had chosen to go to Japan, when in reality, their incarceration and subsequent suffering gave them no other choice. If they hadn't been incarcerated and separated, they would never have considered taking their American-born children to live in Japan.

September 1, 1945
Dear Shizuko,

Thank you, even though you have been very busy, you were still able to make my sweater. It must have been a big job for you to finish such a thing while taking care of two children. I appreciate it very much. I'm hoping that Satsuki won't have to get chicken pox. I've heard that there are many cancellations of repatriation over there and that people are quite concerned about the future. But there is no change in our determination. I think there is no question that what lies before us will be hardships and challenges, but as long as we are determined, we should never worry. I am expecting that the day of our repatriation will be here soon. So, Shizuko, I want you to prepare yourself with that intention. I made a toy tank for Kiyoshi. I painted the chain on the tank, so it will be a little stiff, but it's possible that it will soften if you can get the oil to penetrate the cloth between the chains. It appears that your brother Masami won't have to go to the battlefield after all, and it is a blessing for the Mitsui family.

Ina

Embedded in the following letter from Itaru describing toys he had made for the children are instructions to Shizuko to mend his pants. There, inside the belt lining or pants pocket, he had hidden a letter written on torn bed sheets to evade the censor's razor cuts. I was able to recover four of these cloth letters among my mother's belongings, but it's likely that every reference Itaru or Shizuko made to "pants needing mending" signaled that such a letter had been hidden. The very fact of these letters reflects the constraint my parents felt knowing that their correspondence would be read by censors. In one of the cloth letters, Itaru directs Shizuko to respond with Satsuki's name as a return address to let him know she had hidden a letter inside the package she sent. I never found Shizuko's secret cloth letters.

> *September 3, 1945*
> *Dear Shizuko,*
>   *Some of my books are okay to throw away, but if possible, I'd like to keep the ones on haiku, tanka, literature, drama, art, photography, etc. These are the possessions that took me a long time to collect. Right now it is absolutely unclear whether or not we can be together before repatriation, or how they will be handling our belongings. We may find out in the meantime, but we had better prepare ourselves as if we won't be able to go to Japan together. Please fix the pants because the part that holds the belt has come off. Detach the part around the back and sew it on the inside. If you sew it on the outside, it will look bad. More than anything, hearing about Kiyoshi brings me the most joy. He has certainly become a mischievous boy. Satsuki must be getting big. It has been three months since I've been separated from them. I think Block 68 has now become quite deserted. Until next time.*
> *Ina*

Quoting from the camp newspaper, Shizuko doggedly recorded the words used by the government to chronicle events. To announce the closing of the WRA and DOJ prisons, officials declared "removal of the Military Exclusion Order" to initiate the release of "loyal" prisoners, while those who renounced their citizenship would continue to be detained. Consonant with the language originally used to justify the mass removal and incarceration, these words hid the true atrocity that had been committed. Far from a humanitarian self-correction, it was, in truth, the ending of the government-sanctioned unjust imprisonment of 125,000 people of Japanese ancestry, two-thirds of whom were American citizens and one-half of whom were children. Under the cloud of this false narrative, and with no acknowledgment of government impropriety, prisoners were left with limited options, scrambling to determine what to do next.

One possibility for my parents came from Itaru's maternal aunt, Yoshie Muraoka, and her husband, who were living in Cincinnati, Ohio, and therefore not subject to incarceration. She had stayed in contact with my father and offered to help if my parents were able to avoid deportation.

Wednesday, September 5, 1945 *Rainy*
Extra Issue Newell Star: Military Exclusion Order was removed at midnight on Sept. 5th. Department of Justice continues detention of people who renounced. The current army restrictions will be replaced by the Department of Justice.

September 6, 1945
Dear Shizuko,

I'm glad that Kiyoshi is finally completely well. But you said Satsuki has chicken pox, so this will be another hardship for you. I'll be able to do carpentry work since friends who have repatriated gave me lots of wooden boards. I'm thinking of toys for Satsuki and Kiyoshi to play with on the boat trip to Japan. What do you think will be good? In your letter about your family in Japan, you mentioned that they have become quite poor. Sadly, I think this is something that has become inevitable. When we go back to Japan, I'm sure there will be severe hardship, but I think we will find our way to begin again. [XXXXX ONE LINE CENSORED] Please make sure to answer the questions I ask you in my letter. It seems there are some things unanswered to my questions in my previous letter. Of course, if those were cut out, there would be no way to get it. Hello to Kiyoshi.
    Ina

September 7, 1945
Dear Itaru-sama,

Finally, Satsuki will be through with the quarantine by the end of this week. Because of Kiyoshi's condition, Satsuki had to stay inside for three more weeks, and she has become very

pale and looks quite sickly. Next, as you may know, after mid-
night on September 5th, the military exclusion order that put
us in camp was withdrawn, and all the people on the military
list were freed. For this reason, your kibei friends like Ono-san
and others are constantly fretting about being forced out with
nowhere to go. There has been no announcement regarding the
future of those of us who are on the Department of Justice list.
Today Mrs. Fukami visited me again and said that she sent a
telegram to Haruo because she changed her mind again. She
doesn't know what to do since she wants to go back to Japan but
Haruo has decided to stay. She is so upset that I cannot under-
stand what is what. It seems that these days there are many hys-
terical, crazy internment widows. A young internment widow
in Block 69 became crazy and was taken to the hospital a couple
of days ago. So please don't worry, because I'm not going to be-
come crazy. I don't have time for that. Every day I am busy.
    Shizuko

September 8, 1945
Dear Shizuko,
    [XXXXX SIX LINES CENSORED]
    I've heard that there are many people who are canceling re-
patriation because of the unexpected outcome of the war for the
Japanese. Anyway, our life in camp is finally coming to an end,
and the fear about when and how must be in everybody's mind.
We must not get confused when the time comes. Now we have
to make up our minds clearly and determine a path to take and
proceed without making mistakes. Please let me know your ex-
act desires and thoughts about this. Whether we should, as we
first planned, trouble your grandmother in Japan, who has now
become poor, or we bear the shame for a while and stay with
your parents in Lamona and then move to Japan when the time
is right. Of course there's no change in my thinking, but I won-
der if you might want to stay with your parents. Do not hesitate
to tell me your honest desire. Also this is something I think you
had better keep absolutely secret from Mrs. Fukami and others,
but Haruo has changed his mind and decided to stay here be-

cause he now has no place to go if he goes back to Japan. This is quite different from what he has been repeatedly saying, but I think it is because of the change in his state of mind. Please let me know how our friends are doing over there.

Ina

September 11, 1945
Dear Itaru,

1. I received your letter dated September 1st and September 6th yesterday morning and I felt completely relieved. However, the one dated the sixth had been cut out, and there are some parts that I didn't understand. I appreciate the trouble it took for you to send many things such as the geta, tobacco, tennis ball, *toy top,* toy tank, *etc. I was surprised to see how well you made the* tank, geta, and top. Kiyoshi is very happy. I wish I could show *you his happy smile. Last night he took the* tank *to his* bed *and slept while holding it. I don't know what he was thinking, but before going to sleep, he kept asking me, "Why didn't my Daddy come home with the* tank?" *Then he said an innocent thing to me, "Tomorrow let's go to the* post office *to pick up Daddy." He made me laugh and cry.*

Next, I understand your feelings very well, and I agree with your thoughts that there is no change in our intention and we will look forward to the day of repatriation. As you have mentioned, there will be unimaginable hardship and difficulties that lie ahead of us, but I will be very well prepared for that, and will forge forward with you until my death. So please don't worry about this.

2. Every day around here it is very busy with people who are leaving and those who are sending them off. Since I'm determined, I'm not affected even if I push myself a little harder. After you left, I had some of our friends babysit Kiyoshi for about an hour in the morning, but had to stop since our children got chicken pox. *These days it is especially difficult because there is now conflict between these people. Although the war is clearly over, there is one* group *that doesn't trust the others at all, and they are taking completely separate and senseless actions. It is said that there is no medicine to cure the fool, and it is very upsetting.* Mrs. Yoshida

*in Block 70 is the one who is understanding and is liked by every-
one. She and I are always going back and forth helping each other
as close friends. She is also preparing for repatriation. It's time for
the* mail car *to arrive, so I will close for now.*
  Shizuko

September 12, 1945
Dear Shizuko,
  *You don't have to worry at all about things over here, and least
of all about me. Right now there is nothing that surprises me
about the Japanese situation. I am just realizing the cruel facts
and determined to be prepared for any possibility. Haruo has been
quite strange since we came here. I was surprised, but now there
is no one who wants to be in his company. Itani, who has become the same way, is his only friend. Mrs. Fukami may get angry
about Haruo's decision, but it may turn out to be better for her.
Although he is full of brave talk, he will be unreliable in the future. I heard that the people in the* Block *are gradually moving
out, and it will be a big blow for Kiyoshi when Yamashita-san
leaves. I'm sure he will be lonely for him. Please send my sincerest
appreciation to him. There was reregistration for repatriation yesterday, and I stated my intention to only repatriate together with
my family. However, I don't know if we will actually be able to go
back together or not. The sweater that you sent the other day is
very comfortable to wear. I will write to you again.*
  Ina

September 18, 1945
Itaru-sama,
  *Thank you, I appreciate your kindness and thoughtfulness in
asking about my wishes regarding our future course. Ever since
I found out the war was definitely over, I have thought about
many things and also listened to other people's opinions. But
I believe going back to Japan is the path we should follow. We
are at the crossroads of whether we make Satsuki and Kiyoshi
Japanese? or American? They have Japanese faces, so I don't
want to make them Americans. I feel sorry for the children. The*

fact that my brother Masami was drafted made me feel this very deeply. Also we have to think about your sister Kiyoji-san in Japan, who is your only family. I wonder how she is living nowadays. We must go back as soon as we can and help each other struggle through the suffering and difficulty. How can we stay here living in peace and quiet, and abandon the people living in misery in Japan? It's possible that there might not be enough to eat when we return to Japan, but if that happens, there's nothing to worry about at all if we are determined to die together, the four of us, as a family.

Auntie Muraoka, Ono-san, Akashi-san are all supporting our decision to go back. They said, since we will suffer anyway, there will be more meaning for us to suffer in Japan. Ono-san and Akashi-san will stay here until the last. They are worried that if they are not repatriated, there is nothing they can do but to go out and become beggars. Yamashita-san, on the other hand, is strongly advising that we remain in America. He says taking Kiyoshi and Satsuki to Japan now is the same as all of us committing suicide. He is begging us to stay here because he doesn't want his precious Kiyoshi and Satsuki to suffer. But my thoughts have not changed, and my feelings are the same as yours. With this I know you will truly understand how I feel.

Next, Kiyoshi and Satsuki are well and playing every day, so please don't worry. Satsuki's chicken pox has completely cleared up and her face is now smooth. Recently she has started saying many things, "Kāchan," "Tōchan," "orange hoshii," "iko-u,"[6] etc. Although nobody has taught her, she is saying these things by herself. Day by day she is becoming more adorable. Please take care of yourself.

Shizuko

September 19, 1945
Dear Itaru-sama,

I received a letter from Mrs. Fukushima from Topaz last week. She is worried they will be in trouble if they don't decide about

6. In English, "Mommy," "Daddy," "I want an orange," "let's go."

Shizuko and Itaru, Muir Woods near
San Francisco, 1939

*whether to repatriate, so she lives with worries every day, every
day.*

Today I sent you the photo that you asked for. It's a snapshot
that makes me feel nostalgic.

Mrs. *Itani visited. She asked me, "What has Ina-san been
saying? My husband has not been saying anything, so I cannot
help but worry." And today when Mrs. Yoshida came over, she too
was extremely worried because her husband hasn't written to
her for two weeks. Since we have children, and we have no idea
what's going to happen, even when there is no news, I think it is
common sense to write at least once a week. This morning Mrs.
Fukami came over crying. So the situation here is really getting
worse. She received a letter from Haruo yesterday and brought
it to show me. I wonder why Haruo is so rushed trying to get out.
Because Mrs. Fukami is now on the Justice Department's* stop
list, like me, *she cannot take any steps to get out.*

Right now I'm working hard on knitting sweaters *for our*

children for winter in Japan. There is more to say, but my head
is spinning, so I will stop for now. Good night.
  Shizuko

September 20, 1945
Dear Shizuko,
  I'm glad Kiyoshi and Satsuki have finished the quarantine.
I know you must have gone through much hardship during
this long time. I have finally finished assembling the airplane
that Kiyoshi wanted. I made sure to make it sturdy so it won't
break easily. I sent you back the pants *the day before yesterday.*
Please undo the seams on the back and repair the place where
the belt closes. It is getting cold, so please send it in a hurry.
I received letters from Nagatoishi-san and Okazaki-san. Please
thank them. Nagatoishi-san praised you a lot. He said you are
a sensible wife and quite competent, so you should thank him
profusely for that. Ha ha ha. I think it is understandable that
Mrs. Fukami is anxious during these times. Haruo is depressed
and lonely. Seems like he doesn't have anyone to talk to. Now a
cold long winter in the North Country is about to begin. I forgot
to mention this, but I put a little candy *in with the* pants *I sent.*
Winter underwear *will be issued soon, but when you have time*
please send the ones you have there. It's a pleasure to receive a
package from time to time. Even though I know what might be
inside, until I get to the post office to pick it up, I wonder what
it might be and can hardly wait.
  Ina

September 25, 1945
Itaru-sama
  I just received your letter dated September 20th. Yesterday
I received the package with your pants. *When I told Kiyoshi*
that a package came from Otō-chan, he came running in from
his play. At first he put his hands on the floor and bowed, saying
thank you to Otō-chan and then he opened the package by him-
self, completely believing that it was his new toy airplane. When

he found that it was not, he looked disappointed, but because there was candy, *he seemed to be satisfied.*

This morning he went out to play and came running back home in his bare feet. He had taken off his pants and shoes, so I spanked him hard and scolded him. I asked him why he was in his bare feet and showing his bottom. I couldn't help laughing when he said, "I was doing sumo!" Then he placed his hands on the ground as if he were a sumo wrestler preparing for a match.

Day after day while taking care of the children, I am mending old clothes to prepare for repatriation. I am so busy that I feel dizzy.

The pants *that you sent back are now too small, so it must mean that you have gotten a lot fatter. You seem so carefree. On the contrary, I have lost weight and my clothes have become quite loose. I will write again. Sayonara.*
Shizuko

Thursday, September 27, 1945 Clear
The day before yesterday, I was happy to find another secret note *in the pants Ina returned to me. I was able to understand his situation better.*

From cloth letter pictured at right. Water damage has made part of it illegible:
I'm sure that you would like to see your parents before going back to Japan, but this is now an impossibility. I suppose Mrs. Fukami is angry about Haruo changing his mind about going to Japan, but ultimately I think it's better for them to stay for his sake. If he behaves in such a manner, it may be difficult for him to live in Japan. The other day when I was called in for the hearing [illegible], the officer asked me what I think about those people who canceled repatriation. I don't understand their feelings [illegible] if I were Japanese [illegible] our current life [illegible] twice a week are free movies and then the rest is shakuhachi, work, and reading. And recently I cannot say the food is good, but I think it's better than your life over there [illegible] the past two times about 300 Germans were sent to Ellis

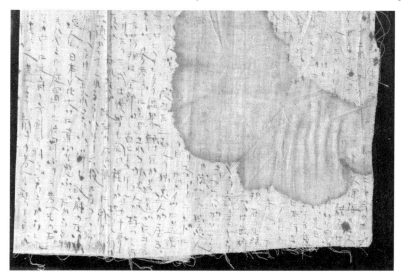

One of Itaru's hidden letters, written on a torn bedsheet and stitched inside the belt lining of the pants he sent to Shizuko to mend

Island in New York. Among them will be some who will be sent back to Germany, and there are still another 300 Germans remaining here. It's likely that, as a result of the hearings, either we will be moved to another place or deportation will be decided. For your reference, the belongings that the deported Germans took with them was a total of 175 pounds and only $90, but it seems that their remaining belongings will be kept in government storage and later will be sent to wherever they return. However, I think it will be very different for the Japanese, whose government has been completely destroyed. So it will be a problem if you dispose of our things carelessly. We will find out the government policy about our belongings in the meantime, so depending on that, let us decide then. Let me know what you think. Because you have been so steadfast, no matter where we go, or what we suffer, I don't have to worry, and this makes my heart strong now. From now on when I send you a package with Satsuki's name, I may enclose a letter, so be watchful. You don't need to send me back these pants, but please send me another pair of thick wool pants. If you sew your letter in the same place, it may not be found, but inspection is quite strict, so you should sew it carefully. Nineteen people are

staying in our room, and most of them are from Ward [illegible]
Yoshida, Yamazaki, Itani, Ikejiri, Imai . . . are together with me.
The elders here still do not believe the recent news of Japan's de-
feat at all, so we try not to talk about it.

October 2, 1945
Dear Itaru,
    I heard that starting from today, the hearings *will finally be-*
gin over here. I'm relieved because my renunciation approval
finally arrived yesterday. Also, I made sure to fix your pants, *so*
please don't worry.
    Last night Ono-san came over and told me that he received a
letter from Watchmaker Oba-san and Oji-san. They moved back
to San Francisco into the house of a Caucasian where Oba-san
is working as a cook, *but Oji-san is looking for a different place*
to live every day. It seems the atmosphere is not very good. They
have been kind to you, like parents. I imagine that you will miss
them since you won't be able to see them again.
    I'm sure you have many things that you need to take back to
Japan, so please let me know. I will write again.
    Shizuko

The collective trauma of years of captivity became painfully evident
with the surrender of Japan and the government's swift movement
to close the prison camps and erase their existence. Prisoners were
now forced to choose between resettlement into an unwelcoming
society or returning to a defeated Japan, all without financial or
material resources to support themselves. They were left to make
this decision in chaos, based only on rumor and hope.

    The trauma of captivity can shrink and distort one's awareness of
the world outside. A kind of magical thinking often occurs under
such circumstances. For some, the decision to renounce was based
on the belief that Japan would win the war and that renunciants
would not only be freed from captivity but also be able to reclaim
their dignity as true patriots. As the reality of Japan's defeat settled into their consciousness, people who believed they had made
the decision to renounce their American citizenship of their own

free will were shaken. Husbands and wives separated in different camps struggled to agree about whether to hold to their decision to be deported to Japan or withdraw their renunciation request. Elderly issei parents, fearing they would be deported, demanded that their nisei children renounce their citizenship so that the family could be deported to Japan together. There were rumors that some women and children were abandoned by fathers who resolutely and without concern for their families left for Japan alone.

Amid the turmoil, emotions ran high. As my parents reaffirmed their decision to go to Japan, the pressure to stay the course among renunciant friends slowly began to dissipate as circumstances of the outside world complicated their lives. To maintain their own sense of integrity and perhaps to strengthen their resolve, Shizuko and Itaru grew uneasy, and critical of friends who chose to remain in the US. To their despair, they learned that the elderly watchmaker and his wife, as well as Haruo and Michiko Fukami and other kibei friends, had given up hope of finding safe harbor in Japan.

October 10, 1945
Dear Itaru,

Last Sunday Kiyoshi had his commemorative photograph taken for Sunday school. The photo was scheduled to be taken at 10, so I took the two children and arrived early. Kiyoshi was excited and got in line with everyone. But the photographer arrived late. By then, Kiyoshi was getting tired of waiting. He couldn't stop crying when the picture was being taken. So I didn't have any choice but to carry him and have our picture taken together. As soon as it comes out, I will buy it and send it to you.

You will be surprised to see that both Kiyoshi and Satsuki have gotten so big. Kiyoshi has become quite a rascal, but Satsuki is also quite difficult to handle. Once a day Satsuki makes Kiyoshi cry. When they fight and she can't compete with her big brother, right away she bites Kiyoshi or pulls his hair to defeat him. Sometimes when Kiyoshi is eating something, she sneaks up and grabs it from him. She's quite quick. This is how it is, so please try to picture this. I am yelling from morning til night. Satsuki is learning the bad things that her brother does and kicks people and spits. Lately Satsuki has started saying people's names, and she is constantly saying, Tōchan, Kāchan, Kiyoshi, Oba-chan [Auntie]. There's no doubt that girls are more talkative. When I tell her to say goodbye politely, she presses her head down hard with her hand and bows, and that makes me laugh. When I ask her where did Tōchan go? She says, "Tōchan, over there, bye bye." She seems to have some memory of you.

Finally people who renounced received their Alien Registration form with assigned alien registration number. Mrs. Fukami canceled repatriation. I think she will be moving out soon. Yamashita-san said he will stay here for us until the last minute. Day by day it is getting lonely.

Please take care of yourself.

Shizuko

Saturday, October 13, 1945
The people who still believe in Japan's victory are creating an uproar, saying that the Japanese army will be arriving here today. They said that everyone is supposed to gather together when they hear the emergency bugle. But nothing happened, and I heard that they were shaken.

Sunday, October 14, 1945
Spent half a day writing a special note on cloth and stitched it inside the pants. I decided to send it tomorrow.

Buddhist Sunday school children and their teachers, Tule Lake Segregation Center, October 7, 1945. Shizuko can be seen carrying Kiyoshi (with *bōzu* haircut) in the second row, far right.

October 15, 1945
Dear Itaru,

I'm relieved to know that you have been doing well.

Mrs. Fukami has come to have the same feelings as Haruo, and she is waiting to leave as soon as possible. She has become a completely changed person. From every block, every day, many people are moving out. The only person that I can talk with is Yoshida-san. When we receive letters, we exchange news and we discuss everything with each other. The other day we laughed so hard together. What Yoshida-san said was, "There's nothing gentle about my husband. Nowadays in his letter everything is a command. How about yours?" So I told her that it was the same for me. Then she said, "Then, we are okay." And we laughed a lot. Until next time.

Shizuko

October 17, 1945
Dear Itaru,

This morning I received the airplane and suitcase. Kiyoshi is so happy. I cannot describe in words Kiyoshi's delighted face. Right away he showed it to Yamashita-san and carefully put it on a shelf and won't allow anyone to touch it. He is saying that he's going to take the suitcase to Sunday School, so he put the books that he takes every Sunday inside. It was unusual that he obeyed me so well today. All of a sudden the tyrant became a lamb.

The other day I mended your old gray pants and sent them to you, so please let me know when you receive them.

Shizuko

October 18, 1945
Dear Itaru,

Tonight suddenly, there was an extra edition of the camp paper. The following was announced:

* This Tule Lake Center will be closed by February 1, 1946.

* Those who are free must make arrangements to move and leave by December 15.

* All the schools will be closed on December 21.

*The administration has not decided the future course of action for those of us who are on the Department of Justice list.

Our future is unknown at this time, but right away I made my request to Washington to allow me to go back to Japan with my husband. National Director Myer has announced that all the internees' families must make notification in this way. When I find out more details I will send you a telegram. Tonight I will send just this urgent information to you. I couldn't sleep worrying about what to do with our belongings.

    Shizuko

October 23, 1945
Dear Itaru,

    Got up this morning at 4 a.m. and asked the neighbor to take care of the children. Went to the dentist to get some temporary relief for my toothache. I was told that I wouldn't be able to have an appointment because of the shortage of staff. There is no help for me. Disappointed. There is nothing to do but to have it taken care of after we go back to Japan. Had a headache from this morning and couldn't do anything this afternoon. I feel sorry for my children when I am like this.

    I'm going to gradually start packing next week. Please don't worry because Kiyoshi and Satsuki are playing as usual. Our neighborhood is becoming more and more deserted. Please take care of yourself.

    Shizuko

October 24, 1945
Dear Shizuko,

    I was very glad that you fixed my pants as I asked. I don't believe things will be confiscated without reason [xxxxx TWO AND ONE-HALF LINES CENSORED] is important. I'm wondering how the people in the block, including Mrs. Kobayashi, are thinking. I may be required to leave for Japan before you, so I'm afraid that I won't be able to take much with me, but by the time you and the children are leaving, you may be able to bring more. I heard that the closure of Tule Lake was decided, but this

is as expected, so we don't need to panic. I'm glad that Kiyoshi received the airplane in good condition. I started making a suitcase for Satsuki right away. I will send it as soon as possible.
Ina

October 28, 1945
Itaru-sama,

Our time to depart for Japan is now close. Yesterday the Department of Justice issued an extra announcement. Repatriation to Japan will begin November 16. And registration for repatriation begins tomorrow. I will make the request to repatriate with you.

I went to the Department of Justice office yesterday and met with a clerk and got more detailed information, so I feel relieved. The clerk said I will be able to meet you on the boat.

Please let me know in detail what things are most important for you to take to Japan. Depending on what you decide, I will need to figure out how to pack everything. Ono-san also has decided to go back to Japan. Please don't worry about our belongings. I will take care of it the best way I can.
Shizuko

October 31, 1945
Itaru-sama,

I received your letter dated October 24 on the 29th, but the letter had a big window in it, so I could not understand your point at the beginning of the letter.

I'm relieved that you wrote to Aunt Muraoka and my parents. I received a letter from my mother, and she said she was glad to hear from you. Yesterday I officially submitted the repatriation application, and I made it clear that all four of us are returning together. We have nothing to worry about now. All we have to do is wait for boarding instructions.

Kiyoshi and Satsuki are well and every day getting into mischief. These days, Kiyoshi is behaving badly and being stubborn, so I can't control him. He keeps making other children cry. He is the naughty boy of this block. It's a problem because he lashes

out at adults and older children. So when I scold him severely,
he runs to Yamashita-san and tells him, "My mommy is mean."
One time he was misbehaving so much that I said, "Mommy is
going far away just like Daddy!" He cried and said, "I'll stop,
please don't go. I'll be too lonely." It's difficult to raise children.

Mrs. Fukami said that Haruo has become a Christian. She
said that he told her that she should read the bible. *People*
change, don't they? I feel very sad about Haruo.

I think you will have finished the repatriation application by
now.

Shizuko

Decisions my parents and others made about their future were
fraught with the constant crisis of urgency and fear. Decisions to
renounce one's citizenship were wrung from people who had been
treated with hatred, demeaned, and denied their human rights. In
the moment, they may not have been aware of it, but their choices
were defined only by the limited options allowed by their captor.
Congress voted to denationalize American citizens in order to legalize "deporting" them to Japan, then, in a repeated pattern of
maintaining power and control over their captive prisoners, required them to register and apply for "permission" to "repatriate,"
much in the same way prison and military authorities had earlier
demanded proof of loyalty after people had already been imprisoned. Motivated by the desire to get rid of dissident troublemakers,
against all moral standards of judgment, deporting American citizens who had been incarcerated without ever committing a crime
was a crime of its own. What appears to be the decision of a willing
victim was, in fact, a final submission to the repetitive infliction of
psychological trauma. Like slaveholders demanding gratitude from
their slaves, prison authorities kept prisoners in a constant state of
fear and placed themselves in the position of granting permission
to people forced to make previously unfathomable decisions.

November 4, 1945
Dear Itaru,

Since closure is soon, everyone is packing or leaving and, like your place over there, this place is full of hustle and bustle. Yesterday Yamashita-san and Horiuchi-san helped me pack, so please don't worry. I'm going to start packing the books. I will write down the title of each book so that you will be able to easily find which book is in which box.

I received a letter from brother Masami. He said that because he is going to Japan as part of the Occupational Forces on December 1, he will take some time off soon and come to visit me. He has fully recovered from illness, so please don't worry.

Shizuko

November 5, 1945
Dear Itaru,

Today it snowed for the first time, and it's so cold that it hurts to the core of my body.

I heard that [xxxxx]-san decided, as we expected, to take the easy way and stay here for a while, and yet he is suggesting that we go back. He's saying that it is the young people who must go back now to rebuild Japan.

Shizuko

November 7, 1945
Dear Shizuko,

The time will come soon when we can go home. It seems that Kiyoshi has become quite naughty, but because of the situation we are in, it is understandable. Satsuki must have become quite a tomboy. It is getting colder, so the children may not find a place to play and it will be difficult. I heard that the cold and shortage of clothing, food, and housing in Japan is devastating. When you are able to send a telegram to Japan through the Red Cross, why don't you contact your grandmother and her family to find out if they are okay? I think that Itani's influence has led Haruo to become a Christian. As I think about it, much has changed. Since the closing date has been decided, I assume that

*everyone is busy. I wonder what other young couples are going
to do. I'm thinking there are still many more people who will be
leaving. How have you been managing the packing? I'm sorry
that you have to do everything by yourself, and that I cannot be
there to help you.*

Ina (watching the first snow)

November 8, 1945
Dear Shizuko,

*Yesterday, for the first time, it snowed all day long. Tonight
four or five of my roommates and I bought sodas, went outside,
and mixed them with snow to make snow cones. We ate them
while laughing hard. The happy faces of grown children is one
of the scenes at the* internment camp. *Have you learned any
more details about repatriation since last time? Over here there
are many rumors, but there is no official announcement. Of
course over here it is very different for us. If we only have two
hours time we can quickly get ready so we don't have to rush
now. I'm looking out the window at icicles that are 3 feet long.*

Ina

November 13, 1945
Dear Itaru,

*I am relieved to hear that you have been doing well. Over here
the first snow has fallen. Although the weather is bad, our children have not caught colds, and they are playing in the snow, so
please don't worry.*

*The preparation for people moving out from here is becom-
ing more and more full-scale. Most of the young couples in this
block want to go out, but they haven't been granted permission
yet. Everyone is anxiously awaiting the announcement, wondering if they will be released or repatriated. Mrs. Fukami also
wants to move out soon, but she is distressed because she has yet
to receive her release notice. Every day it is bustling with the
sounds of hammers making crates and people coming to say
their goodbyes.*

Next, I wanted to send a telegram to Japan through the Red

Cross, but since the war has ended, they are not accepting tele-grams. Also we are getting more information from the letters from nisei soldiers saying that it is extremely cold in Japan and there is a shortage of clothing, food, and housing. Most of the people have canceled repatriation because of this reason.

I stopped packing for a while, and just waiting for an an-nouncement about the limitation on baggage. Maybe it's be-cause I have been packing these days that Kiyoshi keeps saying, "Let's take this and go to Daddy!"

Shizuko

6.

Deportees

K ibei men such as my father had been strongly influenced by prewar Japanese values of loyalty and male-dominated hierarchy. Humiliated by their subjugation in captivity, they found autonomy and pride in dissidence. By refusing to comply with petty demands or ordinances imposed on them, these "troublemakers" resisted psychological domination by their captors. Renouncing their citizenship and facing the mostly unknown consequences of such a decision strengthened connections among like-minded kibei and issei prisoners, binding them to their reclaimed identity as honorable Japanese men willing to make whatever sacrifice necessary to return to their homeland.

In her 1976 book *Japanese Patterns of Behavior*, Takie Sugiyama Lebra explains the importance of group belonging in traditional Japanese culture. A strong commitment to a group, such as the renunciants, gave individuals a sense of community and a shared goal. However, Lebra further explained, a powerful collective identity also meant that if an individual couldn't meet the obligations of the group or decided to stray from its goals, they would be met with shame. For the renunciants, identification with Japanese values such as loyalty and integrity restored feelings of agency and self-worth that had been stripped away when the US government branded them disloyal for standing up for their rights. Wrought from deprivation and loss, the dedication of the renunciants was only remotely and symbolically about Japan and the emperor; the primary bond was really one of brotherhood among men. Their shared commitment required not just hope but a stubborn belief that Japan would win the war and that they would be able to have a good life there.

As the devastation in Japan slowly became known to internees in Bismarck, courage to stay the course in the face of unfathomable nuclear destruction began to falter. And fissures in both the bond among the men and the purpose that brought them together began to fracture friendships and promises. The intense pressure that rose out of a collective value system forged by the incarceration made breaking the bond an excruciating and isolating experience fueled by shame and desperation. As people began to reconsider their intention to return to Japan, those attempting to hold to their resolve experienced a sense of betrayal. The men and women in both the WRA camps and the DOJ internment camps were suddenly faced with yet another convulsive crisis as authorities moved to shut down the prison sites and essentially wash their hands of the altogether disgraceful violation of human rights perpetrated in the name of national security.

Those who were "free to leave" were confronted with frightening uncertainties. Although some were able to return home, most prisoners were facing forced resettlement in an unwelcoming and still hostile country. Many had become impoverished after three years of incarceration. Prisoners who had been released earlier wrote, warning friends and family that housing and employment opportunities were scarce.

Once Tule Lake closed under the authority of the civilian War Relocation Authority, the Department of Justice Alien Enemy Control Unit took over the administration of the prison camp. While all others were being summarily forced to leave, renunciants, now enemy aliens, were placed on the government stop list. But no word of their fate was publicly announced. Prison authorities, tasked with closing the prison camps and ending all budgetary responsibilities, worried that if it became known that renunciants would continue to be detained, another wave of renunciations by people unprepared and fearful of being sent out would likely occur.

Left in limbo, my mother, as well as other internment widows, had no idea how decisions were being made about who would be freed and who would continue to be detained. With the threat of family separation looming, frantically written letters, hacked by censors, escalated the turmoil as family members wavered in their previously determined commitment to make a better life for themselves in Japan. Prisoners were forced to make life-altering decisions while thousands of miles apart, based on remnants of intended messages sent between Tule Lake and Bismarck.

One of the most corrosive psychological effects of captivity is for the prisoner to be forced to betray their fellow resisters and abandon values and principles that have enabled the prisoner to maintain a separate identity from the captor perpetrator. With re-patriation imminent for fifty-five hundred renunciants, each person was faced with a true dilemma: whether to pursue what the government referred to as "voluntary repatriation" to a defeated country and suffer life in war-torn Japan, or to reconsider their decision and live with the disgrace of forsaking their commitment to one another and to the very principles that had served as their moral compass.

November 14, 1945
Dear Shizuko,

Somehow, I feel sad hearing that Ono-san, Akashi-san, and Yao-san all canceled repatriation. When I also hear that there are only seven or eight families left in the block, it even makes me wonder if we have made a mistake. I received letters from your mother in Lamona and Aunt Muraoka in Ohio the other day. In the letter, your mother repeatedly expressed her feelings saying, "Please don't say the sad words that you are going to Japan, but please, please reconsider staying in this country with us. This is our fervent request." I don't know how to respond to her, but by now I assume that your family has been to visit you and that you have talked this over with them. Also, Auntie Muraoka sent me an urgent letter because she heard that repatriation to Japan will begin around the 15th. Anyhow, my aunt understands our feelings well. I'm glad to hear that Masami has completely recovered from his illness. It will be good that he can let you know more information once he arrives at his destination. The closer the time for repatriation, the bigger my worries become. When I read the newspaper about the shortage of housing, of food, of clothing, and limitations on the number of childbirths, I feel more and more disheartened. I don't worry about us, but when I think about our children, I can't help but worry. I cannot say that Mrs. Kobayashi and Mrs. Yamazaki's thoughts about canceling are completely wrong. Since we won't know anything until the time comes, there's nothing to do but to leave ourselves to our destiny. First, we must keep our bodies strong, and we need the determination to bear whatever hardship awaits us. The snow from the other day has yet to thaw. Until next time.

    Ina

On November 13, Shizuko received a letter from the watchmaker Oji-san with distressing news about the belongings they left behind when they were forced into the prison camps. Shizuko and Itaru, along with others who were being removed, had secured their precious possessions, including recently received wedding gifts, in a warehouse owned by Itaru's former employer. The watchmaker had been released; he returned to San Francisco with his wife in search of work and housing, but when he arrived at the warehouse to collect his things, he found that the place had been broken into and everything taken, "except the light bulb and a glass soy sauce bottle." Finding box after box left open and empty, he closed by saying, "I'm at a loss. I think yours, mine, and our friends' belongings will never be returned."

As I read the letter, I wondered whether my mother relived a scene she had witnessed before her own removal. She told me about watching people break into a storage site where Japantown residents had left behind the possessions they couldn't take with them when forced from their homes. In broad daylight, police stood by and watched the thieves running out of the building with arms full of stolen goods. For Shizuko, any hope of someday returning home was further crushed as watchmaker Oji-san confessed that he, like others, had been unable to find a job, while his wife was forced to work as a cook and cleaning lady under unpleasant and difficult circumstances.

Their lives suspended in prison camps about to be closed down, my parents faced the proverbial fork in the road as they struggled, each in their own way, to answer the question, *Where is home?* They innocently, perhaps naively, believed they actually had a choice, albeit a no-win choice, to withdraw their so-called repatriation request to be released back into US society, where they were despised and hated, or to continue moving forward with "expatriation" to a country devastated by nuclear holocaust. As their resolve to go to Japan faltered, regret began to creep into emotional spaces once filled with determined hope.

Concealed cloth letter from Itaru to Shizuko, undated:
I have read your letter that was inside the belt. Now is not the time to be constantly worried. We must seriously consider our future. Right now over here, reregistration for repatriation has started, and I was called in a couple of days ago. I registered to repatriate only with my family. All of us who have families registered in this way. Single men registered unconditionally. That is, they will return by themselves when the government tells them the time and place. Also they are accepting cancellation of repatriation. Both Fukami and Itani canceled repatriation. In the evening before his cancellation, Fukami-san came to my place and said the following things: "Now, since Japan has been defeated, there is trouble with the shortage of food and housing. We who repatriate are useless people and will cause Japan more problems. And because territory has been lost, there is no place for us to return. It will be pitiful for growing children when there is no food. After considering many things, it will be much better for Japan if we temporarily cancel repatriation and stay in the United States to earn even one more penny. Although I think my wife will object, I'm going to cancel repatriation tomorrow, so please understand. Itani has the same thoughts as I do, so

it seems that he will also cancel." For these reasons, Fukami-san canceled repatriation. According to a rumor, I heard that about 200 people will cancel, but as of now there are about 50 or 60 people. I am seeing quite a few people who have started to grow their hair [from the bōzu haircut that signified their dissidence]. What Fukami-san is saying is reasonable, but he is not held in a good light and everyone knows the meaning when they say, "DEEP SEA."[1] Until recently Fukami-san used to come to our room to visit Itani and hang around from morning to night because there was no one else in his room he could talk to. But after he canceled repatriation, his reputation has been damaged, and he hasn't shown up at our place. I heard that he's been sitting alone silently in his room all day. The people who canceled repatriation may return to Tule Lake before long. According to the rumor over here, it is said that the single men will be going to Santa Fe internment camp and those who have families will assemble in Richmond near San Francisco. In truth, when I heard Fukami-san's story, it made me consider many things. When I thought about such possibilities, I wondered what will we do with no place to live when we go back to Japan, or what will happen to our children? I realized that this is a big problem, and I couldn't help feeling shaken in my decision. However, I thought it would be inexcusable to consider returning if Japan had won and not returning if Japan lost. What I am worrying about now is the problem of where we will live. It is constantly on my mind since we won't be able to go to Manchuria now and there is no one we can rely on in my hometown of Yamanashi, so we may even have to go to Hokkaido. If you have any thoughts about this, please let me know. It's necessary for us to plan a course of action. At least I want to send Kiyoshi to university so that he can become a scientist. But this is so much in the future, and I must leave it to his own desires. To be continued . . .

---

1. Transliteration of *Fukami* is "deep sea."

November 19, 1945
Itaru-sama,

I received your letter dated November 14th today. I can sense that you are very distressed. Starting about a week ago, my lower back was in pain. I didn't get much done, and was just getting by, and then, two days ago, I got a terrible flu. Now I'm in bed and the neighbors are taking care of me. Kiyoshi has recovered from a bad flu, but now he has a rash on his face, and I wonder if it might be measles. Right now, the clinic is busy and only giving shots to the people who are going to Japan. They will not accept sick people.

As you say, there would be nothing to worry about if it were just the two of us returning [xxxxx] we cannot let our children starve to death. [xxxxx] Please cancel repatriation. [xxxxx] so we can temporarily stay at my mother's place. It was timely that [xxxxx]-san came to see me this evening, and after discussing different things with him, I decided to send a telegram to you. It's still not too late to cancel repatriation. Please answer right away. I will take whatever action you decide.

Shizuko

November 19, 1945
Shizuko-san,

Suddenly on the evening of the 16th the repatriation order was announced with instructions for people who have applied for voluntary repatriation. Baggage and money limitations are as follows. Baggage is up to 175 pounds and includes 60 pounds of carry-on. Carry-on baggage is limited to one per person. The total amount of money is $60. The government will keep the rest of the money, but it is likely that they will not issue a receipt. Also it is likely that the government will not be responsible for the rest of our belongings. So after you buy necessary goods, you have to take care of the remaining money as you think best. Next, if you can make arrangements, please send me about $70 right away for repatriation shopping expenses. Also if you have time, please send me my clothes and other everyday things. But don't send any valuable things such as my suit because it may *be a problem if for some reason I am no longer here and we miss each other. I will let you know more details by airmail or telegram.*

Ina

November 20, 1945

Dear Itaru Ina,

My friend's daughter living in Japan wrote to me about the truth of the current Japanese situation, and it is even more devastating than what is reported in the newspaper. Lately Kiyoshi is not eating very well, and as I said in yesterday's letter, he has a rash. Today, although I'm up, taking care of the children, I must force myself to do the house chores. There is talk that the next repatriation will be this coming 27th, so Kobayashi Oba-san is busy. I just can't be still and rest. I have been pushing myself too much lately and am not well. [xxxxx]² since I am in such bad health, please [xxxxx] repatriation. I understand that it will be [xxxxx] difficult for you to hear me asking you to cancel now, but I am begging you. [xxxxx] hasn't come yet. I'm [xxxxx] thinking that probably she is waiting for your response.

This is my once-in-a-lifetime request, so please cancel.

Shizuko

P.S. Today there were many telegrams from Santa Fe, and I heard Mike Nishimoto, Yamakido, and Yamasaki-san from this block have decided to leave for Japan. Mrs. Yamasaki was crying, saying that she doesn't want to take her small children.

Caught in an ever-tightening vise of pressure from family and friends, while hearing disturbing news of conditions in Japan and struggling to care for the children and prepare for removal to Japan, Shizuko collapsed from physical exhaustion and illness. Afraid that going to Japan would be disastrous for the children, and determined to keep the family together, she dared to change course,

2. Shizuko wrote this letter on airmail stationery that folds into an envelope. Censors cut the stamp on the outside, thereby cutting segments of the letter on the inside.

sending a telegram to my father, asking him to cancel repatriation. My honor-bound father, taken by surprise, responded with concern for her health yet urged her to delay cancellation of repatriation for as long as possible. For him to make an about-face on his decision would be a disgrace, a sign of weakness and a betrayal of his fellow Hoshidan members who had committed themselves to return to the mother country as "true Japanese."

Shizuko may well have sensed that Itaru was wavering but that he could not be the one to make such a decision. A torturous exchange of letters followed, with Shizuko repeating her request that Itaru cancel repatriation, while at the same time fearing that he might leave for Japan without her and the children as other men had done.

The desperation I hear in my mother's letters during this time stirs painful emotions for me. I reflected on the losses she suffered as a child when her mother died and her father left her and brother, Isamu, in Japan to be raised by a grandmother she had never known. When Isamu died a few years later, she had lost everyone in her family. Falling in love with and marrying Itaru was powerfully healing for her. When they were briefly separated during their engagement, she wrote emphatically, with a tinge of humor, "*no matter how much you dislike me, I will hold on to you, and never, never let go.*"

Despite her effort to reassure Itaru that she was doing well, over time her difficulties managing the children and her worsening health issues seeped through the letters and ultimately led to her abrupt message to Itaru imploring him to cancel repatriation. In spite of the intensity of her request, she was willing to sacrifice it all to avert the possibility of further separation from Itaru.

November 22, 1945
Dear Itaru,

Last night I received your telegram response. If you are going back to Japan, I will take our children and go with you. First of all, the reason why, all of a sudden, I thought about cancellation is because I was exhausted in my mind and body. I felt desperate and thought that there would be no way that I could get on

board because of my poor health. Also, Kiyoshi has been suf-
fering with a high fever, so when repatriation was announced,
I had only finished half of the packing. I was alone having a dif-
ficult time and I was sick in bed, and then Ono-san came to say
goodbye. Just at the same time I had received your disheartened
letter dated November 14th. I showed it to Ono-san, and after
I talked to him about many things, I felt afraid, but I made up
my mind to have him send you a telegram. Ono-san repeatedly
advised that we should cancel for the time being. He said, "I feel
sorry for Ina-kun to have to go back to Japan with such insecu-
rity. It will be awful to take your precious children to Japan in
the devastation and not be able to feed them milk or eggs."

Also, the limitation on the amount of baggage is too cruel,
and in such cold weather we would not be able to take enough
warm clothing for the children. I wondered what would become
of Kiyoshi and Satsuki if we go to Japan where there is a shortage
of housing, food, and clothing.

I heard that on the ship there is no milk given to children who
are Kiyoshi's and Satsuki's age. As a mother I would feel more
pain than death to hear our children every day asking me for
their favorite milk *that they can't live without.*

In your telegram you say I should go to my parents in Lamona,
but it is too coldhearted. Every day Kiyoshi is missing his daddy
and waiting [xxxxx six words censored] *asking me when*
you will be back. So are you saying that you are going back
[xxxxx] *abandoning our precious children and me? Although*
it is to be expected if this were during the war, but [xxxxx] *is*
different.

Please [xxxxx] *think carefully about this once again. Please*
think carefully, if not for me, [xxxxx] *for the sake of Kiyoshi*
and Satsuki. If [xxxxx] *not going to cancel I will go with you,*
no matter what will happen to me. I want you to clearly under-
stand this.

In the next couple of days I think I will get much better, and
I'm going to start packing again. It seems that Kiyoshi had heat
rash from his high fever, but today I am relieved to see that his
skin is drying up. I sent your corduroy pants *by separate mail,*

*so please look carefully where I have repaired them and make
sure you are satisfied. Every day I will send your clothing little
by little.*

   *Now please for the future of the four of us, calmly think this
through. A representative of the Department of Justice was saying that we could cancel at any time. Please let me know when
you receive the* pants.

   Shizuko

The agony of separation my parents felt was exacerbated by censored communication. Letters were often delayed, arriving in random sequence and fueling misunderstanding and frustration as
their contents became more anxious and repetitive. When Itaru
pushed back against Shizuko's request to immediately cancel repatriation, she appeared to try to hold back her anxious wish and continue preparing for repatriation. Yet Itaru's message also showed
that he was beginning to realize that repatriation was not, after
all, the best solution to the crisis of their displaced lives. Shizuko's
anxiety spilled over. Waffling between being the obedient wife,
accommodating her husband's reluctance to change course, and
her now overwhelming fears of the consequences, she appealed to
him, *"We have been easing our minds by thinking that things will be
better by going to Japan, but now, I am worried and afraid about the
future so much that I cannot sleep at night. Because of this I haven't
slept well for over a month. . . . Let's gather up our courage and make
up our mind to cancel this time and repatriate in two or three years.
Please answer right away. Please don't get angry, and try to consider
this objectively."*

   The secret cloth letters made it possible for my father to explain
in more detail his reasons for not wanting to cancel repatriation
until the last minute, and enabled him to strategize with Shizuko
about how best to avoid losing face while accommodating her ad-
amant plea. Prisoners with no control over their circumstances
and little information about the consequences of their decisions
were repeatedly traumatized by the shifting sands of government
whims. Although their ingenious cloth letters helped my parents
bypass the censorship that wreaked havoc on the lives of separated

families, I'm struck with the realization that they must have been in a constant state of anxiety. It not only took a toll on their emotional and physical well-being at the time but also greatly influenced how they would cope with life in the future. Their nervous systems forever altered by chronic trauma, they lived within narrow confines, where safety and acceptance ruled their choices. By accommodating, complying, and enduring, they could maintain some modicum of control over their lives. To be strong and not cry was how they survived. They expected no less of me and my brothers. Therein was the intergenerational transmission of their trauma. Outwardly I was seen as a striver, someone who would succeed, fulfilling whatever my potential was to be, but inwardly, I was driven not by a sense of self-mastery but by fear that if I failed to do what was expected of me, to comply with the rules of authorities, bad things would happen.

Concealed cloth letter from Itaru to Shizuko, undated:
What you said in your telegram and response to my letter is reasonable, but as for me, I'm absolutely not able to cancel at this point because of my connection with the people around me, and my own feelings. However, we have two paths in order to reach our purpose. The first one is that when I return to Tule Lake, we can talk everything over thoroughly again and make our decision based on Kiyoshi's health. The second one is, if I get ordered to repatriate instead of being sent back to Tule Lake, I think you will receive the same order at the same time, so when that happens, I want you to send me a telegram with the message, "Kiyoshi is sick, so please postpone repatriation" (KIYOSHI NOT WELL PLEASE POSTPONE UNTIL NEXT). *Anyway, no matter what it says, it will be best if the message has reasons that would not be considered wrong when others hear about it. The reason for this is because there is no privacy with telegrams here. They are left open and passed on from one hand to the next so that everyone knows immediately what telegram is sent to whom. This is exactly what happened to the last telegram that you sent me. It was an extremely bad experience for me. However, I made the excuse to people that "my wife thought that I might go back*

by myself on the next ship so in a panic she sent me such a telegram," but I told them that I would absolutely not cancel repatriation. *After all, even though we will cancel for the time being, we'd better absolutely keep it a secret from others until the last moment, and when the time comes, we can request post- ponement of repatriation by making the right excuses such as "Kiyoshi is very sick" or "our doctor advised that we should not put him on the ship." If you have already told others that you want to cancel repatriation, tell them, "Ina absolutely objects, so there is nothing to be done but to follow him," and make it ap- pear to people as if you are preparing for repatriation (except for Ono-san). And meanwhile it may be a good idea for you to tell people that Kiyoshi's health condition is not good. So if at the last minute we postpone, I think it won't look bad in other peo- ple's eyes. I want you to consider fully my present situation. Al- though it is a little dramatic, please use your head and do things carefully in every respect. This is my fervent effort because I love you and I love our children. Kiyoshi's poor health because of measles or something will be perfect as a reason. If we have any other reason, people will look down on us. Also absolutely never tell people like Mrs. Yoshida about the cancellation. Since Mr. Yoshida is in the same room, even though I tell him things that make sense in order to save face, I will be extremely humiliated if a different story came from over there. In any case don't bring up the cancellation again. If people ask you, tell them, "Ina absolutely objects." I know that I'm repeating myself, but if I am able to go back to Tule Lake, we can talk more easily. According to rumor, it is said that we will go back to Tule by the middle of December, so then we will be able to have a much better talk. If I'm not able to go back to Tule Lake, you must send me the telegram that I mentioned earlier. Until that time, I will be pre- paring for repatriation along with everyone else. Therefore in my regular letters, I will continue to write as I have been writ- ing. When you read this letter, you should write, "Satsuki said, 'I want to see Daddy.'" That will be your response to this letter.*

As Shizuko continued to press Itaru to cancel repatriation, he was caught in a double bind. Concerned for his wife and the welfare of the children, as well as his own faltering trust in his repatriation decision, he attempted to avoid losing face with his fellow repatriates by delaying his cancellation until the last minute when staunch critics would have already left for Japan. But with letters delayed and crossing in the mail, confusion and frustration brought my parents to a painful exchange. Itaru conceded that his family's welfare must be the priority, but his request for delay rather than immediate cancellation pushed Shizuko to express with increasing urgency why cancellation was necessary. To minimize the confusion of out-of-sequence messages, these final letters of 1945 are significantly excerpted.

November 29, 1945
Dear Itaru,

I read your letter thoroughly, and I understand very well your position that you do not want to cancel repatriation until the last minute.

If Kiyoshi and I are fully recovered by the time the last ship is leaving, I will board the ship as you wish. At that time I will send you a telegram, so please respond so that there will be no misunderstanding that would cause our paths to not cross.

I don't know what happened to Kiyoshi, but this morning a lot of grainy pus came out of his nose, and one of his nostrils is closed up. So right away I'm going to take him to the doctor. My mind is racing and I'm feeling dizzy, and I don't know what to do.
Shizuko

December 2, 1945
Dear Itaru Ina,

Over here we are dizzy with busyness because some people are moving out and others are going to Japan. The office announced that 5,000 voluntary repatriates will go on this ship.

If you say that you will stay in the US for now for the sake of our children, I will pack our remaining belongings and write letters to our friends who have moved out and ask them to help us after we leave camp. Whatever we do, we cannot escape suffering, but at least we will be able to give our children enough milk if we stay here. According to one soldier who recently returned from Japan, it is such a horrible situation that it was devastating to see. Because small children don't have anything to eat, they are malnourished and they fight over someone's leftover bread. More and more children are succumbing, and there are riots all over because of the food shortage.

Whether we go back to Japan or stay here, as long as we are together, we will endure the hardships, but at this moment I am full of regret. When I think about causing you such pain by pressuring you, I feel so sorry, and I don't know how to apologize to you. I'm pleading for you to not be angry with me. Destiny for the four of us will be determined by whether we repatriate or not, so please think about this thoroughly and give me your clear answer.

Tomorrow is Kiyoshi's birthday, but I can't do anything for him because the canteen *is closed. Please take good care of yourself.*

Shizuko

December 3, 1945
Dear Itaru-san,

Kiyoshi's toy horse arrived just in time for his birthday, and it turned out to be a good present *for him. I wish I could show you his happy face.*

From today's letter I understand very well how you are thinking. I am very sorry that I spoke to Mrs. Yoshida. I ask that you not be angry with me and please forgive me. When I was sick and in bed she came to visit me. It was wrong, but because I was so discouraged, I confided in her about many things. Mrs. Yoshida understood me very well. She said these encouraging words to me, "Each person will repatriate based on their different situation, so think this through, and don't worry too much about what others think because this is your life to do what you need to do."

Knowing that my thoughtlessness is causing you to suffer and that you are losing your appetite and not sleeping at night, I feel like I want to die. I beg you. Please forgive me.

I completely understand why you feel that you must hold on until the last minute, and I am no longer worried. Please persevere and cheer up by thinking about our precious Kiyoshi and Satsuki. Every day, every day, Satsuki is saying she wants to see her daddy.[3] I believe it won't be too long before the four of us will live together in laughter. Please cheer up and try to eat a lot. I fixed your pants immediately and sent them to you, so please try them on right away.

    Shizuko

December 5, 1945
Dear Shizuko,

I received your letter dated the 29th yesterday evening, and I was disappointed. You do not understand at all what I'm trying to say. My point that we won't cancel until the last minute doesn't mean at all that I will force my will. I would like to do as you wish. Hearing that you and Kiyoshi are still not feeling well, I don't remember that I said a single word to force you to repatriate under those conditions. I would like you to think a little more deeply about what I said. It will be extremely difficult for me to cancel right now, so what I mean is that I would like to wait until the last ship departs. I don't remember that I said to force yourself to pack or to repatriate at any cost while you are in poor health. I don't think I am such an obstinate person. It's hard to express how shocked I was when you asked me to cancel all of a sudden, after we had been so determined to repatriate. Now I'm able to put my thoughts together and calm down. For a while I was at a loss with no one to talk to, and I was having a hard time by myself. After that, with each letter I learned about yours and Kiyoshi's health condition and came to the conclusion that cancellation is unavoidable and that I would do as you wish. Please keep this in mind and recover as soon as possible by

---

3. Code words agreed on to let Itaru know that a concealed letter is enclosed in the pants she is sending.

not pushing yourself, and plan *thoughtfully for the future. I just want you to think about my situation and my position and act cautiously. I was thinking of not sending a letter today because I just wrote to you yesterday, but since yours was such a disheartening letter, I decided to write again. Until next time.*

Ina

December 10, 1945
Dear Itaru Ina,

Today I received your airmail letters dated the 4th and 5th. Please don't scold me so angrily. I understand very well your feeling that it is not possible for you to cancel suddenly because of your position and situation. I was too insistent, but I sent you letters one after another so that you would decide firmly to stay here temporarily for the sake of the children. But in your two letters today, I was relieved to learn of your clear intention. I will not write to you for a while.

Now that I know that we are going to stay for sure, and since you asked me to make plans for the future, I am going to take action now. Please take care not to catch a cold.

Shizuko

7.

Internees

For more than four decades, Japanese American community members have organized pilgrimages to the Tule Lake incarceration site in Northern California. Earlier informal social gatherings had been led mostly by nisei former incarcerees in cities on the West Coast as a way of reconnecting with classmates and friends from their prison camp days. With time, younger sansei college students, along with some who were children in the camps or descendants of former prisoners, began organizing Tule Lake pilgrimages, at first informally, then later with more intention to educate and address the historical injustice of the incarceration. Eventually the issue of the collective trauma resulting from the many losses suffered by the thousands held in the high-security Tule Lake Segregation Center became a focus of the pilgrimage. Survivors and their descendants sought answers, as well as healing for the trauma that had been woven into their lives. Gathering with others after visiting the site where family members had been held and hearing stories of life in the camp shared by aging survivors often brought on tears that had been held back for generations.

It became evident to organizers that pilgrims needed a space to process the experience of visiting the site, feeling the searing heat and choking dust, and remembering moments of their own incarceration or stories shared with them by their parents or grandparents. I was asked to facilitate Reflections Groups, which were organized at the end of each day of the pilgrimage. We were all surprised by the large number of pilgrims who chose to participate. Here survivors who were willing shared their stories of loss, strength, and survival. These firsthand accounts provided the human context for decisions prisoners had been forced to make while held captive. For those who had for decades silently endured the stigma imposed on them by the government and continued by members of their own community, the shame of being a disloyal No-No or renunciant could finally be shed. Slowly, the story of the Tule Lake dissidents, victims of government manipulation and race hatred, could be heard above the rancor of those who had vilified them.

During these pilgrimages I began to see the powerful impact of healing while in community. Our trauma was a collective trauma; our friends, families, and neighbors were all deprived of their rights. Through these pilgrimages and the Reflections Groups specifically, I recognized that collective trauma required collective healing—being together in our shared experience, validating one another's experiences, and providing context that only those who lived it could fully understand.

In July 1945, President Harry S. Truman set forth deportation Proclamation Number 2655, which stated,

> All alien enemies now or hereafter interned within the continental limits of the United States . . . who shall be deemed by the Attorney General to be dangerous to the public peace and safety of the United States because they have adhered to . . . enemy governments . . . shall be subject upon the order of the Attorney General to removal from the United States and may be required to depart therefrom.

By the end of 1945, what officials had referred to as "voluntary repatriation" was clearly a plan for forced deportation. For my parents, facing one uncertainty after another, the threat of deportation loomed large. As soon as they found some resolution, yet another action by the authorities upended their plans, and their resolve.

Because prisoners and internees were led to believe that repatriation to Japan was on a voluntary basis, renunciants had never been informed, nor ever themselves considered, that their resulting alien enemy status would make them ineligible for release and resettlement. Shizuko and Itaru, like others, believed they could cancel their request to repatriate to Japan at a later date, even after their release from captivity. When Shizuko previously inquired about the possibility of canceling her repatriation request, she was assured by a high-ranking official that she could remain in the US as an alien resident. She had no idea that the Department of Justice, again in the absence of any semblance of due process, had labeled her a dangerous enemy alien and issued orders to detain her indefinitely, to be deported at the will of the US government.

On October 10, 1945, the Department of Justice took control of the Tule Lake Segregation Center, classifying all prisoners who had not yet been released as federally held "internees of war," subject to deportation and/or removal to Immigration and Naturalization Service (INS) internment camps. Renunciants were not officially informed of the deportation plans for months, and this lack of transparency fueled anxiety that overwhelmed the minds and hearts of prisoners, especially the women and children left behind in Tule Lake.

December 16, 1945
Dear Itaru Ina,

A couple of days ago there was a rumor that all the people who are interned would be deported. But I got more information and learned that those who wish to stay must submit a RE-HEARING APPLICATION to determine whether they will be released or deported. I am prepared for the worst case, so please don't worry. I have packed the dishes, books, radio, baby buggy, etc. in a total of 23 boxes, and yesterday morning I sent them out to my mother's place. I stayed up until 2:00 in the

morning and finally finished packing. I felt a great relief, and today I began to feel a letdown and suddenly I am very tired.
   Shizuko

December 18, 1945
Dear Shizuko,
   We heard that it was announced in Tule Lake *that even though people canceled repatriation, they will still be deported. Haruo and other people are beginning to prepare for the worst case. I'm not sure how much I can believe this, but if it is decided that we will be deported, no matter how sick our child is, there will be no way to escape it. Haruo is saying that if he is forced to go back to Japan, it would be best for the family if he goes by himself, leaving Mrs. Fukami and his child behind. I haven't canceled yet. I will wait until the last minute and send a telegram when it becomes inevitable. I'm praying that you and Kiyoshi will recover completely by then. Hearing that you are prepared enough for the worst case, I am relieved. Please don't worry at all, because I am determined to make the best decision for the sake of our children no matter what hardships we must face. Anyway, the majority of the people here will be going back on this ship, so after that we won't have to worry about what others think. We just need to persevere a little longer.*
   Ina

December 21, 1945
Dear Shizuko,
   I am very disappointed that after we decided to stay in this country for the sake of our sick child, now the Department of Justice has announced that we internees will definitely be deported. When I think that our innocent children have to suffer because I was interned, I feel so much pain that I cannot even cry. As we hear more details of the true situation in Japan, it seems that we who return to Japan without homes, farms, or money will be a burden to others. And as I think about the misery of having a sick child with no place to live, I am hoping now that we will be allowed to stay in this country for a while, no matter what it

takes. However, for us internees, once deportation is decided, it will be inevitable. It was a misfortune that I was interned. If it is decided, then we must get through this misfortune taking perfect steps. You may disagree with this, but if I am deported, then I'm wondering if I should go back by myself first, while you go to your mother's to stay with the children for one or two years. Of course, living apart from family is what we never wanted to experience again. It would be painful and worrisome, but if we think about the children, don't you think that we should endure this? If I am by myself I can manage even if I don't have a home, and in another year Kiyoshi will get healthier and Japan will be more settled. If the four of us repatriate, it will be suicidal and it will all be for nothing. Let's consider this thoroughly and do what we can to keep this from happening. The joy of having children, the pain of having children, the longer we are apart, the more I think about the children day and night. For the sake of our children, let's endure whatever hardship. We must try not to worry so much and just wait for our coming destiny.

Ina

December 24, 1945
Dear Itaru Ina,

I heard that the re-hearing to cancel repatriation will start over here at the beginning of January, then everyone will be sent out before the WRA closes this place.

Mrs. Fukami is saying she will take her child to her mother's and let Haruo go back to Japan by himself. But I will absolutely never do such a thing. We could endure, but it would be cruel for the children. If the father is not around, it's likely that the child will grow to be timid. It's been six months since you left, and Kiyoshi has missed you so much that I have cried many times. I believe that if we must suffer, it will be better for all of us to suffer together.

Shizuko

My mother was a modest, unassuming woman who almost always deferred to my father, but as I read and studied these letters, I realized how strong and determined she could be, especially when it came to protecting her children. She seemed to have had no qualms about actively seeking out prison officials for information and assistance. I came to understand how proactively she managed difficult situations while still maintaining her role as a dutiful wife. She was a risk-taker, willing to leave her grandmother's home in Japan to embark on an adventure as a Silk Girl to the World's Fair. And her moving to San Francisco and starting life anew when she married my father was no easy adjustment.

When assaulted by threatening and inconsistent government policies, my mother was fiercely determined to protect me and my brother. She sent multiple repetitive letters and telegrams, even more than those included here, to my father to make sure he would stay the course. She launched a major letter-writing campaign to people outside, including government officials, friends, former teachers, and family members to garner support to stop the pending deportation of her family. She helped other non-English-speaking women fill out forms and write letters, often advocating for them to prison officials.

My mother's toughness was something I failed to see while growing up. Always loving and patient with us kids, accepting of my father's poetic self-absorption, she was strictly rule bound, kind, and accommodating to others, often at her own expense, especially in her interactions with white people, whether store clerks, employers, neighbors, or our schoolteachers. She deferred to others, worked hard, avoided conflict, and rarely complained even when treated unfairly. Her eagerness to speak up and take risks had been beaten back by the trauma of captivity and the racism and discrimination that continued long afterward. I understand now that her strength remained in her ability to quietly endure hardship, to make life work and move on. Like others who had survived the punishment of mass incarceration, she passed on to her children survival lessons that required us not only to respect authority but also never to challenge it, to work harder than others to prove we were worthy, to keep our heads down and not bring attention to ourselves, and above all, to make whatever sacrifice necessary *kodomo no tame ni*, "for the sake of the children." It was a narrow path, in some ways a razor's edge for successful living, for survival, for a person who was so unjustly victimized by her own country. For a good part of my life, I lived anxiously, true to my mother's precepts.

> *December 26, 1945*
> *Dear Itaru Ina,*
>
> *What a lucky thing happened to me this morning. After the announcement was made about deportation, I went to the Department of Justice many times and tried to meet the head person, but I didn't get a chance to see him. All the other people have also been unlucky, but finally, this morning I was able to meet him, so I was very happy. I was relieved to learn more detailed information. I will not write all the details, but according to this man, the first thing that you and I need to do is cancel repatriation, so I canceled immediately while I was there. He said that you must cancel right away, so please trust him and make sure that you do it.*
>
> *In your recent letter I sensed that you might be thinking about going back by yourself if you are deported. After reading that, I thought about many things and couldn't sleep or eat very well. But today I found out for sure that you will not be deported if you file for cancellation, so I felt completely relieved. Please trust me and share this happiness with me.*
>
> *Yesterday about 1,800 families who are repatriating left for Portland. Tomorrow the same number of people will depart.*
>
> *Every day wherever I go there are people who are packing and people who are coming to say goodbye, so the air is filled with anxious excitement. It seems like our children have a feeling of "going somewhere," and every day, every day they are making a fuss saying that they are going to Daddy's place soon.*
>
> *Yesterday was Christmas, so I bought our children's favorite chicken and made dinner and set a place for you to celebrate Christmas in a small way. Kiyoshi and Satsuki put some pickled radishes [takuan] and beans [mame] on your plate and said,*

"Daddy, you like this, so please eat a lot." When I saw that they were not eating much, while putting their food on your plate, I cried about their innocence.

Soon the day will come when the four of us will live together in laughter.

Shizuko

December 28, 1945 [From Itaru, no greeting]
Yesterday I sent a package to Kiyoshi. One box of gum, a box of chocolate, and one "sea horse" that I carved. Finally there are only 3 days left of this year, and because many of my friends have repatriated, I am even more lonely. This is the first time that we will be apart on New Year's, but let's stay in good spirits and look forward to the coming day when we will be together and let go of this year full of difficulties.

Ina

December 31, 1945
Dear Itaru Ina,

It's been more than a month since Kiyoshi caught his cold, but the bumps on his face haven't cleared up, and his cough hasn't completely stopped. I am treating it as much as I can, but I'm having a hard time because he won't let me put the medicine on him. I try to hold him down by myself, but he is quite strong and I am often defeated. He doesn't seem to feel sick, and he is in good spirits and playing. These days, since you left, I think he has gotten smarter, and there is not a day that he doesn't say, "Daddy, Daddy." Sometimes when he comes running home from playing I'm surprised when he says things such as, "Mommy, little Nobu's daddy is at home so why did my daddy leave me? What did he leave for?" He asks me for such details, and I can't put him off anymore and it's difficult to answer him.

When we have children there is no end of worrying. I'm sure when you see Satsuki next time that you will be surprised. She has grown up a lot. She is already able to say anything. When the three of us are sitting at the table for our meal, she feeds herself, holding her spoon, just like us. When she's not happy she says bad words to me such as "stupid" [bakatare], *"poop head"* [unkotare], *and "pee-pee head"* [shikkotare], *and she rivals Kiyoshi in this.*

From time to time when I watch them play together, it's quite entertaining. Kiyoshi is always using Satsuki as a servant. There are times I burst into laughter when I see him ordering her to bring him a pencil *out of a box or as he peels an orange, he has her carry each peel and put it into the* can. *The day will come soon when you will enjoy watching our dear children as they grow.*

I heard that the closure of this place will be postponed for another month and will occur at the end of February. The current population is about 7,000. About 3,500 people out of this population are renunciants *who want to stay in the US, and the rest are* free *and must move out by the time of closure. I heard that the* WRA *will relocate all the* renunciants *to another place at the* WRA's *expense by the end of February.*

Finally, in another two or three hours, the year 1945 is about to end. Although it is New Year's Eve, I'm not able to be in such a mood. I will welcome the New Year praying that the day of our reunion will be here as soon as possible.

Our action of 1945 was a once-in-a-lifetime mistake. This was my fault because I wanted to go back to Japan so badly. But I think it has been a training of the mind for each of us. I am prepared, even beyond what we have suffered already, for whatever hardships await us in the future.

I will close *this as the last letter of the year 1945. 10 p.m. Sayonara.* Happy New Year!

With Love Always,
Shizuko

I met Wayne Merrill Collins at the biennial Tule Lake Pilgrimage in 2014. He had been invited to speak about his father, Wayne Mortimer Collins, the attorney who must have seemed to appear from nowhere for people like my father, isolated in a North Dakota prison camp in 1945. As I listened to Wayne Merrill offering a spirited account of his father's undeterred effort to challenge the legitimacy of the Renunciation Act of 1944, I had the chilling sense that the man who advocated for my father was actually in the room. As he passionately disputed the US government's justification for denationalizing thousands of Japanese Americans, the son, Wayne Merrill, could easily have been the man who finally offered hope to the prisoners waiting to be deported to war-torn Japan.

It was a profound experience for me to reckon with my own unease and confusion about my parents' decision to give up their American citizenship. Like the renunciants themselves and, later, many of their descendants, I had gotten tangled up in the web of distortion spun by the government to justify the ugly, racist legislation that ultimately separated families, denigrated dissidents, and further traumatized innocent captive people. With great clarity and indignation, Wayne Mortimer Collins had declared that renunciation was a result of government-created duress—not a confirmation of disloyalty and, most important, not a decision deriving from the "free will" of imprisoned people.

The Renunciation Act of 1944 was essentially a mass denationalization plan to be rid of dissident "troublemakers," but in its provision, the law required that such renunciation must be made on a voluntary basis. Tule Lake prisoners were manipulated into experiencing a false sense of self-efficacy when informed that they could "apply" to give up their US citizenship in order to "repatriate" to Japan. Again, in yet another government sleight-of-hand language perversion, "voluntary repatriation" implied that prisoners were returning to their country of origin, though many nisei renunciants had never been to Japan. And because it was "voluntary," prisoners, including my parents, believed they could change their minds if they decided to stay.

Victims of coercive government control, they were never informed that renunciation could lead to prolonged detention, designation as "dangerous" enemy aliens, or forced deportation. They were, in fact, now prisoners ineligible for release and resettlement in the US. The powerless victim, in the absence of any other point of view, will inevitably come to see the world through the eyes of the oppressor. Wayne Collins, with the unblinking eye of a dedicated civil libertarian, challenged the legality of renunciation and presented that much-needed other point of view.

As historian Donald E. Collins (no relation) surmised in his book *Native American Aliens*, Wayne Collins was probably the first person outside of Tule Lake, the DOJ, and the WRA to learn that mass renunciations of US citizenship had taken place within the prison confines. In August 1944, the Northern California branch of the ACLU tasked him with representing men being held in a prison stockade at the Tule Lake Segregation Center. Dissident prisoners had been undergoing random arrests, informal trials, and isolation. Collins demanded that the stockade be shut down and the men held there released. His threat of habeas corpus proceedings forced administrators to comply. Almost a year later, in July 1945, the ACLU was informed that the stockades had been resurrected; Collins returned with a vengeance, and the illegal isolation area was finally permanently dismantled.

During his 1945 visit, Collins first learned of the legalized renunciation of US citizenship making it possible to remove prisoners to DOJ internment camps as alien enemies. When he spoke with family members who described the so-called voluntary repatriation of renunciants, he famously exclaimed, "That's ridiculous! You can no more resign citizenship in time of war than you can resign from the human race."

I came to understand that Collins was not only a legal advocate but also the quintessential compassionate witness for people who had suffered the pain of unjust incarceration. He had the authority and status, separate from the perpetrator, to be able to clear the psychological dust that tormented my parents' prison existence. With this standing, he imbued a new meaning into the renunciation process inflicted on the prisoners at Tule Lake. Having been seduced by the language of government euphemisms, as I listened to the younger Wayne Collins speak about his father, my feelings of shame lifted, my doubts were resolved, and my anger rose, fresh, taut, and righteously owned.

Without Collins's counternarrative, I would never have fully grasped the extent to which government and civilian authorities exploited their power to disguise the racist intent of the entire renunciation process. As Wayne Merrill made his closing remarks, my heart raced as we all offered a standing ovation to the father who had served as compassionate witness to our Japanese American families, and to the son who gave voice to the long-distorted truth that dissidence is not disloyalty. I felt such deep sorrow for the shame my parents and others suffered from the long reach of the government narrative that continued even beyond the barbed-wire fences of place and time. Being held in captivity results in the loss of agency and even the ability to distinguish between the individual's perception and the perception being imposed on them. The shame often held by the victim is the shame that rightfully belongs to the perpetrator.

On returning home from his visit to shut down the stockade for the second time in 1945, Collins received photographs showing horrific images of officers in uniform wielding bats and batons, dragging helpless, imprisoned men inside a newly constructed concrete "jail within a jail" at Tule Lake. When I asked Wayne Merrill about the source of these photos, he said his father had never disclosed his source; however, the son of Robert H. Ross has acknowledged that the photos were taken by his father, an administrator and the designated photographer at Tule Lake. Only a person in such a position would have been permitted to be present at the scene of such violence. Apparently sympathetic to the victims, Ross documented the abuse and passed the uncensored photos to Collins sometime after his July 1945 visit. The photos Collins received and subsequently made public included the photo of my father inside the Tule Lake Segregation Center jail—the very same photo I stared into at the Smithsonian Museum in 1988. Sometime between that jail photo and the mug shot taken of him in Bismarck two days later (shown on page 163), my father had been assaulted. As disturbing as it was to see the insult my father endured being photographed for the mug shot, I was even more sickened by the sight of the cuts and bruises on his face and neck.

8.

Alien Residents

S oon after control of Tule Lake was transferred from the WRA to the Department of Justice, it was announced that all who had renounced their citizenship would be deported to Japan. Only a few government officials offered lukewarm opposition to the mass removal, concerned about the public appearance of such actions, but Wayne Collins was outraged. With the backing of the Northern California ACLU, three months after his visit to Tule Lake to finally shut down the stockade, Collins filed lawsuits on behalf of renunciants to prevent the DOJ from carrying out its plan. These suits required that renunciant plaintiffs be set free, deportation orders be canceled, applications for renunciation be voided, and citizenship be restored. Collins obtained a court order during these proceedings, which forbade removal until a decision had been reached.

The DOJ, halted from carrying out its mass deportation plan, was determined to continue to detain and ultimately deport all "troublemaker" renunciants. Authorities also feared the expenditure of millions of dollars to keep the prisons open during what could be years of legal proceedings arguing the justification for deportation. To bypass the question of the legality of the proposed mass removal, the DOJ announced on December 10, 1945, that individual "mitigation" hearings would be held. These hearings would give the appearance that there was some degree of discernment about who should be deported as risks to national security rather than a carte blanche removal of anyone who had opposed or criticized the incarceration. The hearings were purportedly designed to identify mitigating factors that could lead to release, but renunciants were never informed of the criteria that would be used to determine the outcome of the proceedings.

While WRA camps moved rapidly toward closure, prisoners' concerns were left unanswered: How would they survive if they were deported to Japan? Would wives and mothers be reunited with the men held in separate internment camps? And what would happen to families fractured by the continued detention of some members and not others? The situation was particularly difficult for those family members—mostly women, children, and elders— held at the WRA prison camps, who were forced to resettle outside without knowing the fate of their interned husbands and fathers in the DOJ internment camps.

Hearings were held between January 7 and April 1, 1946, in all of the DOJ camps where renunciants were interned, first at Tule Lake, then at the Bismarck and Santa Fe internment camps. DOJ officials stated that although citizenship would not be restored, any renunciants who could prove they were victims of duress at the time of renunciation would be freed from detention. Prisoners were denied any form of legal counsel during these hearings, and there was no protocol established for them to present their individual cases or to access information held in dossiers referred to by hearing officers.

January 3, 1946
Dear Shizuko,

   This morning I officially signed to cancel repatriation, so there's nothing for you to worry about. At the same time, along with 150 other people, I submitted a petition to the attorney general. We are in the process of following the best procedure as advised by an attorney whose name is Collins. *Regarding this,*

I need the letter that approved *my renunciation. I think it is in my leather briefcase, so please find it, and send it to*—WAYNE M. COLLINS, ATTORNEY AT LAW, MILLS TOWER, 220 BUSH, S.F. *I think the cost to pay the attorney is about* $20 *per person.*

   Ina

January 6, 1946
Dear Itaru Ina,

   Today I received your postcard. I am relieved to hear that you officially canceled repatriation. The hearings *over here started this morning. Six people went from this* Block. *I learned from Hamai-san what it was like. In any case, we should* mention *that my brother Masami is a soldier. I heard that this would be of great* help.

   Next, I received a detailed letter from Uncle Muraoka today, and he told me that no matter what, I should move out and bring the children to Cincinnati as soon as possible, whether or not you are deported. He said there are many jobs. I've looked into many possibilities, and I think it will be best for us to go there. If you are deported, I think you will be able to go with your mind at ease knowing we are with Auntie and Uncle Muraoka. And if you are allowed to stay in the United States, you will have more chances *over there. Anyway, my* hearing *will be over in the next couple of days, so if I can move out, I will make up my mind to go to Auntie Muraoka's. If you agree with this plan, please reply right away.*

   Shizuko

January 7, 1946, Evening
Dear Itaru Ina

   Those who had their hearing *today will be given notice within a couple of days whether they can move out. So I think it will be my turn soon.*

   The other day I went to the social welfare office and heard about the situation in San Francisco. I was told that the people who left earlier are having trouble because there are no jobs or housing available to them. I was advised that we should go east. *Let's rely on Uncle Muraoka's words and go to Ohio. We can ask Auntie to take care of the children so I can go to work. Let's not go back to San Francisco.*

Some of the young couples on this block who have *renounced joined the "$100 case" with the same lawyer, Mr. Collins. They are involved in the movement to reclaim their citizenship. According to Mr. Collins, those who are* interned *will never be deported, and those who have nisei children should* strongly state *at their* hearing *that they have to be in the United States to raise their children, who are American citizens.*

Shizuko

January 10, 1946
Dear Shizuko,

As I said in *my previous letter, I officially canceled repatriation on January 3rd. The other day all the issei* internees *who decided to cancel repatriation were handed notices of repatriation. These were, in fact, "deportation orders." If they oppose the order, and they request it, they will at least be given a* hearing. *They will be released or deported based on their* hearing *results. We submitted petitions to the attorney general to withdraw our renunciation and have our US citizenship returned to us. Of course now that we have retained an attorney, it will cost money, but our budget is less than $20.00 and nobody can afford more than that. As internees we* feel *that we can't trust the outcome by just canceling repatriation, so it will be a wise strategy to do the* best *we can within the limits of what is permitted, so everyone is taking the same action. If I am* released, *I would like for us to make up our minds to go to Cincinnati. Although it is quite a distance, and it will be very difficult for you to take the two children from there, I think it will be convenient in many ways to live close to my aunt. Please let me know what you are thinking.*

Ina

January 13, 1946
Dear Itaru,

  Kuwada-san is visiting here now. He is working as an interpreter for the hearings.

  Let's decide to go to Auntie Muraoka's. I'm worried about taking our children on the train trip all the way to Cincinnati, but I'll be able to manage as long as I prepare myself not to sleep for 4 or 5 days. And when I think about you arriving soon after, I feel strong, and this small suffering will be nothing.
  Sincerely,
  Shizuko

January 20, 1946
Dear Itaru Ina,

  Today is Sunday, and Kaoru-san's older brother,[1] *whom you've known, visited me unexpectedly. I heard details about many things, so please be relieved that there is nothing to worry about.*

  I heard that our hearings here will be over next week, but still, I haven't gotten my notice yet. I think you will be given quite a hard time at the hearing, but no matter how difficult it is, for the sake of our precious Kiyoshi and Satsuki, I'm begging you please do not lose your temper. As long as you keep this in mind, there is nothing for you to worry about. Let's keep in mind that it was our big mistake that we renounced, and that we want to raise our children in the United States as good citizens. We don't want them to have the same hardship that we suffered as children in Japan.

  I'm certain that we will be reunited in February. Please take care of yourself and wait for this. Kaoru-san's older brother sends his best regards to you.
  Shizuko

---

1. To avoid the censor's cut, Shizuko is avoiding naming Itaru's kibei friend K. Kuwada, who was working as a censor/translator for the government.

January 22, 1946, Morning
Dear Shizuko,

Attorney Collins arrived in the evening the day before yesterday. He met with us in the auditorium from 10 a.m. until a little after 3 p.m. yesterday. He kindly explained to us much of the preliminary information regarding the hearings and answered our questions. I felt greatly relieved because we heard this information from a very reliable person, unlike information given to us in the past. The thirteen people who came here with me have already signed the request for their hearing, and they are just waiting for their time to come. I don't think there is anything to worry about in preparation for the hearing because of Mr. Collins' remarks and explanations yesterday. Also, when you have your hearing, please let me know how it was. In any case, I don't think there is anything much to worry about.
Ina

Finally persuaded by Shizuko to cancel his repatriation request, Itaru would now have to justify his reasons for wanting to remain in the US. Officials said that prisoners who could prove they gave up their citizenship under pressure would be released to settle outside. Renunciants would soon learn that those who were not successful in convincing the hearing officers would be deported. Caught in the jaws of a monstrous government plan to be rid of dissidents under the artificially constructed banner of disloyalty, prisoners were in turmoil not knowing what it would take to escape deportation.

Shizuko, fearing that the family would be separated, and consumed with guilt for pressing Itaru to renounce in the first place, gathered her courage and did whatever she could to prevent Itaru's deportation. Somehow never fearing or considering the possibility of her own deportation, she met with prison camp administrators and hearing officers to explain Itaru's innocence, and gathered information on how best to respond during questioning. In the process, she also supported and encouraged other internment widows to do the same.

Shizuko first sought help to petition for Itaru's release from Louis M. Noyes, the Tule Lake Segregation Center attorney, who listened to her story and composed a letter for her to sign. The letter included the difficulties Shizuko suffered from her arrest, her subsequent pregnancies, and the illnesses that led her to plead with Itaru to renounce so that they could take their children to Japan in hopes of a better life. Interestingly, the letter went further to make the case that she had urged Itaru to renounce because she was fearful of the pressure groups who threatened harm to those who did otherwise. However, in her diaries and letters to Itaru, it was clear that my parents' decision to renounce was in response to the cruel and unjust treatment they suffered at the hands of their own government. Certainly, extremist factions had a hand in pressing some prisoners to renounce, but for my parents, renunciation was a decision made in despair and in fear of the racism reflected in America's inability to distinguish between the enemy at war and innocent American citizens of Japanese ancestry. Shortly after Itaru was separated from the family, Shizuko had written to him, saying, "We must decide about the future for our children. Because they have a Japanese face, I don't want them to be American."

Perhaps, sympathetic to my mother's plight, Noyes actually took the liberty of writing the letter, probably knowing what justification would more likely lead to Shizuko's desired outcome. The letter is clearly not in her voice. In the letter, Noyes blamed other prisoners for Itaru's decision to renounce. Further, he made false claims: that she and Itaru were never active in the Hoshidan and in fact were opposed to the goals of the organization. "My husband was against the group," Noyes wrote on her behalf, "but he . . . was afraid to resign because of the threats." The letter went on to specifically name known leaders of the Hoshidan and an elderly couple who had already repatriated as the people responsible for the threats.

This position clearly established a point of view that blamed other prisoners for the duress leading to the decision to renounce, rather than the grievous injustice of the government-imposed mass incarceration. In Shizuko's hearing responses and, later, Itaru's, it's evident that they both relied on Noyes's justification that duress inflicted by other prisoners contributed to their decision to renounce. In the end, this perspective would be the most acceptable rationale for hearing officers and other government officials to allow prisoners to withdraw their renunciation requests and avoid deportation. It would be considered the strongest "mitigating" factor for being released.

Shizuko's first hearing lasted only thirty minutes and even included a moment of light-heartedness with the hearing officer, but she was later called back again to undergo a two-hour interrogation, most likely in order to address the discrepancies between what she said and what was recorded in her file.

January 23, 1946
Dear Itaru Ina,

When I told the Tule Lake attorney, Mr. Noyes, about my circumstance, he wrote a letter for me, which I am enclosing. He told me that it would be good for me to send this right away to Bismarck and to Mr. Ennis in Washington. Here is a copy, so please read it thoroughly, and if it's OK, please respond by telegram and I will send it right away. Please write your response as follows: "Soon you are released, please go to Ohio."

If you don't agree, you don't have to send me a telegram. Also please show this letter to Yoshida-san and tell him that Mrs. Yoshida wants him to let her know right away if he wants her to write the same letter. If so, then she will write it.

Shizuko

January 25, 1946
Dear Shizuko,

Haruo's case seems to be extremely complicated, and he is losing heart. I am at a loss because there seems to be no way to comfort him. I don't think it's likely that he will be deported. I believe he will have his hearing after the rest of us are finished. I am expecting that the hearing will be quite hard on me. I'm worried, but I'm not afraid because I believe that it will be best to just tell the truth as it is. When I think about the whole situation, I realize that neither Haruo nor I have done anything wrong, and yet we have fallen into such a mess. I heard that Kuwada-kun visited you, so I'm sure you heard about his fam-

ily situation. When you see him again, please give him my best regards.

Ina

January 26, 1946
Dear Itaru Ina,

I had my hearing *at 9 a.m. yesterday. I was questioned for about 30 minutes and was able to answer well and give details without regrets, so I feel relieved. The following are the main questions and my honest answers:*

1—Do you have a family member who is in the American mili-tary?—My younger brother Private Masami Mitsui.
2—When was he drafted?*—March 1945.*
3—What is Masami's address?—Maebashi Gunma Prefecture in Japan.
4—Why and when was your husband interned?*—Because my* husband's *name was listed as a member of the Hoshidan, but he was not* active *at all. He was taken away last July.*
5—Why did you and your husband *join the Hoshidan?—When we joined it was not called the Hoshidan. We were simply people who wanted to repatriate, and there was no other mo-tive. And without our knowing, some* leaders *named it Hoshi-dan. Although my* husband *was against joining the group from the beginning, I forced him to join. At that time most of our friends and neighbors were members and so there was nothing else I could do in my position.*
6—Why didn't you resign *from the group right away?—I just couldn't do it because one of the* strong leaders *lived next door. We saw him every morning and evening and I couldn't bear be-ing* criticized. *And as a Hoshidan members we were not* active *at all, and we never valued the group at all.*
7—Have you and your husband *attended the morning ritu-als?—*No, *we did not, although the group members* criticized *us as* lazy *or* cowards.
8—How many years did you receive Japanese education?—8 years.

9—Were you mainly taught to be loyal *to the emperor?*—Yes.
10—Do you believe that the Emperor is God?—No. *He is a human being.*

11—Why did you renounce?—*Because I wasn't treated as an American citizen.* When I was 4 months pregnant and suffering from morning sickness, I was ordered by forced evacuation to Tanforan *on a severe rainy day, thrown into a filthy,* windowless, *smelly horse stall. My morning sickness became worse, and I was very sick and bedridden for most of the time. I will never forget for the rest of my life how much I suffered during that time. Then, I was sent to Topaz, a place with terrible* dust storms, *and I suffered from nose bleeds, diarrhea, and I was about to miscarry my baby. This pain during my pregnancy had been imprinted in my brain after that, and I felt bitter about everything. I thought that there was no hope for my future in the United States, where we who are American citizens were put through such a terrible experience, and I urged my* husband *to go to* Tule Lake *so we could* expatriate. *My husband saw me suffering during my pregnancy, and he cried a man's cry. I don't think you could understand my feelings unless you get pregnant and experience what I did. (The* hearing officer and his secretary *burst into laughter, agreeing that they haven't had the experience of pregnancy. Until then I was tense, but all of a sudden it seemed funny, and I laughed with the* officer.*) The reason why I* renounced *was the forced evacuation and the atmosphere at* Tule Lake *at the time.*

12—When you renounced, *didn't you say you would be* loyal *to Japan?*—Yes. *Even if I'm not loyal, I thought that I wouldn't be allowed to renounce if I didn't say so.*

13—Are you loyal *to the United States now?*—YES. *For the first time my eyes are open. The path that I had taken up until now was very wrong.*

14—When you renounced, *did you want Japan to win?*—I was *praying for world peace to come as soon as possible whether Japan won or not.*

15—Why did you cancel repatriation?—During my pregnancy *I was put in a horse stall, and it was so cold that even after child-*

birth I still haven't recovered yet, and especially when it's cold, I have severe back pain and have been in and out of bed until recently. It would be suicide to take our children to Japan at this time in my weakened health condition. For the sake of my children's happiness and in order to raise them to become good American citizens, there's no other place but the United States. When I was a child I had no choice about being sent to Japan, and there I fell into such misery because I was partially educated in both countries. I'd like to raise our children in America so that I can make sure that they won't have to suffer what I suffered.

16—How did you feel when Japan attacked Pearl Harbor? —I couldn't believe it.

17—If your husband is deported, will you be going to Japan with him?—No. I will remain in the United States for the sake of the children.

18—If you remain in the United States, where will you go?—I will go to either my parents' or my husband's uncle's place, and I will ask them to take care of our two children while I go to work to support them.

19—Do you have any close relatives in Japan?—No. My husband's younger sister and my grandmother.

20—Do you have anything else you want to say?—My husband was interned because I listed our name with the Hoshidan, but he is not guilty of anything, so I would like him to be released as soon as possible. In any case, because of my poor health after childbirth, I've been so nervous that I caused my beloved husband and children to suffer, so it is my fault.

I was asked many other questions, but these are the main ones.

To the Person Who Is Censoring This:[2] I'm so very sorry, but please do not cut this letter regarding my important hearing and deliver it to my husband.

I'm begging you to do this.

---

2. This note to the censor was written on a separate sheet of paper enclosed in the envelope.

Although Shizuko's mitigation hearing results were recorded on January 29, 1946, it would be weeks before she would learn the hearing officer's recommendation that "Her renunciation was her own voluntary act and without duress. Her testimony that she and her husband were members of the Hoshi Dan and affiliated organizations in name only is discounted. It is recommended that she be removed to Japan."

Once again, Shizuko's fate was determined in the absence of any form of due process. Trapped by war and their captor's racist intent, prisoners had no idea on what basis decisions were made. Shizuko's responses under questioning were guided by what she believed was the key to her freedom, rather than the truth. The so-called mitigation hearings were not designed to discover whether or not the decision to renounce was a result of duress as Collins argued, but instead were a means to justify deporting people who dissented, accusing them of being a national security risk.

No mention was made of what was to become of my mother's American-born children. I did locate, however, a copy of my own records from Tule Lake. Eighteen months old, born in an American concentration camp, I was formally listed as an enemy alien. My birthright deleted with the stroke of a pen, I was anointed an enemy of the state.

As Tule Lake emptied and friends and neighbors were released, Shizuko, yet to be notified of the outcome of her hearing, continued to hope and prepare for release. She finally got word that the letters of support she requested for Itaru had begun to arrive in time for his hearing in Bismarck. Her younger brother, PFC Masami Mitsui, sent a letter from his army post in Japan, and Tule Lake block manager Mr. Yamashita strongly vouched for Itaru, along with others who confirmed that Itaru's decision to repatriate was a reflection not of disloyalty but of his concern for the welfare of his family.

Kay Kuwada was a longtime kibei friend of Itaru's dating back to their bachelorhood in San Francisco. My parents were initially shocked to learn that Kuwada was serving as a translator for the administration. This meant he was one of the censors, using his Japanese language skills to surveil letters written by prisoners and excise the "sensitive" information they contained. Prisoners distanced themselves from known censors to avoid being seen as collaborators. Dissidents viewed censors, who were granted special status by the authorities, as despicable traitors to their own people.

Although my father had been good friends with Kuwada before the war, their affiliation was strained by the circumstances of their incarceration. Throughout their letters, Itaru and Shizuko referred to Kuwada using the English translation of his name, "mulberry field," or as "Kaoru-san's elder brother." At one point, Shizuko cautions Itaru about his friend's new hobby using scissors. Kuwada had been stationed at the Santa Fe internment camp in New Mexico, where Itaru and other Bismarck internees were to be transferred. When the mitigation proceedings began, he was temporarily assigned to Tule Lake to serve as interpreter for issei men brought from Bismarck for their hearings.

Ever determined to prevent Itaru's deportation, Shizuko managed to meet with a hearing officer named Shevlin just before he left Tule Lake to conduct hearings for renunciants at Bismarck. She implored him to consider Itaru's circumstances, and in the process mentioned Itaru's friendship with Kuwada, who worked with Shevlin. He advised her to have Kuwada write a reference letter on Itaru's behalf. On February 7, 1946, in spite of the awkwardness in their relationship, Kuwada wrote from the Santa Fe internment camp, describing his association with Itaru since 1934. He concludes,

> I can vouch for his loyalty to the United States. He obeyed all laws; performed no acts contrary to regulations; uttered no disloyal word nor revealed any subversive acts toward the United States. . . . I was indeed surprised to have heard that Itaru Ina had renounced his citizenship. His past records show the man who lived a normal life in a free environment. His present records show the man who, due to evacuation and external influence, is leading an abnormal life. I am confident Itaru Ina still possesses those pre-war qualities that made him a good citizen. If these pre-war qualities would extenuate his present situation, I am confident that Itaru Ina,

after returning to normal life, will do his utmost to redeem his mistakes.

January 31, 1946
Dear Itaru Ina,
  Right after I am released I am going to take our children to your aunt's as you said, so please don't worry. However, please never do such a thing as to go back to Japan by yourself because you feel relieved that we are at your aunt's or because you are worried that your hearing will be so relentless. No matter what, please do your best to hold on until the very end. Because the hearings will vary depending on the person, I don't think the hearing will be so difficult for innocent people like you.
  Please take care of yourself.
  Shizuko

February 1, 1946
Dear Shizuko,
  Attorney Mr. Collins *said that there will be* hearings *here for sure and that we don't need to worry, so I'm sure it will happen sooner or later. Over here everyone is very busy gathering* rec-ommendation letters *rather than worrying about the* hearings, *but I haven't made a request of anyone. If I am to be deported, even if I have* 100 *recommendations, it will be useless. Even if we request these, especially since our acquaintances are issei and are aliens, it won't mean much. I remember that the* 5th *is your birthday. I am enclosing just a* card *because in my life as an* internee, *I'm not able to give you anything. If I am released, then I will be able to do something for you.*
  Ina

February 3, 1946
Dear Itaru Ina,
  Yesterday ten people out of the entire camp received their re-lease papers, *so it has caused great excitement. It's rumored that most people will receive* release papers *by next week, so we are all anxiously waiting.*

Finally renouncees *have started full-scale packing. We have all been going through uneasy days, but now we can see our future getting brighter.*

Yesterday I met Mr. Shevlin, *who is going to conduct a* hearing *for you and the others. I asked him if I could talk to him about testifying as your* witness. He said, *"Write a detailed letter and bring it to me." So I wanted you to know that I wrote it immediately and gave it to him. In this letter I wrote about the* mitigation facts *you sent me in your letter³ that prove that you are clearly* innocent.

Since I am to blame and feel responsible, I've tried everything I could do on my own, hoping that it would help *you even a little at your* hearing.

In a few days, I think Mr. Shevlin *will be going over to your place.*

Also Uncle Muraoka wrote to me and gave me details regarding things over there. He said I should go there as soon as I am released *and he will come to pick us up in* Chicago, *but I declined his offer because it is too much trouble for him. I can manage by myself on a four-to-five-day train trip. I'm planning to stop at your place on my way to* Ohio *so that I will have no regrets in case you are to be deported.*

Shizuko

February 11, 1946
Dearest Ina,

Just received your air-mail post card dated February 7th and very much disappointed to hear that all of you are going to be transferred to the Santa Fe Internment Camp. Wherever you are send, please, please do not give up your hope. After all, you are innocent, so you will be coming back to us very soon.

Whether you will be sent to Santa Fe, I shall visit you on the

3. These facts include Itaru's purchases of war bonds and war stamps, as well as his registration for the civilian defense and the fact that he voted in every election and never went back to Japan after 1930.

way to Cincinnati. Your son is asking for you all the time, so I must see you for sure.

Your mitigation hearing is going to start from today? Wishing you a good luck!

Please take good care of yourself and keep your chin up.

With love always,

Shizuko

February 13, 1946, Evening
Dear Itaru Ina,

I want to let you know right away. Today I received a letter from Kuwada-san. He said that on the 5th he sent a recommendation letter for you to Mr. Shevlin so that it will arrive in time for your hearing, so please expect it. He said that there is nothing for you to worry about, so he wants you to wait patiently for a little longer until you receive your release and to not apply for repatriation.

Also last night there was a notice for the 352 renouncees over here. We could either go to Japan as volunteer repatriates on the ship leaving this coming February 21st or be interned at the Santa Fe internment camp. Everyone is feeling defeated.

Even though you are being sent to Santa Fe, I believe that you will be released for sure, since Kuwada-san and Masami have been vouching for you. I am also doing whatever I can, so please be patient and wait.

Shizuko

February 19, 1946
Dear Shizuko,

I received the recommendation letter from brother Masami yesterday. I'm glad that it arrived just in time. Yesterday was the fifth day of the hearings over here, and not even half have finished. Until the hearings began, everyone was very optimistic, but once they started and we learned more about the situation, everyone was shocked and worried that they were not as expected. In every room, everyone seems worried, and all they talk about is the hearing. Of course it is my intention to persevere until the last moment, but at this point, I'm not able to be optimistic, so I want you to be prepared for the worst, especially if people like you at Tule Lake *are to be interned somewhere else. Our future will be full of difficulties even if we are released. We are scheduled to move to* Santa Fe *in ten days, but there is no definite announcement yet. If you and the children are released and it is the end of the month, it will be the worst time for a visit. Why don't you cancel this visit and take the shortest route to your destination? We can make plans for you to come visit me at another time. As much as I want to see the children, it will be an ordeal to* stop over *with two children. In addition, the departure over here could be changed at any time and for any reason, so it could turn out that you come all this way and arrive after I have left. When I find out my departure date, I will send you a telegram if I can. If I go to* Santa Fe, *you should write to me in English to avoid having to be read by censors. If you have an urgent message after the 24th, you should send it to* ALIEN INTERNMENT CAMP, SANTA FE, N.M. *Over the past couple of days, it has been very warm over here and the snow has melted quite a bit.*

Ina

March 4, 1946
Dear Shizuko,

By the time you receive this letter, we will have arrived in Santa Fe. *I received your letter dated the 20th, and since then, I haven't heard from you, so I'm worried that something has happened. It was July 5th when I was sent to* Bismarck *and March 5th that I am leaving, exactly 8 months, and yet I have no idea when I will be released. This is my final letter from* Bismarck, *but since there is nothing special to write, I will write a little about my* hearing *because I think you might be worried about it.*

1—The reason for renouncing—My wife's *influence was the primary reason.*
2—Why did you answer No-No *in* Topaz?—When I was at the *meeting regarding the registration problem, everyone was trying*

to agree on a group decision that we should definitely say "no,"
or we shouldn't register at all. I objected to this and insisted that
we leave it to individual free will. As a result I was perceived
extremely negatively by others, and I was called traitor [inu].
Also because there had been incidents of assault at some places,
I decided to take the same action as the majority in order to keep
my family safe, so I wasn't able to express my free will. Especially
because our Block 23 in Topaz was composed mostly of people
who moved to Tule Lake, I couldn't do much. Therefore, until
we arrived at Tule Lake, we had no intention to return to Ja-
pan, but because of these circumstances we decided to apply for
repatriation.

Other questions were, why did I join Hoshidan? Why didn't
I quit the group sooner, etc.? And those are pretty much similar
to the questions you were asked, but the question that gave me
the hardest time was regarding the record of my renunciation
hearing. *Because I was told by Uncle Kobayashi that I wouldn't*
be allowed to renounce *unless I gave extremely* tough *responses,*
I had said a lot of things that make me sweat when I think about
it now, such as, I had been a Block *board member of the Seinen*
Dan when I wasn't even a member of the board. *I found out that*
a stupid statement about suicide that I don't even remember was
kept in the record. I was disgusted with myself.

Otherwise there was nothing else particularly different. Most
of the questions were the same as the ones over there. Because
it is true that you had quite an influence *in every aspect, I pre-*
sented it in this way, so I'm worried now, you may end up being
interned. As soon as I arrive in Santa Fe *I will let you know my*
exact mailing address. I think I will be bumping along on the
train this time tomorrow.
  Ina

Immediately after his interrogation, Itaru was flagged for deportation. Once again, there were no known criteria for determining
whether a prisoner should be released or deported, and no effort
to obtain evidence of loyalty or disloyalty or to hear testimony from

witnesses. No mention was made in the report regarding any letters of reference. In the absence of any form of due process, hearing reports show that decisions were preemptively made based on previously gathered information from government documents. Among the stated reasons for Itaru's recommended deportation were his No-No answers to the loyalty questionnaire, the charge of sedition for making a statement that the US government should treat prisoners equally to free people, and a response he gave during his renunciation hearing when asked whether he was willing to commit ritual suicide if Japan were to lose the war. (This last statement he made believing he would not be allowed to expatriate unless he emphatically demonstrated his loyalty to the emperor.) From this perspective, the cards were stacked against him before his hearing even began.

The "Report and Recommendation" from the hearing officer, Howard E. Scheppler, was dated February 21, 1946, the same day as Itaru's hearing:

> The subject lived in Japan for approximately twelve years, from 1918 to 1930. Received education in that country and attended school in the U.S. three years. The subject appears to be an intelligent, well-informed individual who was fully capable of making his own decisions although I believe it is possible that his wife who was an employee of the Japanese Silk Company and made numerous trips to Japan, the last trip in 1940, exerted an influence on him. He claims that he did not withdraw from the Hoshi Dan because of pressure and influence on him and stated that he never on any occasion attended or participated in any of the activities of that organization. I find this very hard to believe. In regard to his statement to the renunciation hearing officer that he would commit Hari Kari[4] if Japan lost the War he tried to laugh it off at this hearing and said he considered the hearing officer was "joking" with him. I consider this a Class I case and recommend removal.

4. Anglicized reference to *hara kiri*, ritual suicide.

By spring of 1946, six months had passed since the end of the war. Tule Lake was the last of the WRA camps to close. Closure of the DOJ internment camps soon followed. My parents had yet to be informed that they were destined to be deported. On March 5, my father, among the 188 internees from Bismarck, departed for the Santa Fe internment camp in New Mexico. The Ft. Lincoln internment camp was officially closed on March 6, 1946.

The INS detention camp at Santa Fe, New Mexico, located two and a half miles west of the city center, had previously served as a Civilian Conservation Corps camp. To detain issei in the initial sweep of community leaders immediately after the bombing of Pearl Harbor, the INS had obtained permission from the New Mexico State Penitentiary to use this facility to hold DOJ internees. A twelve-foot-high barbed-wire fence surrounded the twenty-eight-acre compound, which was equipped with eleven guard towers.

As instructed, Shizuko wrote letters to Itaru in English to avoid delays routing them through Japanese-language censors. As her hope for release began to fade, resignation began to permeate her diary entries and letters to Itaru. Around this time, Shizuko's letters to Itaru became uncharacteristically sporadic, then stopped.

March 8, 1946
Dear Shizuko,

After I left Bismarck *the evening of the 5th, I continued on with an unexpectedly pleasant trip, then today at 3 p.m., I arrived here safely. I am so exhausted from the train trip that I don't feel like writing anything, but I wanted you to know that I arrived safely. Although it was brief, I was able to meet Kuwada-kun.*

Now that I am separated from [xxxxx], *I'm at a loss because I have no one to talk to. I heard that the climate is better here than* Bismarck.
Ina

March 9, 1946
My dearest husband,

I have received your last letter from Bismarck yesterday. I am

sure you are safely arrived to your destination by now. Change
of climate might affect your health so please take good care of
yourself. Especially be careful about drinking water.

I should have written to you more sooner but I was waiting
for my result of hearing day after day. There are several hundred more to be release so probably I might get it next week
for sure.

This vast camp of Tule Lake is now a Ghost Town. Even in
the day time, make you a creeps. Most barracks are deserted
with litters around and just cats and dogs are snoofing around
for something to eat. Only you see a people here and there.
When the night comes, it's so dark without outdoor light and
I could hear only squeaking of the doors which cause by the
night wind. So nowadays I go to bed with children around 7
p.m. and lock the door firmly. In Block 68, there is only Mrs.
Kobayashi and I with children and rest of are 11 bachelors. So
you could imagine how quiet around here. Sometimes I volunteer to clean up latrine and laundry room and also make a
fire at boiler room for laundry. 69 Mess Hall have been closed
long ago and since we are going to 70's Mess Hall. Everything
is very inconvenient but I am sure it won't be long now.

Poor Kiyoshi, his friends have all gone out so his best play-
mate is a dog called Queenie. He takes dog around for hunting
junks all over the vacant rooms. I wish you could see his collections! Honestly, he is asking for you every single day. And
it's very surprising, how he remembers what you did at home.
He mentions most of all is the time you climbed up to attic
with light, searching for window's screen. Also the time you
took him to baseball games. These things he mentions quite
often. I hear that the boys are more for his father than mother.
I found that out since you have gone. I have read that story
called "MY SON DOESN'T KNOW HIS FATHER." But
you need not worry about your son. When you see him soon,
you will be proud of him.

Satsuki is fine too. Several days ago, while I was doing my
packing, she disappeared suddenly. Block 68's boys help me
with searching for half an hour and finally I found her way

over the ground of Block 74. Certainly she made me frightened. Usually she is never been out of my sight but within 10 minutes, she disappeared.

I have enclosed all the snapshots which I took it on March 1st. It's not so good but you could see how much children have grown up since you went away.

I am not optimistic about your release or my future life. I have been thinking things very seriously and it might be better for me to volunteer to go to Crystal City family internment camp after I get my release and wait for your final disposition. What do you think? Please let me know your decision right away.

I just got finish packing 12 freights. Suppose to send out to Ohio tomorrow but I think I better wait for my release and your final decision. You might think, again Shizuko is in doubt at last minutes.

If I don't get your answer on time, I shall be going to Ohio anyway and plan to visit you on the way. I do not care how trip is hard, long as I could see you.

Mrs. Yoshida is planning to go to Portland and Mrs. Itani is to Los Angeles. Many internees families have been released this week so we will be fixed in no time.

Please take good care of yourself and praying for our happy reunion.

With love, Always Shizuko

March 14, 1946, Morning
Dear Shizuko,

Yesterday evening I received your letter dated the 9th and the pictures of our children. Because of the limited space, I will only write about business. If you are released, you should make arrangements right away to go to Cincinnati. My aunt said in her previous letter that she is waiting for you to be released as soon as possible. Of course, if you think it's better to go to Crystal, I'm okay with that. However, for the sake of the children, this is a good time to end life in camp. Also I'm not going to object to your desire to visit me on the way, but traveling with

Shizuko with Kiyoshi and Satsuki, Tule Lake
Segregation Center, March 1, 1946

*two children is not going to be easy, and I'm concerned about
the stopover and the roundabout route. However, if you decide
to come, I think we can ask Kuwada-kun to make arrangements
to find a place for you to stay. So, even if I'm deported, I will feel
relieved that you are with my aunt. Or, if I'm released, we will
be able to modify our plan, so you should decide to go to Cincinnati in any event.*

    Ina

March 22, 1946, Morning
Dear Shizuko,

    *Since I moved here I have only received one letter, so I don't
know at all how you are doing. According to conversation with
Kuwada-kun yesterday, I found out that you and others are supposed to go to* Crystal City *internment camp, so this may be*

*better at this point. It was decided that this place too will be
closed soon, and all the people who aren't released will be sent
to Crystal. If I go to Crystal and we are together, it will be easier
for us whether we are released or deported. However, if we end
up going to Crystal, we cannot be optimistic about our future
at all. I was going to write when I received a letter, but it doesn't
seem like it will arrive soon, so I have nothing else to write.
I have no idea where you are or how you are doing at this time,
so I will stop for today.*

    Ina

More than three thousand renunciants at Tule Lake had applied
for hearings, but on February 12, 1946, after only half of these hearings had been granted, the DOJ announced that 449 applicants
had been rejected and would be deported. Even as the rest of the
hearings continued, this number remained the same. In his ongoing litigation effort, Wayne Collins charged the government with
bad faith. The 449 had been chosen arbitrarily, and the continu-
ation of the hearings was to give the false appearance of fairness
and legality. By the time Tule Lake closed on March 28, 1946, the
prisoners listed for deportation, including my mother, brother, and
me, boarded the train to be interned at the Crystal City Family Internment Camp in Texas or Seabrook Farms in New Jersey. Some
prisoners were notified of their release just hours before the last
trains were pulling out, and releases continued to be made as the
train stopped in San Francisco and Los Angeles.

An exhausting four-day train trip brought us across miles of swel-
tering, flat, empty plains to the small desert town of Crystal City
at the southern tip of Texas, just thirty miles from the Mexican
border. I don't have any memories of that train ride, but I can only
imagine what it must have been like for my mother—not just the
grueling experience of having to travel with two toddlers for several
days, but the hopelessness she must have felt as all her efforts to
secure our release had been to no avail. Designated as dangerous
enemy aliens, we were brought to Crystal City, a gathering point
for those awaiting deportation to war-ravaged Japan, not knowing
whether we would be reunited with my father.

The Crystal City internment camp was the largest INS prison camp, and the only "family internment camp" administered under the DOJ. Armed guards stood watch in six guard towers at the corners of the ten-foot-high barbed-wire fence surrounding the 290-acre compound. My mother had once described men, likely border patrol guards, surveilling the perimeter of the fence on horseback. The Crystal City internment camp also held German and Italian nationals who had been in the US at the outbreak of war. One day, an unexpected contingent of internees arrived. Hoping to see familiar faces, my mother joined others to greet and assist the new arrivals, but she was surprised to hear the names, especially of the children, during the roll call as people offloaded from the train. She gave examples of names such as Jose Nakamura, Miguel Hirota, and Carmen Iwama. The families spoke to each other in both Japanese and Spanish. My mother was later shocked to learn that these Japanese Latin American mothers and their children had been arrested and deported from thirteen Latin American countries. They were to be reunited with fathers kidnapped in 1941 by the US government in a secret agreement with their respective Latin American governments, to be used in a prisoner-of-war exchange with Japan. Another injustice beyond belief.

Surveillance at the Crystal City internment camp was constant. Temperatures regularly reached 115 degrees. An internal security force patrolled the Japanese section of the camp. Jan Jarboe Russell, author of *The Train to Crystal City*, captures in an interview with a former internee the highly regimented structure of life in the camp: "The roll calls seemed endless. Three times a day a whistle blew, and all had to run back to their cottages and huts, form lines, show their faces, and stand still for the count in the presence of armed guards."

Housing units included prefabricated "Victory Huts," which were bungalows with small kitchens, as well as barracks and mess halls. The water reservoir used for irrigation for the prison farm needed to be dredged and lined with concrete. The administration reached an agreement with internees, allowing them to use it as a swimming pool in return for performing the necessary labor to rebuild the reservoir.

During a brief train stop in El Paso on the way to Crystal City, Shizuko sent Itaru a hastily written postcard:

March 23, 1946
Dear Ina,
    Mrs. Yoshida's and my cases are still pending. We are on the way to Crystal City Internment Camp. Expect to arrive tomorrow morning.
    Love, Shizuko Ina

March 25, 1946
My dearest husband,
    Hello! to you from way down Texas. We have reached here yesterday morning at 6 A.M. Childrens are fine but I am completely worn out from 4 days on the coach train. No time to rest, busy getting our baggages, straighten out our house, washing and so on since arrived here. From tomorrow we have to start cooking our meals at home so everyday must go to marketing. Mrs. Yoshida lives at same building so we are planning to cook together and eat together until you folks will join us.
    I have met Mr. Ikejiri at El Paso, Texas and heard everything about you. Looks like you might get release earlier than I am. If you do, I wish you could visit here before you will go to Ohio. Kiyoshi is so anxious to see you. Before we left Tule Lake, I was told by dept. of justice's officer that you folks will be at Crystal City before we will so I wrote letter to you addressing Crystal City. Also many people were released before got on the train at Tule Lake so I was waiting for mine until last minutes at Tule Lake. I certainly had a dizzy time.
    Now I am at Crystal City Internment Camp so I am not bit optimistic about my future. I might as well ease myself until they release me. I do not know when I will be able to see you again but lets keep our chins up. Take good care of yourself.
    With love Always, Shizuko
    p.s. I have sent you a telegram by C.O.D. because all my money have been confiscated at Tule Lake before got on the train so I am penniless.

March 30, 1946, Morning
Dear Shizuko,

I received your letter dated the 25th yesterday evening. Since I hadn't heard from you for a long time, I was worried about what was happening, but now I feel relieved to know how you are doing. The release from over here is now official, and because some people are going to California and some are going east, every morning, every evening, there are fewer and fewer people. Everyone including Midori's Papa and Haruo have been released uneventfully and departed for their destinations. My hearing was late, but if things go the way they have been, I may be able to be released reasonably soon. Yesterday morning I presented myself at the administration office to ask if I could be permitted to be transferred to Crystal City where my wife and children are because I am planning to go east and will ultimately be heading in the direction of Texas.

I doubt whether this is likely to be permitted, but if you want to be with me before our release, you must say that the reason is that we are planning to go east. I think it will be a good idea for you also to make this direct request immediately by stating that taking our two children by yourself on a long trip will be extremely difficult. If I am released before you and, if I am allowed, of course I want to make every effort to go east with you. Also if I can visit you over there, I will do that too. If you get released, you should do what you can to wait for me so then we can make arrangements to leave together. This place will be closed the middle of next month, and if I don't get released by then, it's likely that I will go to Crystal. Because time is running out, I will write to you next week. Say hello to Mrs. Yoshida.

Ina

April 4, 1946
My dearest husband,

I have received your letter which dated March 30th last evening. So many people are getting their release over there. Never can't tell, might be one of the lucky person next time!

Few people are getting their release here in this camp too. But no luck for me.

How is weather over there? I imagine it's hot as here. Really it's too hot for us. Every evening, I take children for walk and sometimes to movie show. We have a nice movie twice a week at outdoor theatre. Also we have nice swimming pool. Kiyoshi wanted to go swimming but I promised him if daddy comes home he will take to swimming. So he is waiting for you all the time.

I am having very busy times compare with Tule Lake life because I must do cooking and marketing everyday beside caring for children and housework. Hoping to see you soon.

With love, Shizuko Ina

April 8, 1946
My dearest husband,

Post card dated April 3rd and the package of salted fish have been received this afternoon. I give some to Mr. Ikejiri and Mrs. Yoshida. It's so hot down here so its nice to have some salted fish. We must have lots of salt in order to keep ourself well.

I thought you might worry so I didn't tell you this but Kiyoshi have been confined in hospital for week with [xxxxx]. And he got well so I brought him home today. Also Satsuki had a light fever for few days and she is also getting better so please do not worry.

Everything is fine here but this heat is getting me down and certainly I wish I could get out of here soon. Otherwise I might going to pass out this summer.

Rumors are flying around here that you folks will be coming here this Sunday so most of the internee widows are anxiously waiting. Hope it comes true.

With love, Shizuko Ina

April 10, 1946, Morning
Dear Shizuko,

Yesterday evening I received your letter dated the 4th. The closure of this place is scheduled for the 19th, but I think if I'm not released *by the 15th, I'll be sent to* Crystal, *so I will make this letter the final one. If everything goes as planned, I'm supposed to arrive there on the 16th. Since the* elevation *here is 7,000 feet, I can still see the snow on the mountains. However, no matter what, spring is spring and the buds on the trees are becoming more green and the peach blossoms have begun to bloom. I don't have anything in particular to write, so I'm going to stop for now. If I'm not* released *by the 15th, I think I will be able to see you next week.*

    Ina

Even as Itaru made his way to Crystal City, just as Shizuko had days earlier, it was clear that neither had been informed of the results of their hearings, and though the possibility of their release was slowly slipping away, each held hope that they could be released and reunited as a family. It's not clear exactly when my parents were finally notified of the results of their mitigation hearings, but records show that they were both issued deportation orders on the same day, March 28, 1946, days after our arrival at Crystal City. Each deemed "to be an alien enemy dangerous to the public peace and safety of the United States because [he/she] has adhered to the government of Japan or to the principles of government thereof," they were ordered by Attorney General Tom Clark to depart the US for Japan within thirty days of receiving notice. They were to depart of their own accord, but if they failed to do so, they would be removed by authority of the commissioner of Immigration and Naturalization.

    Itaru arrived at Crystal City from Santa Fe within a week of his last letter to Shizuko, dated April 12, 1946. I have imagined the scene hundreds of times: Mom, Kiyoshi, and I standing in line near the fence along with other mothers and children, searching faces as the 188 men stepped off the bus or truck that brought them from the train station to the gates of yet another barbed-wire enclosure. My brother, shy and reticent, but recognizing the father he remembered and maybe even holding the toy tank made for him by his otō-chan. My mother, exhausted by long months of uncertainty and frantic effort to keep the family together, waiting, tears slipping from her eyes, to stand beside Itaru as he takes Kiyoshi's hand. As for me, I cry, turn away, and refuse to be held or touched by the stranger whose presence was creating so much quiet commotion. It's a moment that stirs me deeply even as I write today.

Within a few weeks of our reunion, my mother began writing in her diary again. Conditions were better. We lived in a small "cottage," where we could cook and eat together as a family. She carefully noted every cent spent on food and necessities purchased from the camp commissary using government-issued tickets in exchange for goods. Her entries are brief but disquieting. On May 3, she wrote, "Nearly 100 Germans received their last deportation notice from U.S. Attorney General yesterday. Probably our fate will be the same."

By September 1945, about a thousand renunciants had banded together to form the Tule Lake Defense Committee. They approached Wayne Collins to represent them. Collins, the only attorney who would take on cases of people who had renounced their US citizenship, initiated class-action suits for the cancellation of renunciation of citizenship and the prevention of forced removal to Japan. Despite opposition from the Department of Justice and the national office of the ACLU, and refusal of support from the National Japanese American Citizens League, Collins and the Tule Lake Defense Team were undeterred. On behalf of the 5,589 Japanese Americans who renounced their birthright between 1944 and 1945, Collins argued that all evacuees, particularly those at Tule Lake, were victims of duress by the US government, which made their renunciation invalid.

What had originally been planned as a program of detention of enemy aliens during time of war became more draconian and deportation oriented when a new attorney general, Tom C. Clark, took office. Even at war's end, he concluded that renunciants were dangerous persons and should not be allowed to remain in the US. Faced with the impending forcible deportation of all renunciants to Japan, Collins filed four suits against the government on November 13, 1945. The most urgent at the time was the writ of habeas corpus, demanding freedom from detention and prevention of deportation. Of the 5,589 renunciants, eventually 4,754 persons signed on as plaintiffs in the mass suits.

Collins advised plaintiffs to submit requests to reopen their cases while the issue of renunciation under duress was pending in the US District Court in San Francisco. Among my father's DOJ files, I found a copy of his handwritten letter stating why his case for deportation should be reconsidered. He explains that he was not represented by counsel at his mitigation hearing, nor was he allowed witnesses to speak on his behalf. Further, that decisions were made based on secret data kept in a dossier to which he did not have access, and that the hearing itself was not conducted under oath, nor was any evidence presented justifying the denial of his release from detention.

Temporarily blocked from implementing mass deportation by Collins's writ of habeas corpus, the Department of Justice, intent on removing the renunciants, opted in January 1946 to conduct individual "mitigation" hearings in an effort to give the appearance of due process for deportation decisions. Because the hearings had a direct bearing on Collins's case, the US District Court in San Francisco moved to delay the trial that would have determined whether renunciants would be freed from detention and deportation. My parents were among the 449 renunciants who received unfavorable verdicts in the hearings, but rather than having them deported immediately, the court ordered all 449 to be held in specific DOJ camps, including the Crystal City internment camp.

Because my parents' correspondence had ended once they were reunited and Shizuko's diary entries had over time withered due to a feeling of purposelessness or sheer despair, I don't know just how much they were aware of their status at this time. Shizuko continued her desperate attempt to persuade administrators to release her family. She began yet another concerted letter-writing campaign, asking Caucasian family friends, a former teacher, and friends who had been released earlier to write letters to the attorney general pleading for the family's freedom and rescue from deportation. In one letter to her Caucasian former teacher, she closed her entreaty with, "Please help me. I am desperate."

In response to letters attesting to Itaru's and Shizuko's good standing as citizens, Thomas M. Cooley II, director of the Alien Enemy Control Unit, wrote on May 8, 1946, "After careful consideration of all the relevant facts in this case the Attorney General made a finding that Mrs. Ina had adhered to the Japanese Government and its principles and by an order dated March 26, 1946 directed her removal to Japan . . . it will not be possible to reconsider her case."

Among the last of the many boxes in my mother's tiny apartment, I found a family portrait taken by a German photographer in a studio setting inside the Crystal City internment camp. The photo seems to say it all: we are finally together, but the four years of incarceration have taken their toll on each of us.

Saturday, June 8, 1946
9 A.M. whole family took a picture by German photographer.

In the same box was what appeared to be a page torn from a notebook, similar to the ones my mother used as diaries. On June 19, 1946, she wrote:

Wednesday, June 19, 1946
WHAT A JOYFUL DAY! RELEASED!
We have received notice from the office to come to office right
away on 11:15 a.m. We thought we are going to get our 30 day
deportation notice but instead we are released. Believe or not
but it's true. Can't express in words.

At the administrative office, my parents were each handed copies
of orders signed by Attorney General Thomas C. Clark on June 19,
1946, stating in part, "it appear[s] from a reconsideration of all the
evidence bearing on this matter that said alien enemy should now
be released."

I was unable to uncover any official rationale for this sudden
"reconsideration," from declaring my parents "a dangerous risk
to national security" to this point, after more than four years of
incarceration, suddenly deciding to free them. The word "evidence" suggests that the rule of law had been applied, when in
fact no due process had been granted to any of the 125,000 people
of Japanese ancestry, from the time of their initial incarceration
and throughout the war. One can only surmise that without actual basis in fact, and in tacit acknowledgment of Wayne Collins's
claim of duress, any further efforts to deport American citizens
would not succeed in the courts. The war was over, and again, not

one person of Japanese ancestry had been convicted of sabotage or fifth-column activity. The cost of housing and maintenance of thousands of innocent people in confinement had become too burdensome to continue. My parents were released not on the basis of their proven innocence but for the protection and convenience of the US government.

On further research, I came upon a memo that at first looked unremarkable, initiated by Ollie Collins, likely a subordinate of Thomas M. Cooley II, assistant to the attorney general. A second document signed by Cooley and initialed by the attorney general instructs that paperwork be processed for the release of my parents. All of the facts listed in support of their release were ones my parents had previously given in their final hearings, which had been disregarded at the time. As the government grasped at straws to now justify release of hundreds of prisoners, the word of a fellow Japanese American working as a censor ultimately led to my parents' release.

Memorandum recommending the release of Itaru and Shizuko Ina

TO: Mr. ~~Cooley~~ Morison
DATE: June 14, 1946
FROM: Ollie Collins
SUBJECT: Itaru and Shizuko Ina—Husband
                 and Wife—File No. 146-54-167

I believe these cases should be reconsidered. There are two small citizen children involved. The wife has a brother serving in the U.S. Army and stationed in Japan. All of her relatives are here. She was a member—in name only—of Hoshi Dan. The husband was a member but not an officer, of Hokoku Seinen Dan.

I am impressed by the letter from Kay Kuwada concerning the husband. Kay has been employed by the INS at Santa Fe for about 3 years, as I recall, and Ivan Williams "swears by him". Kay acted as Interpreter at Tule Lake during the mitigation hearings. He is personally acquainted with a great many of the renunciants, and I frequently asked his opinion concerning the loyalties, etc. of the renunciants, and Kay was very careful about making recommendations, and in only one instance was he willing to vouch wholeheartedly for a renunciant. Kay's letter convinces me that subject's actions are the result of evacuation, camp life, etc. The two infant children constitute a hardship. I think both should be released.

On June 28, 1946, my parents received a letter of final disposition signed by J. L. O'Rourke, head of the Crystal City internment camp, authorizing their release and detailing arrangements for them to proceed to Cincinnati. The irony of the closing statement could not have escaped my father's attention: "Mr. Ina, you are further advised that it will be necessary for you to report to your Draft Board immediately upon arrival in regard to your change of address and occupation."

Four years and two months after my parents were removed from their home in San Francisco, on April 30, 1942, having never committed a crime, our family was finally free, heading by train to Cincinnati, Ohio, the occasion of my earliest childhood memory.

Sometime after our arrival in Cincinnati, my mother, fearful that our family would be accused of any wrongdoing, wrote to O'Rourke. Her letter is polite and proper, yet nearly every word she writes reflects the aftermath of her trauma.

> Dear Mr. O'Rourke,
>
> During our trip to Cincinnati, our train have been delayed for three hours so we did not used our meal tickets on Baltimore & Ohio Railway Lines. Therefore I am sending it back to you.
>
> We have arrived in Cincinnati on July 10th safely and enjoying back to normal life again. I wish to thank you for everything during our four months stay in Crystal City Camp.
>
> Sincerely yours,
> Mrs. Shizuko Ina

It has taken me a lifetime to understand that my parents had lived for years after their incarceration as "alien residents"—Americans without American citizenship. Released from physical captivity yet still not free, they kept their heads down and worked hard without complaint, ever vigilant that without citizenship, their standing in America was tenuous and fragile. Not unlike undocumented immigrants to the US today hoping to acquire asylum, my parents lived in fear that somehow any misstep could lead to deportation or detention. Without conscious awareness, my brothers and I shouldered the burden of securing our family's future through our good behavior. My parents never dared to express any bitterness or anger, yet the unspoken shame and insecurity underlying the pressure they felt to be 110 percent loyal Americans was passed down to us children. It was this inherited trauma response that defined who we were, how we looked, and what we deserved in life. We learned not to complain, to avoid being vulnerable, and to feel a never-ending need to strive.

The intergenerational transmission of trauma takes place at many levels of communication between parent and child. Trauma, particularly repeated and chronic states of trauma, such as captivity, alter the structure and functioning of a person's nervous system. Victims develop a hypersensitivity to threat that manifests in specific emotional responses, behavior patterns, and cognitions expressed in fixed values and attitudes, all in the service of survival. Mostly unconscious, these coping strategies can often result in problems regarding human attachment and intimacy, and in some cases, mental health problems including chronic depression and anxiety. Not always toxic and destructive, these coping strategies can also reflect the resiliency and psychological tenacity of victims. In any event, so imperative are these attitudes and behaviors for survival that they often continue to be unconsciously called on even for generations after the trauma has passed. For Japanese Americans, many of the coping strategies adopted during imprisonment were in sync and intertwined with Japanese cultural values such as stoicism, conformity, conflict avoidance, and respect for authority, which made those strategies more deeply entrenched and difficult to recognize. Children of trauma victims often grow up observing and absorbing the silence. The shadow of secrecy and shame follows the trauma of unrelenting humiliation.

In 2019, four years after my initial foray to the Karnes County Residential Center, reports of the tragic detention of people from Central America seeking asylum in the US continued to appear in the newspapers almost daily. My heart felt heavy knowing that an increasing number of innocent women and their children were being criminalized for escaping life-threatening circumstances in Guatemala, El Salvador, and Nicaragua. After traveling miles of torturous terrain with babes in arms and toddlers in hand, mothers arrived ever hopeful of rescue and safety in the US. Instead, they were greeted with vicious dogs and handcuffs, and suffered disrespect, abuse, and indefinite detention. Like my own family detained in 1946 in a Texas prison camp, these families were subjected to the stress of interminable delays and lack of information or access to legal assistance while awaiting hearings to determine whether they would be freed, further detained, or deported. With impunity, government officials declared that "detention as deterrent" could serve to stop others from crossing borders into the US. In order to further punish and deter those who were seeking asylum, the government adopted a cruel policy of separating children from their parents.

That year, a small group of friends and cohorts, including survivors who had been incarcerated as children during World War II, began planning a pilgrimage to the site of the former Crystal City Family Internment Camp. It had been almost seventy-five years since we were sent there to be reunified with our fathers after months or years of family separation. From the very beginning of our discussion, we spoke with great concern about the crisis taking place at the border. Innocent Central American children were being held in mass detention just forty miles east of our pilgrimage site at the South Texas Family Residential Center in the town of Dilley. Their plight resonated too much with our own childhood experience for us to ignore.

As we gathered for our planning meetings, survivors shared their family stories. Many of us, now in our seventies, eighties, and nineties, spilled long-held tears, grieving in ways we had never allowed ourselves before. Being in community with others who shared our experience, offering their empathic presence as compassionate witnesses, made it possible to speak our truths. We were determined to find a way to bring light to the trauma we knew so well, and how it was being repeated once again for thousands of children of color. We were reminded of the silence that prevailed in our neighborhoods and throughout the country when we were disappeared from our homes into remote prison camps out of sight and out of mind for the rest of the citizens of America. We would not be silent bystanders. Our grief had transformed into meaningful and productive outrage.

As our plans began to unfold, we reached out to others who had been held at Crystal City and to younger members of our communities, many of whom were fourth- and fifth-generation descendants of World War II prison camp survivors. They brought their organizing skills, their energy, and their (to many of us unfamiliar) audacious expressions of outrage. Some even brought their reluctant parents. The labor of this remarkable intergenerational collective resulted in a unique, culturally meaningful protest plan. Not only would we create a spectacle to catch the attention of the press but, like the Quaker woman who tossed the quilted blanket over the fence to my mother at Tanforan, we also wanted the children inside the prison to know that someone outside cared.

We survivors had been brought up to stay out of the limelight, keep our opinions to ourselves, and certainly not risk our own security by speaking out against those in power at the highest level of government, yet Japanese American communities across the country were stirring. Our collective, latent trauma was being activated by the inhumane actions of our current government. With the energy and boldness of the next generation of yonsei millennials serving as the wind beneath our arthritic wings, we decided we would bring our stories and raise our voices to demand that our government stop repeating history.

At the pilgrimage site in Crystal City, Texas, we were warmly welcomed by mostly Hispanic local officials and dignitaries. We were heartened to learn that many of them knew our history, and some of them shared their own stories. One elder said he remembered his father pressing tortillas through the chain-link fence to Japanese American prisoners. We held brief Buddhist and Christian ceremonies to honor our parents and grandparents and all who had suffered and died in confinement at the Crystal City internment camp. My tears flowed as I reflected on the sacrifices my parents made and how their love for me and my brother guided their every decision during those grievous lost years of their imprisonment.

Returning to the site of shame where many of us had witnessed our parents coping with the fear of deportation, we connected to our own long-suppressed trauma as we retraced their steps, our eyes landing here and there on a rusted pipe or a crumbled remnant of concrete. For the many of us who were too young to remember, we imagined moments with our families, filled in by the scene around us—the heat, the mosquitoes, the trucks and cars rushing by. I needed this time to be alone with my thoughts, to reconstruct even a tiny fragment of memory. I found myself seeking a secluded space somewhere so I could lie face-down, my heart touching the earth in communion with the only eternal witness to my community's suffering.

Coming back to where we had lived as children was a way to un-wind our history, to understand how we became who we are today. There had been generations of silence, stories that were taken to the grave or that disappeared in the ashes of cremation. Although I was there at the pilgrimage with my brother and many good friends, I was consumed by an aching loneliness. Perhaps only in that loneliness could I experience such deep sorrow.

After the pilgrimage program ended, we headed to the Dilley fa-cility. We had honored our family, our ancestors. We remembered what we could, and we wove the threads of our memory together to shape some sense of wholeness out of the destruction of our family histories. As we traveled by bus and car forty-five miles to the cur-rent site of shame, the mood began to shift.

Coming out of our introspection and silence, the group seemed to awaken, revitalized with purpose as we approached our next des-tination. We were going to protest—something my parents were punished for, something they came to believe could only bring disaster and defeat. It was something many of us had never be-fore dared to do. Protest was outside the narrow confines, the psy-chological concentration camp that dictated how we could find acceptance and therefore safety in this country—by remaining compliant, passive, silent. We were going to do something nobody had done for us. We were going to show up en masse, this time on the outside of the fence, to protest the unjust incarceration, the criminalizing of innocent people because of the color of their skin.

Through our protest, we would bring a message of hope and car-ing to the families behind the chain-link fence crowned menacingly by barbed wire. In homage to our ancestral heritage and to offer symbols of hope and compassion, we asked our family and friends to fold ten thousand origami paper cranes to hang from the fence that separated us from the children. We wanted them to see from the distance the brightly colored wings that symbolized freedom. By the time we arrived in Texas, more than thirty thousand paper cranes had been folded and sent from all parts of the country. Taiko drummers from Denver and New York arrived to sound the beat of our hearts. We made signs; we sang children's songs in Spanish and Japanese. We chanted, shared our stories, and spoke to the press demanding that all detention facilities holding innocent people seeking asylum be shut down. Imprisoning innocent people, let alone children, is inhumane and traumatizing. We stood strong and loud, claiming our moral authority as survivors and descendants of racist mass incarceration. We had for years proclaimed "Never again," but that day, our mantra was "Never again is now!"

Just as my parents had experienced a renewed sense of dignity when they chose to protest their incarceration, seventy-five years later we felt purpose burn through our cloak of compliance, conflict avoidance, and silence—symptoms of our own trauma. We were on fire with intention to use our history, our stories, to bring light to what was being done to innocent people, to mothers and children at the Dilley site. What we didn't realize at the time was that protest was our healing, bringing to life the part of us that had been deadened by trauma. It was exhilarating to feel that our stories had purpose, that our voices were no longer muffled by fear. The state violence inflicted on us had fractured our families, our hearts, and our spirits. In protest, we felt strengthened and connected. It was as if we all had to be together, to speak with one voice, to stand up for others targeted by racist injustice. Only then could we reclaim our wholeness and fully realize who we were always meant to be. Every child in detention today is my brother, my community. I am every child in detention.

Life in Ohio was not easy for my parents. Having lost everything—their home, belongings, jobs, and most important, dreams for a better life—they had to start from scratch, relying on extended family for support and assistance. We were finally free, but my parents, with no citizenship status, were "resident aliens." They lived with anxiety about their future. They couldn't vote or buy a home. They dared not travel out of state, jaywalk, or argue when shortchanged. They never spoke with us about having to live under the shadow of their prison life. Yet they did what they could to provide a nurturing, loving home life for us. My father was finally able to return to photography, capturing hundreds of precious moments of our childhood freedom.

Kiyoshi and Satsuki one year after release, Cincinnati,
Ohio, 1947

Renunciants like my parents would have carried on their lives
forever in an indeterminate state of limbo without citizenship if it
hadn't been for the heroic effort of attorney Wayne Collins, who
continued to challenge the plight of those condemned to stateless-
ness. Charles Wollenberg, Wayne Collins's biographer, describes
the attorney's presence at Tule Lake in the summer of 1945 as "an
impetus to activism" against the Renunciation Act of 1944. With
the support of the Tule Lake Defense Committee, Collins fought
for the renunciants, arguing that they were "under the duress of incarceration, subject to threats of violence, and acting on the basis
of false rumors and inaccurate information."

On April 29, 1948, more than three years after the war with Japan had ended, federal court judge Lewis E. Goodman handed Collins a complete victory, which stated that it was "shocking to the conscience that an American citizen could be confined without authority and that while so under duress and restraint, for this government to accept a surrender of his constitutional heritage." He further declared "the plaintiffs to be citizens of the United States."

It would take until 1959, thirteen years after my parents' release, to officially have their American citizenship reinstated.

In 1948, my younger brother, Michael Takeshi, was born. Unlike with Kiyoshi and me, Michael's Japanese name was relegated to a middle name. Soon after we entered school in Cincinnati, teachers met with our parents and advised, "If you want your children to be real Americans, they need to have real American names." Suddenly Kiyoshi ("pure and noble") became Kenny, and Satsuki ("child of the fifth moon") became Sandy. My poet father, who took pride in carefully selecting meaningful Japanese names for us, must have winced at the erasure of our Japanese identity. When I was in my thirties, I took a job that required me to present my birth certificate. It was only then that it dawned on me that Sandra, nickname Sandy, was not my name at all. I had always thought that Satsuki was my middle name.

I realize now that reclaiming my birth name was my first act of dissidence. My father was silent when I announced that I wanted, from then on, to be called by my real name, but my mother was distraught. She repeatedly said to me, "Don't do it. Bad things will happen." In my life, she was the only one who could never quite call me Satsuki. Anything seemingly "un-American" would trigger her fear for our safety and security. Even when we traveled to Japan together several years later, where it would only be appropriate for her to use my Japanese name, she would verbally stumble when introducing me to family and friends. Other Japanese American friends and cohorts whose names had been Anglicized teased me about "going native."

In 1950, my father was offered a job with his former employer at the Nonaka Trading and Import Company as a bookkeeper, so we left Cincinnati and returned to his birthplace, San Francisco's Japantown. My parents continued to follow instructions from Wayne Collins, submitting a detailed affidavit regarding the duress they experienced leading to their decision to renounce their US citizenship. In 1959, thirteen years after living as "alien residents," my parents received a curt and officious notice stating, "In view of the determination that your renunciation was null, void and without legal effect, you are entitled to the return of your birth certificate." Included in the notification letter that reinstated their status as American citizens was each of their birth certificates, surrendered at the time of their renunciation.

9.

Healing

As I reclaimed my identity as a Japanese American, my name became ever more precious to me. But it would take decades longer for me to finally find my anger and my voice about what my family had to endure because of our ancestry.

Without being consciously aware of why I made the career choices I did, as I look back now I see that I have long been in search of my identity, my history, and, most important, my healing. I understand now that the World War II prison camp experience has been like a ghost, elusive yet haunting every aspect of my life. I went to college before there were any ethnic studies classes. I majored in psychology focused on the theoretical work of exclusively white European scholars. My community's experience of incarceration was absent from my American history classes. The silence and invisibility of our families and our history left many of us adrift, longing to be white, hiding ourselves to avoid being viewed as the forever foreigner. My mother would tell me to stay out of the sun so I wouldn't get any darker. Freshman girls at UC Berkeley talked about applying Scotch tape to their eyelids to make themselves look more beautiful. I wished I had bigger breasts, longer legs. My parents didn't hug us or say "I love you" like the families

283

we watched on TV. Many of us wanted to rid ourselves of the characteristics that had led us to be cast out. More than anything, we just wanted to belong.

It was only in the last half of my forty years as a psychotherapist that I began to study the effects of trauma. The concept had never been used to describe our prison camp experience, nor had the idea that the effects of trauma could be passed on to the next generation. A whole world of understanding opened up for me when I realized that false imprisonment of an entire community could have a profound and intergenerational impact. The silence and unconscious coping responses of a generation that experiences such an overwhelming and life-changing injustice can lead to an "other" orientation to life, lasting for generations. We survivors and descendants become vigilant about how we are perceived by others, and meeting the standards set by the dominant culture for beauty, success, and belonging becomes our paramount goal, leading us to inhibit, even abandon, our true selves. These attitudes and behaviors are crucial for victims' survival, but as with other forms of trauma, they often remain even after the immediate threat has passed. Sadly, for people of color today, the threat of being unjustly targeted has far from passed. The US continues to enact racist policies of incarceration, deportation, and travel bans. In a social system fraught with anxiety about the COVID pandemic and seeking a scapegoat, violent anti-Asian hate crimes have proliferated.

Our 2019 protest at Dilley, Texas, was the beginning of what has grown to become a national Japanese American social justice organization, proudly channeling our cultural heritage into a mission of solidarity. Tsuru for Solidarity would become our moniker, combining *tsuru*, the Japanese word for cranes symbolizing peace and hope, with our commitment to reach out to work together across communities to bring social change. Breaking down the walls that have purposely divided and alienated us from one another will be essential for building a true democracy in America.

An important component of Tsuru for Solidarity's work today is to conduct Healing Circles for Change. This group process was inspired by a precious moment we experienced while visiting a service center in Laredo, Texas, near the Mexican border. Through our allies in South Texas, we had heard about the Laredo Immigrant Alliance, where families recently released from both Karnes and Dilley detention facilities could find temporary shelter while awaiting their asylum hearings or searching for family members in the US. Providing care on a shoestring budget, volunteers, including undocumented students, offered food, shelter, and information to families, mostly mothers with young children.

Our intention was to bring a small donation collected from our group to cover the cost of a washing machine so that families could wash diapers and clothing. There were twenty of us, a Buddhist minister and several survivors and descendants. We parked our rented cars and walked along wooden fences with laundry hung to dry in the sun. As we entered the worn and modest building, we could hear the laughter of children playing games and the gentle sounds of mothers quieting crying babies. They had all just been released after weeks or months of incarceration. Among the women, worn and anxious, and the men, silent and sullen, we were afraid of being seen as intruders. Grief weighed heavily in the room.

Volunteers welcomed us warmly, and in an impromptu attempt to connect with the families, we created a circle of chairs around the room. Curious about the motley crew of Japanese Americans who had traveled from California, mothers with children in their arms joined the circle along with volunteers. We brought strands of colorful paper cranes that lit up the faces of the children. Often when Tsuru for Solidarity members debriefed after a protest action, we would sit in an informal circle to share our experience. Now, that process magically unfolded in a room full of strangers. One of the volunteers served as translator. We began by briefly sharing our stories and our purpose for being in Texas. My brother Kiyoshi, usually quite shy and reticent, stood up to speak. He talked about having been incarcerated as a child for four years; deeply moved by the situation, he offered these words of hope: "I'm almost eighty years old now. I want you to see that I survived, that I'm okay. You must be strong. Do not give up hope. You too will be okay." The woman beside him, carrying a toddler in her arms, stood up to speak. Black strands fell from the rubber band holding her hair back; her clothes were rumpled and faded, and tears streamed down her face. As she spoke, the translator struggled to keep her own composure. "I have just spent four months in a terrible place," she said. "I feared for my children. We were hungry and afraid every day. When I hear that you were in prison for years, my heart aches for you. I cannot imagine your suffering."

It was an incredible moment of connection. She was crying for us. Her empathy knew no bounds. I had never felt so seen. An ocean of love seemed to fill the room as we sat side by side, quietly letting the tears flow. We were crying for them. We were crying for ourselves.

I had conducted groups for Japanese Americans over the years at various pilgrimage events and in my own psychotherapy practice. These group experiences were always stirring and emotional, yet this moment felt especially sacred, as compassion flowed from this woman who had suffered horrific trauma herself. It was a moment of true humanity. Gathering to listen with deep empathy across the divide of language and culture, to share our stories and our parallel experiences of oppression, brought a powerful healing. We came wanting to offer help, yet we were the ones who received the most profound gift.

It was love for their children that guided my parents' decisions, some of which had painful consequences. It was with deliberate intention that they left their letters, diaries, and poetry—concrete proof of their love, their life, and their struggles that would allow this story to be known by their children and grandchildren. My parents were ordinary people facing extraordinary forces meant to destroy and eliminate their very being. Yet they endured and found a measure of strength and dignity in their resistance. Pummeled by their experience, they unintentionally passed on to me dire lessons for how to live and survive in an unsafe world. These lessons were taught not so much consciously or through direct instruction but more through their actions and behaviors and their deep instinct to protect. These lessons of caution and risk avoidance were woven into every facet of my life. In the process of researching and writing my parents' story, I learned that, thanks to their courage and love, my life today no longer has to be about survival. Instead, it can be about using my voice and taking action to challenge injustice, and serving as compassionate witness to those who have been forced to live in fear.

I arrive at the end of my family story with deep reverence for all who endured the World War II incarceration. It is my hope that this one story will encourage others to discover and claim their own family stories. In this way, we collectively challenge the distortions and lies that have suppressed the truth and the facts of our traumatic history. Each story will add to a multifaceted accounting of how democracy failed and how some of us, not all of us, managed to survive. When we weave our stories into the fabric of our American history, unfettered by euphemisms, distortions, and denials, truth and healing will follow.

Acknowledgments

Okagesama de is a shortened response in Japanese social greetings to the inquiry, "How are you?" It reflects the interdependence of all relationships, translating as "in your shadow" or "thanks to you." This book has only been possible, okagesama de, to many people over the twenty years who have helped, guided, and supported me to bring this story forward.

Okagesama de, first and foremost, to historian, scholar, and sister badass, Barbara Takei of the Tule Lake Committee for her bold and visionary mission to challenge and rewrite the government's false narrative about the dissidents and renunciants at Tule Lake. Other scholar historians who have provided invaluable resources include Frank Abe, Jeffrey F. Burton, John Christgau, Donald E. Collins, Wayne M. Collins Jr., P. Scott Corbett, Roger Daniels, Mary M. Farrell, Art Hansen, Yuji Ichioka, Tom Ikeda, Karen Ishizuka, Gwenn Jensen, Tetsuden Kashima, Junko Kobayashi, Cherstin M. Lyon, Wayne Maeda, Eric Muller, Donna Nagata, Brian Niiya, Greg Robinson, Jan Jarboe Russell, Jere Takahashi, John Tateishi, Sandra C. Taylor, Nancy Ukai, Michi Weglyn, Sensei Duncan Ryūken Williams, Charles Wollenberg, Hiroshi Yanagisawa, and Ikumi Yanagisawa, along with many others. Invaluable resources include the *Report of the Commission on Wartime Relocation and Internment of Civilians* and the Densho Digital Repository and the *Densho Encyclopedia*.

Okagesama de to writers who have shared or narrated first-person accounts of the World War II Japanese American incarceration: Motomu Akashi, Gordon H. Chang, Brian Komei Dempster, Louis Fiset, Rev. Yoshiaki Fukuda, Kimi Cunningham Grant, Mary Matsuda Gruenewald, Kimiko Guthrie, Lily Yuriko Nakai Havey, Brian M. Hayashi, Lawson

Inada, Tatsuo Ryusei Inouye, Mike Ishii, Akemi Kikumura, Minoru Kiyota, Junko Kobayashi, Lawrence Matsuda, James Mitsui, Edward Miyakawa, Toshio Mori, Kyoko Oda, John Okada, Mine Okubo, Chizu Omori, Emiko Omori, Noboru Shirai, Yoshiko Uchida, Melody Miyamoto Walters, and Karen Tei Yamashita.

Okagesama de for psychological insight and perspective, Judith Herman, Peter Levine, Amy Iwasaki Mass, Alice Miller, Donna Nagata, Lisa Nakamura, and Naina Sodhi.

Okagesama de to former internees who so generously shared their stories with me: Mitsuye Fukuda, Hank Naito, Bill Nishimura, Art Ogami, Tom Umemoto, and Tad Yamakido.

Okagesama de to research assistants Kim Ina, Tadao Koyama, Elizabeth Uno, and Devon Yoshikawa.

Okagesama de to Frederick Crews, for your thorough read and feedback on the early unformed mass of a manuscript. Your words of encouragement have been the light at the end of the tunnel.

Okagesama de to coconspirators giving birth to Tsuru for Solidarity, Mike Ishii and Nancy Ukai.

Okagesama de to Heyday publisher Steve Wasserman, managing editor Emmerich Anklam, developmental editor Mia Nakaji Monnier, and copyeditor and proofreader Michele Jones. Out of the granite mass, you were the stonecutters.

Okagesama de to the Jonathan Logan Family Foundation for your generous funding and years of patience. You provdied the mallet and chisel needed to carve the stone.

Okagesama de to Abby Ginzberg for your generosity of heart and encouragement to seek funding.

Okagesama de to my spirit daughter, Naina Sodhi, for her unstinting love and support.

Okagesama de to my brothers, Kiyoshi and Michael, and all my Ina and Mitsui family for urging me on.

Okagesama de to my sons, Dylan Tomine and Adrian Tomine, for the inspiration to write.

And finally, okagesama de to the memory of my soulmate and forever compassionate witness, Carey Covey.

About the Author

Satsuki Ina is a consulting psychotherapist specializing in trauma. She helps victims of oppression to claim not only their voice but also their power to transform the systems that have oppressed them. She is co-founder of Tsuru for Solidarity, a nonviolent, direct-action project of Japanese American social justice advocates working to end detention sites. Ina has produced two documentaries about the World War II incarceration of Japanese Americans, *Children of the Camps* and *From a Silk Cocoon*. Her work has been featured in the *New York Times*, the *Los Angeles Times*, *TIME*, *Democracy Now!* and the documentary *And Then They Came for Us*. A professor emeritus at California State University, Sacramento, she lives in the San Francisco Bay Area.